SHAKER LIFE, ART, AND ARCHITECTURE

Hands to Work, Hearts to God

SHAKER LIFE, ART, AND ARCHITECTURE

Hands to Work, Hearts to God

❖

SCOTT T. SWANK

PRINCIPAL PHOTOGRAPHY BY BILL FINNEY

ABBEVILLE PRESS ❖ PUBLISHERS

NEW YORK ❖ LONDON ❖ PARIS

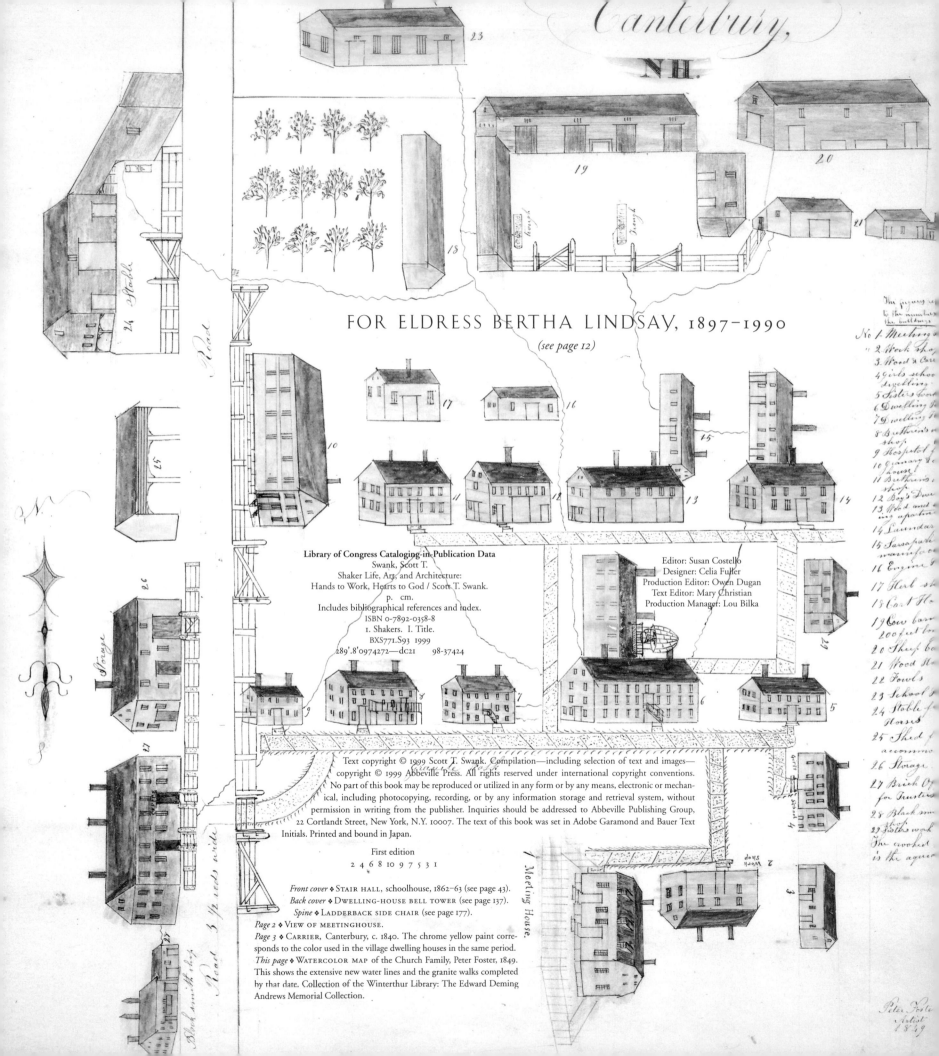

FOR ELDRESS BERTHA LINDSAY, 1897–1990

(see page 12)

Library of Congress Cataloging-in-Publication Data
Swank, Scott T.
Shaker Life, Art, and Architecture:
Hands to Work, Hearts to God / Scott T. Swank.
p. cm.
Includes bibliographical references and index.
ISBN 0-7892-0358-8
1. Shakers. I. Title.
BXS771.S93 1999
289'.8'0974272—dc21   98-37424

Editor: Susan Costello
Designer: Celia Fuller
Production Editor: Owen Dugan
Text Editor: Mary Christian
Production Manager: Lou Bilka

First edition
2 4 6 8 10 9 7 5 3 1

Front cover ❖ STAIR HALL, schoolhouse, 1862–63 (see page 43).
Back cover ❖ DWELLING-HOUSE BELL TOWER (see page 137).
Spine ❖ LADDERBACK SIDE CHAIR (see page 177).
Page 2 ❖ VIEW OF MEETINGHOUSE.
Page 3 ❖ CARRIER, Canterbury, c. 1840. The chrome yellow paint corre-
sponds to the color used in the village dwelling houses in the same period.
This page ❖ WATERCOLOR MAP of the Church Family, Peter Foster, 1849.
This shows the extensive new water lines and the granite walks completed
by that date. Collection of the Winterthur Library: The Edward Deming
Andrews Memorial Collection.

CONTENTS

❖

PREFACE

Detail of the HENRY CLAY BLINN MAP OF CANTERBURY, showing an eagle holding a banner with the words, "Plan of Canterbury by Henry Blinn 1848."

Shaker Life, Art, and Architecture: Hands to Work, Hearts to God presents Shaker design in the context of the Shaker community in Canterbury, New Hampshire. The study would have taken a different shape if I had not had the opportunity to live in the village as director and president for the past eight years. During that time I have been able to observe the effects of daylight from sunrise to sunset; experience the four seasons in the village landscape; explore every room in the twenty-five remaining original buildings of the Shaker Church Family; follow Shaker footpaths, fencerows, roadways; walk through fields and woods; discover spatial patterns; listen to the sounds and silences of buildings and landscape; and peel back the layers of time and memory. My greatest thrill is not even the discoveries I have made; a deep satisfaction lies in knowing that this publication will stimulate a new wave of discussion and learning, as we try to push Shaker studies to new levels. Such a dialogue of the past and present is the essence of historical scholarship and the greatest reward for its practitioners.

People often tell me that they have never forgotten their first visit to Canterbury. Part of that memorable character is embedded in the authenticity of the village. Canterbury Shaker Village, a National Historic Landmark site, has been preserved and conserved with a rare degree of architectural integrity.

Overlaying the historic village landscape is the aura of the last generation of Shakers who resided here. The village, founded in 1792, was a thriving Shaker community for two hundred years; the era of continuous Shaker occupation of the property ended in 1992, with the passing of the last Canterbury Shaker, Sister Ethel Hudson. Many people today believe that Shaker spirits still inhabit the village, and a few even claim to have experienced direct benevolent encounters. To be sure, in many parts of the village there is a sense that the Shakers have only momentarily stepped away.

Then there is the sheer beauty of the place—the setting of the village on a high ridge; the placid millponds; the patterns of fields and forests; the vistas; the mystery of archaeological remains in the form of stone dams, walls, and mill foundations; the many types of gardens; and the remnants of ancient orchards. There are magnificent trees: endangered elm and butternut, native white pine, sugar maple, ash, hemlock, and oak. Many exceptional non-native trees were also planted by the Shakers, notably tulip poplar and Chinese elm. Unfortunately, the great American chestnut no longer grows here, but it lives on in some of Canterbury's early framing timbers and cabinetry.

Canterbury Shaker Village is special in a scholarly sense as well. It is the best vantage point from which to observe and study the original architectural and spatial intentions of the Shakers and to reconstruct intellectually and visually the architectural program that was called the "pattern from the Mount," the official plan sanctioned by the early Shaker leadership in New Lebanon, New York. The entire early community plan is still formally intact, in spite of Shaker alterations over many generations.

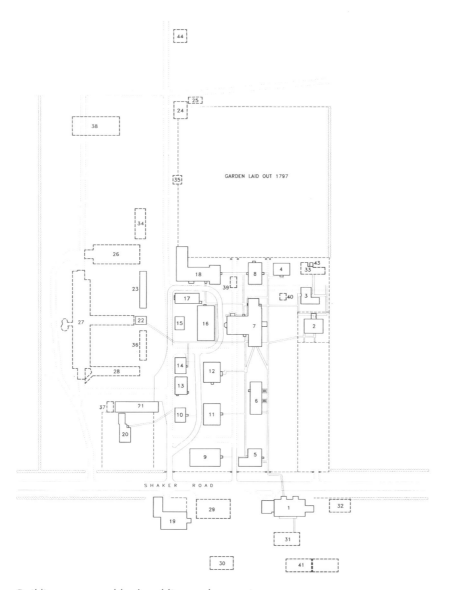

Buildings represented by dotted lines no longer exist.

From the beginning, the Shakers intended that their village would be a living, growing organism, with buildings and spaces emanating the spirit of the Shaker life in community and contributing to the development of that spirit. This may help explain why the site seizes the attention of even those who have very little understanding of the Shakers.

My goal in writing this book is to help demystify the Shakers, not contribute further to an uncritical, romantic image of them. Although I no longer believe much of what previous scholars have said about Shaker "perfection," I am still in awe of their original audacity and purpose, as well as their achievement. The aim of this book is to explain Shaker intent and to present in text and pictures the results of the Shaker effort to realize their visions.

ACKNOWLEDGMENTS

My introduction to the Shakers came in an academic setting—a course in American religious studies at the University of Pennsylvania taught by Dr. Don Yoder, a scholar of far-reaching erudition, who steered me to the writings of Daniel Patterson on Shaker music, Edward Deming Andrews on Shaker spirit drawings, and Charles Nordhoff on American communitarian movements. From there I began to explore the early writings of the Shakers and their detractors. Yoder also introduced me to the Shakers themselves. He encouraged me to attend the 1974 Shaker Bicentennial Conference in Cleveland and saw to it that I met Eldress Gertrude Soule of Sabbathday Lake and Canterbury, and Eldress Bertha Lindsay of Canterbury. I was intrigued and charmed by these lively, modern Shaker women, and shortly afterward I made my way north for an unforgettable visit to the Shaker community in Canterbury, New Hampshire. This book, then, owes most on the one hand to Don Yoder, a master teacher who opened my mind to the rich complexities of American religious life, and on the other hand to the Shakers, who opened the doors of their community for discovery.

In April 1990, when I became director of the Canterbury Shaker Village, I had an all-too-brief time to learn from the founders of the museum. Eldress Bertha died in the fall of 1990, and Sister Ethel Hudson died in September 1992. Charles "Bud" Thompson—a longtime non-Shaker resident of Canterbury, a founder, and the first curator of the museum—retired in 1990. Fortunately, by that time the village was well established as a museum, with a remarkable archive of original Shaker manuscripts and photographs.

The surviving Shakers in Sabbathday Lake, Maine, have also provided much wisdom for this book. By being true to their Shaker heritage and faithfully carrying on their way of life in community, they have inspired me to keep my focus on Shaker design as the product of the Shaker community, rather than as the achievement of individual Shaker leaders, builders, cabinetmakers, artists, or members. The Shaker way still works for those at Sabbathday Lake, and the demonstration of their faith made me want to understand how it had worked at Canterbury for two hundred years.

Many former and current staff members at Canterbury Shaker Village have contributed to the research and development of this book. My deepest appreciation goes to the chief curator, Shery Hack (architecture), Jean Burks (furniture), Mary Ann Sanborn (textiles), and Darryl Thompson (chronology and bibliography)—all of whom contributed written material that has been incorporated into the final text. Renée Fox tracked down historical photographs, checked facts, turned up unknown manuscripts, and called my attention to new dissertations and books. Judy Livingston endured eighteen months as my research assistant; she organized files, researched specific documents, and managed the growing collection of new photography for the book. Karen Redd patiently typed the manuscript and guided it through all its permutations before it reached Abbeville Press. Canterbury's museum interpreters were also very helpful, especially Darryl Thompson and Michael Pugh, and building research by the Village property department, particularly by Donavon Freeman, Dan Holmes, and Jon Norling, led to important discoveries.

As Shery Hack, Judy Livingston, and I visited research libraries, we accumulated an enormous debt of gratitude to the directors and fine staffs of the Sabbathday Lake Library, New Gloucester, Maine; the Shaker Museum and Library, Old Chatham, New York; the Hancock Shaker Village Library, Hancock, Massachusetts; the Dartmouth College and University of New Hampshire Special Collections; the State Library of New York at Albany; the Western Reserve Historical Society Library, Cleveland, Ohio; and the Winterthur Library, Winterthur, Delaware, where Richard McKinstry and Neville Thompson work their special brand of library magic.

Collectors and dealers have also contributed to this book by generously sharing their knowledge and access to their collections of Shaker material. A few collectors contributed photographs for the book, and several dealers helped the village locate rare Shaker artifacts, manuscripts, and photographs. I especially wish to thank Bob and Kathy Booth, Bob Hamilton, Steve Miller, Joan Sherman, Erhart Muller, Gerald McCue, David Newell, Scott DeWolfe, Mark Reinfurt, and Doug Hamel for their assistance.

Photographer Bill Finney is the real hero of this book. For more than twenty years he has taken remarkable photographs of Canterbury's Shakers and their village. The photographs in this volume, primarily taken over the last four years, are the product of his long hours at the village and in the darkroom. His vision of Canterbury is apparent in the artistry of his work.

This project would not have been possible without a benefactor. Research, writing, and photography have been underwritten by a generous grant from the Henry Luce Foundation. My deep gratitude extends to Ellen Holzman and to the president and board of the foundation for their confidence that our small museum could deliver a book that would contribute to the understanding of the Shakers and American art and culture.

I am grateful to my own Canterbury Shaker Village trustees, especially the former chair, Charles DeGrandpre, for generously permitting me to set aside other duties to keep this book on schedule. The entire board provided enthusiastic support for my work and recognized the importance of this project.

Once the raw materials were assembled, the editors and designers at Abbeville Press took over. Their work has improved the book immeasurably. Editorial Director Susan Costello had confidence in the project from the outline and concept stage, and gave clear directions to my writing. She assembled a remarkable professional team including the text editor Mary Christian, the production editor Owen Dugan, and the designer Celia Fuller.

Lastly, I must acknowledge Philadelphia architect Richard Conway Meyer, whose penetrating questions and astute observations preceded nearly every major intellectual discovery in this book. As the architectural consultant for this publication, he challenged, provoked, and pontificated, all to our great delight and benefit. He is not afraid to leap, nor to be wrong, and in the process he has led us to places we never thought of going. He has the ability to look through the physical to read the invisible—a nifty talent for any mortal, even an architect.

INTRODUCTION

Leap and shout, ye living building!
Christ is in his glory come,
Cast your eyes on Mother's children,
See what glory, fills the room!
Full of glory, all in motion,
Skipping like the lambs in May
Dancing in their sweet devotion
How the blessed virgins play!

"Ye Living Building," a hymn from the Shakers' first songbook of 1813, *Millennial Praises*, captures much of what was so shocking to outside observers in the late eighteenth and early nineteenth centuries. To establish their new faith, the Shakers developed strategies—such as this rousing hymn and the leaping Shaker dances of worship it suggests—to jolt their followers from old Protestant beliefs and practices. Today we have come to associate the Shakers with the serene minimalism of their furniture and interiors. But as the exuberance of their hymns and dances suggests, and contemporary accounts confirm, theirs was a revolutionary Christianity, and their communitarian way of life often astonished contemporaries. The Shakers separated themselves from the outside world, but not in contemplative withdrawal. In their communities they pursued work and worship to build the "living building," which was their term for the collective body of Shakers.[1]

The Shakers, who eventually named themselves the "United Society of Believers," were followers of Ann Lee, a charismatic Englishwoman who in 1774 led a group of eight radical "Shaking Quakers" to America and by 1779 established the Shaker movement in what is now Watervliet, New York, near Albany. By 1783, as a result of two years of itinerant evangelism by Mother Ann, her brother William, James Whittaker, and other Shaker preachers, new converts were meeting regularly in loosely structured communities throughout New York and New England. Mother Ann and her brother died within months of each other in 1784. James Whittaker emerged as the successor and consolidated the preaching gains of the early 1780s by encouraging the development of the Shaker communal society in New Lebanon, New York. Upon Whittaker's death in 1787, Father Joseph Meacham and the New Lebanon community asserted leadership as the Central Ministry, the governing body for all Shakers, and began what they termed the "calling to order" of other communities. Under the direction of the Central Ministry, groups of Shakers were gathered into organized societies on Shaker communal lands—to the east in Massachusetts (including Hancock, Harvard, Tyringham, and Shirley), Connecticut (Enfield), New Hampshire (Canterbury and Enfield), and Maine (Alfred and Sabbathday Lake), and to the west in Ohio and Kentucky.

Opposite ❖ EARLY WINTER VIEW OF THE MEETINGHOUSE HILL, looking north toward the 1792 meetinghouse.

After Mother Ann's death and the establishment of the new communities over the next decade, the movement grew rapidly. By its peak in 1850, the Shaker movement comprised approximately five thousand members in eighteen communities.[2] Today, six Shakers still live in the last remaining village at Sabbathday Lake, Maine.

Shaker religious belief and practice was unacceptable to most American Christians in the eighteenth century, and alarming to those with few religious convictions. To be sure, there were fundamental differences between their beliefs and those of most Protestant groups. First, the Shakers rejected the basic Protestant concept of the Godhead as the Trinity. Instead they posited a male/female duality of God as expressed by Jesus Christ and Mother Ann Lee. They rejected the concept of the resurrection of the body, and focused instead on the spiritual nature of their believers. They repudiated all sacraments, even baptism and communion. Their millennialist beliefs—and the concomitant social order that embraced communal ownership of property, celibacy, pacifism, restructured families, and dance as a form of worship—were seen by many outsiders as a threat to moral, religious, and social order.[3]

Within a few years of their arrival in the American colonies, the Shakers were fueling social and religious fires. Firsthand accounts of Shaker life by outsiders capture the separatist, revivalist qualities of Shaker culture that alarmed their contemporaries. James Thacher, a young doctor in the Continental Army, learned of the Shakers in 1778, and entered the following in his journal:

> *We are just informed of a new order of fanatics, who have recently introduced themselves into our country, pretending to be a religious sect; but if reports be true they are a disgrace both to religion and to human nature. . . . The methods which they practice under the idea of religious worship is so obviously impious, as to*

This book is dedicated to Eldress Bertha Lindsay (1897–1990), shown here in her sitting room at the trustees' office, 1988, with a bouquet of ninety red roses to celebrate her ninetieth birthday. She was instrumental in establishing Canterbury Shaker Village as a museum.

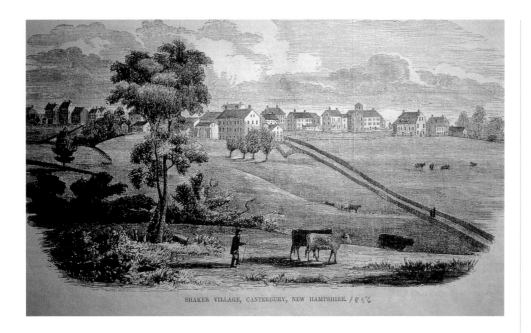

SHAKER VILLAGE, CANTERBURY, NEW HAMPSHIRE. 1856

CANTERBURY SHAKER VILLAGE'S earliest published image, a woodcut, appeared in several national magazines before 1860.

exceed the bounds of credibility; but we have the particulars from eye witnesses who have been admitted to their midnight orgies. They spend whole nights in their revels and exhibit the most unbecoming scenes, violating all rules of propriety and decency. Both sexes, nearly divested of clothing, fell to dancing in extravagant postures, and frequently whirl themselves round on one leg with inconceivable rapidity, till they fall apparently lifeless on the floor. . . . No imagination can form an adequate idea of the extravagant conduct of these infatuated people—a burlesque on all moral and religious principle.[4]

In the years after the American Revolution, two powerful currents, revivalism and industrialization, swept over New England. Although these generally have been interpreted as antithetical, since one is spiritual, the other materialistic, both were rooted in cultural modernization. Focus by previous writers on the Shakers' rigid Millennial Laws and the classic period of Shaker art and history from 1815 to 1860 has led to interpretations of the Shaker movement as a separatist utopian religious movement—that they were revivalists, thus reactionary anti-industrialists embodying a lost spirit of American innocence. Yet it is a mistake to interpret the Shakers as a folk culture steamrolled by American modernization.

In fact, the Shakers were agents of change, active and enthusiastic participants in the modernization of American society. After all, they formed a revolutionary social movement as well as a new religion, and it was through a series of social inventions that they hoped to achieve their millennialist goal. Chief among these inventions was the Shaker village, the communal society where religion, village planning, and community behavior were constructed as a harmonious whole.

A half century later, the Shakers' communitarian social order began to arouse more interest than their startling religious practices. Many foreign observers visited Shaker communities to see this American success story for themselves, but not all were favorably impressed. Charles Dickens, eager at first to visit the Shakers, left us with this sour account:

> *We walked into a grim room, where several grim hats were hanging on grim pegs, and the time was grimly told by a grim clock, which uttered every tick with a kind of struggle, as if it broke the grim silence reluctantly, and under protest. Ranged against the wall were six or eight stiff, high-backed chairs, and they partook so strongly of the general grimness, that one would much rather have sat on the floor than incurred the smallest obligation to any of them.*[5]

After the Civil War, communitarian aspects of the Shaker movement became the subject of more intensive scrutiny by journalists and political thinkers. Political commentator Charles Nordhoff and reformer John Humphrey Noyes wrote seminal comparative studies of American communitarian movements. The Shakers also caught the attention of political theorist Friedrich Engels; his *Socialism: Utopian and Scientific* (1880) recognized Shakerism as an important utopian socialist experiment. For Engels, the community was a forerunner of scientific socialism, the emerging Marxist movement that he predicted would eventually triumph over industrial capitalism.

By the twentieth century the Shaker movement was diminishing, and American society was no longer interested in the Shakers' religion, nor even their communitarianism, for after World War 1 American scholars placed a social premium on individualism and America's unique characteristics. The Shakers' "rediscovery" in the 1920s was spurred by two fresh currents: a revival of interest in American folk cultures and an accelerating appreciation for the modernist aesthetic in art. As "folk" objects became collected and exhibited, the Shakers were increasingly esteemed for the "simplicity" of their design aesthetic.

Faith and Edward Deming Andrews, who in the 1930s led the movement to study and collect Shaker art, themselves reduced the Shakers to a one-word concept: "simple." To the Andrewses, as characterized by the title of their study *Religion in Wood: A Book of Shaker Furniture* (1966), the extraordinary religious purity of the Shakers turned them into artisans of perfection—pious minds and hearts creating rarefied, minimalist forms. In the landmark 1986 exhibition *Shaker Design* at the Whitney Museum of American Art, curator June Sprigg essentially continued in this vein of linking moral integrity and aesthetics. She selected a range of Shaker art to illustrate the Shakers' visual environment of "quiet power" derived from the harmony of all parts in achieving a balanced, well-proportioned whole. She reaffirmed earlier writers' admiration for the simplicity of the Shaker ways, based on what she identified as the underlying "optimism" of Shaker design. For Sprigg, the result of Shaker design was American art of the highest order, profound in its spirituality, yet of direct visual appeal.[6]

But as this book examines, Shaker design cannot be fully understood in twentieth-century stylistic terms, because it is primarily an expression of the larger social structure of Shaker order. Life in a community, lived according to a code of rules, is a relatively obscure and alien concept today, as we value individual creative expression and achievement. The Shakers, as millennialists with a belief in progressive revelation, were committed to

Opposite ❖ SECOND FLOOR, SYRUP SHOP. This building was the location of Dr. Thomas Corbett's distillery for making Shaker medicinal syrups. In later years the first floor was used for food canning and the second floor for drying herbs.

community rule in their specially designed environment in which they could perform a wide range of activities and ritual acts that were designed to accentuate their solidarity and de-emphasize the individual.[7]

Shaker Life, Art, and Architecture: Hands to Work, Hearts to God examines Shaker art, architecture, and design in the context of the daily lives, beliefs, and behavior patterns of the Shakers, not as a separate, purely aesthetic phenomenon. The Shakers invented a whole new social structure, with new forms of architecture and community planning, new definitions of family, behavior, methods of worship, symbols, clothing, and furniture forms. This book explores how their visual expression was inseparably woven into their community structure. Their art, architecture, and village design was shaped by the actions of the community. Every aspect of their daily lives was reinforced by Shaker ideas.

While the discussion here pertains to all Shaker communities, this book focuses on the community of Canterbury, New Hampshire—one of the oldest, most typical, and most completely preserved of all the Shaker villages. In 1792 it became the seventh Shaker society, and it remained prominent until Sister Ethel Hudson died in 1992. For a study of Shaker art and architecture, Canterbury's position and resources are unrivaled by any other Shaker community: it has surviving architecture from all periods of its long history, and—most important for a study of architecture, art, and community planning—it is the only Shaker community that retains an intact first-generation Shaker meetinghouse and first dwelling house on their original sites. As a result, Canterbury is a unique resource for discovering Shaker architectural intent and early Shaker community planning and design.

The Shakers' way of life in their community radiated from their core belief in what they called "gospel order." Although this concept evolved over time among Shaker communities, gospel order was a fundamental defining principle of Shakerism that included official rituals such as the signing of the covenant affirming Shaker beliefs, communal concepts and structures such as the organization of communities into "families," and practices such as the construction of villages that separated the Shakers from the rest of the world. Gospel order assured that the covenanted membership would lead disciplined lives in harmony with God and Shaker rules. It also established a pattern for the smaller ordering systems that regulated day-to-day aspects of Shaker life.

"Village Life," part I of this book, delineates the Shaker-built environment and its religious, economic, and social structure. "Community Order," part II, examines the Shaker response to community life and emphasizes the relationships between people and the spaces in which they lived. Following this contextual study, part III, "Shaker Style," is a reassessment of Shaker "style" in art and everyday objects. The chapters in these three sections examine how the Shakers' behavior, beliefs, and concept of community order are the keys to understanding Shaker architecture and design.

❖

Opposite ❖ MEETINGHOUSE LANE GATE, looking south. The granite wall along the east side of Shaker Road (1797) is the first stone wall constructed by the Shakers at Canterbury. The wooden fence is set on iron pins leaded into granite stones, which are deeply embedded in the ground. Both stone wall and fence were designed for beauty and permanence. Note the graduated width of the rails from bottom to top of the fence, which terminates into a molded handrail.

VILLAGE LIFE

THE BUILDING PROCESS OF A PLANNED COMMUNITY

When Nathaniel Hawthorne passed through the Shaker village in Canterbury, New Hampshire, while on a horse-trading mission with his uncle in 1831, he was impressed with what he saw:

> *I walked to the shaker village yesterday, and was shown over the establishment and dined there with a squire and a doctor, also of the "world's people." On my arrival, the first thing I saw was a jolly old shaker carrying an immense decanter, full of their superb cider, and as soon as I told my business, he turned out a tumbler full and gave me. It was as much as a common head could cleverly carry. Our dining room was well furnished, the dinner excellent, and the table was attended by a middle aged shaker lady, good-looking and cheerful, and not to be distinguished either in manners or conversation from other well-educated women in the country. This establishment is immensely rich. Their land extends two or three miles along the road, and there are streets of great houses, painted yellow and topt with red; they are now building a brick edifice for their public business, to cost seven or eight thousand dollars. On the whole, they lead a good and comfortable life, and if it were not for their ridiculous ceremonies, a man could not do a wiser thing than to join them. Those whom I conversed with were intelligent, and appeared happy. I spoke to them about becoming a member of the society, but have come to no decision on that point.*[1]

The prosperous village that Hawthorne observed was the result of nearly forty years of continuous construction by the Canterbury Shakers. Hawthorne visited Canterbury as the Shakers were erecting their brick trustees' office, their largest and most expensive building.[2]

But that was only one of many major construction projects at Canterbury. The pace of construction, which began in 1792, continued unabated until the late 1850s, when the main agricultural complex was greatly enlarged by the building of a two-hundred-foot-long cow barn, the largest frame barn ever built in the state of New Hampshire. Although the scale of most of their buildings was still residential, Shaker dwelling houses also must have appeared massive to contemporary visitors. By 1840 Shaker dwellings at Canterbury and Enfield, New Hampshire, were among the largest in the state—comparable to the institutional buildings of Dartmouth College, the State Capitol in Concord,

Pages 18–19 ❖ AERIAL VIEW, CHURCH FAMILY BUILDINGS IN ROWS, as laid out starting in 1792. The meetinghouse is located at the southern edge of the village (at the far right).

Opposite ❖ MAP OF CANTERBURY SHAKER VILLAGE, Henry Clay Blinn, c. 1848. This map shows the three principal social units of Canterbury Shaker Village, namely the Church Family (bottom), the Second Family (middle), and the North Family (top)

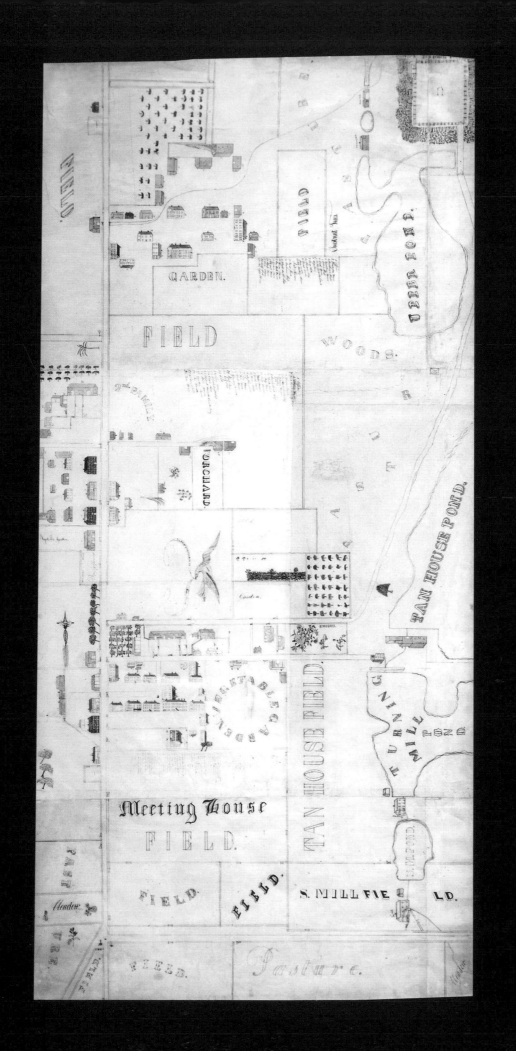

VIEW OF CANTERBURY CHURCH
FAMILY AREA from the south, c. 1855. This is
how Nathaniel Hawthorne would have seen
the village in 1831. The large brick structure on
the left is the trustees' office. The south row of
buildings dominates the hilltop. The meetinghouse
sits to the far right. This is the earliest known
photograph of the village.

the warehouses and mansions of Portsmouth, and the new mills of the southern New
Hampshire river towns.

Early-nineteenth-century visitors during this peak were also impressed by the
density of Shaker buildings at Canterbury's Shaker community, whose population was
matched by few central New Hampshire towns in the 1840s. At one point during the
1820s the community consisted of four organizational social units, known as "families"—
the Church Family (so named because the meetinghouse was located there) and the
Second, North, and West Families. Each had its own set of buildings; in all, the four families built approximately one hundred structures for themselves. Many of these buildings are visible on a monumental, detailed map completed about 1848 by Henry Clay
Blinn, a Canterbury Shaker whose many learned pursuits, which included chronicling the
community and establishing an early Shaker museum at Canterbury, have contributed
immeasurably to our knowledge of Shaker community life. By 1848, nearly three hundred Shakers lived at Canterbury, but the number of short-term visitors and religious
inquirers in fact pushed the total annual population figures much higher—in the 1840s
the Shakers served several thousand free meals annually to visitors and those wishing to
try the Shaker life for a time.

The origin of the Shaker community at Canterbury lay with Benjamin Whitcher and his family, who first settled the site in the mid-1770s. Other families followed Whitcher to the fertile ridge in Canterbury, but none of them would have yet heard of the Shakers, who were still getting established near Albany, New York.

In the ferment of the postrevolutionary 1780s, New Light Baptist revivals in Massachusetts, New York, New Hampshire, and Maine were a source of converts to Shakerism. Whole families of Baptists helped to establish communities in New Lebanon and Hancock, Massachusetts. The New York Shakers sent missionaries to northern New England to present the Shaker faith. The Shaker missionaries had great success in Loudon and Canterbury, New Hampshire, where Free Will Baptists had established several congregations.

Whitcher and his family were among the earliest converts to Shakerism, and their farm became a meeting place for the Shakers. By the 1790 census, Whitcher had thirty-five people in his household, with larger numbers who came for worship only.[3] We can trace the beginnings of Canterbury's Shakers to the unanticipated but welcome flood of new converts to Whitcher's farm, but how and when did the planned Shaker community begin?

When in 1792 Canterbury was "called to order" by the Central Ministry at New Lebanon, the new Church Family (the first and most authoritative "family" in a new Shaker community) began to erect their first building—their meetinghouse—but it was not without considerable influence from the seat of Shaker authority.

The Central Ministry at New Lebanon (a village situated on the side of a small mountain in eastern New York, thus also called "the Mount" and after 1861 "Mount Lebanon") dictated the design and construction that took place in all Shaker communities. When the Central Ministry officially sanctioned a design or model for buildings, furnishings, or objects, it was known among the Shakers as the "pattern from the Mount." The Central Ministry also established further guidelines for community planning and the design and construction of particular building types.

These unwritten building standards were already developing by the late eighteenth century, when the new communities were called to order, and would be entrenched by 1820, when Shaker buildings exhibited a "Shaker style" of architecture that was essentially a streamlined Federal or Neoclassical idiom. These were not the only orders to come from New Lebanon: in 1821 the Central Ministry recorded a host of Shaker rules known as the Millennial Laws; these were greatly expanded in 1845 and revised further through the nineteenth century. These regulations, which touched on every aspect of Shaker life, were an attempt to further codify Shaker practice and bring consistency to the numerous scattered Shaker communities. Their instructions for building design made precise specifications that may have been unwritten assumptions in early Shaker building history; for example they prohibited "beadings, mouldings and cornices, which are merely for fancy" and "odd or fanciful styles of building."[4]

Canterbury was planned according to the general guidelines conferred by the Central Ministry and shaped by the needs and social structure of those living in a celibate and communal order. The three core buildings of any Shaker community were the

CANTERBURY CHURCH FAMILY BUILDINGS

Year	Building	Year	Building
1792	meetinghouse tan house	1812	carding mill wood mill
1793	dwelling house blacksmith's shop	1813	warehouse clothes house
1794	ministry stable office second dwelling house	1814	sheep barn turning mill
		1816	sisters' shop
1795	spin shop brethren's south shop wash house corn house coal shed hog pen	1817	swine house
		1819	horse barn
		1822	wood house
		1823	schoolhouse
		1824	brethren's north shop
1797	garden shop granary horse mill (grist)	1825	yellow building
		1827	garden barn
		1828	clothing mill timber house bacon house
1798	wood house horse barn		
1799	woodshed cider house	1830	cider mill
		1830–33	trustees' office
1800	sawmill and gristmill	1832	new sawmill and gristmill
1801	cow barn	1834	horse stand
1802	cow barn enlarged	1840	cart shed
		1841, 1848	syrup shop additions
1804	fulling mill	1841	north shop
1806	building for visitors	1848	new ministry shop
1808	ministry shop	1850	cheese house
1810	new office	1850	pail house
1811	house for visitors new blacksmith's shop	1858	new cow barn

meetinghouse, the dwelling house, and the office—spaces for worship, life, and work.[5] Those were among the earliest to be built at Canterbury. We will see that as the village building progressed, the plan of the community was obliged to yield to some practical considerations of existing, functional buildings on the Whitcher farm. As the community flourished, later building accommodated the expansion of the Shaker community and industries.

FORMATION: 1792–1858

The highly symbolic meetinghouse could not be built by non-Shakers, so when it was time for Canterbury to erect one, the Central Ministry sent Shaker builder Moses Johnson to supervise the project. The Canterbury meetinghouse, completed in September 1792, was Johnson's sixth for the Shakers and the only one of the first six to survive virtually intact. He had built meetinghouses in New Lebanon in 1785; Hancock in 1786; Watervliet in 1791; Enfield, Connecticut, in 1791; and Harvard, Massachusetts, in 1791. (New Lebanon's and Harvard's have since been given gable roofs and converted to other uses; a seventh, built at Shirley, Massachusetts, in 1792–93, now stands at Hancock Shaker Village; the Sabbathday Lake, Maine, meetinghouse dates to 1794.)

At Canterbury, in the hands of Father Job Bishop, an accomplished woodworker, as ruling elder, and Moses Johnson as master builder, the first Shaker building was constructed "of the exact size, shape and style of finish as the one at New Lebanon."[6] Bishop was from one of the founding families of New Lebanon, and had won the confidence of Mother Ann, whom he saw for the last time just three days before her death in September 1784. His loyalties to Mother Ann, the Central Ministry, and the Shaker faith were unswerving throughout his life.[7]

The Canterbury meetinghouse has several unusual features. The first-floor interior is completely open, with no supporting posts. The frame is chestnut, unlike most other extant village buildings. The building was roofed with old-growth pine shingles with birchbark weather stripping, remnants of which survive around doorways, windows, dormers, and along the ridgeline of the roof. The floor structure consists of a heavy double frame, set on stone and floored with two overlapping layers of one-inch (2.5 cm) hard pine, making it able to support synchronized group dancing. The gambrel roof construction was the first of its type in the Canterbury area. Although the Shakers in New York would have known both the English gambrel tradition of Connecticut, and the Dutch gambrel of the Hudson River Valley, the specific design source for early Shaker meetinghouses is still unknown. One fact is certain: the two-and-a-half-story gambrel was a rare house form—or meetinghouse form—in central New Hampshire in the late eighteenth century.[8]

The design of a Shaker meetinghouse departed from the architectural norm in at least three other respects: it functioned both as a house of worship and a residence for the Shaker ministry (two elders and two eldresses); it introduced a ritual dance floor into a house of worship; and the design eliminated all ecclesiastical focus in the worship area in

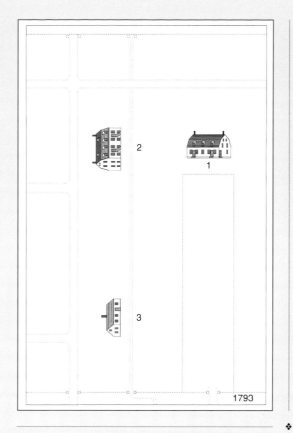

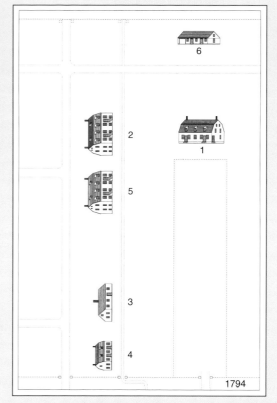

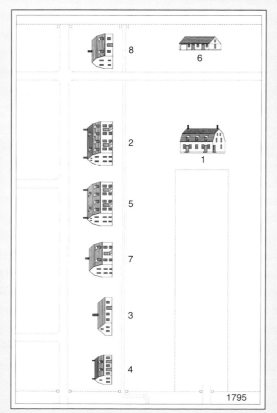

CANTERBURY CHURCH FAMILY PLAN,
1790s. These plans show the original intent of the
Shaker community layout. Buildings, numbered to
correspond with the plan, are:

1 meetinghouse (1792)
2 first dwelling house (1793)
3 blacksmith's shop (1793)
4 first office (1794)
5 second dwelling house (1794)
6 ministry stable (1794)
7 brethren's south shop (1795)
8 spin shop (1795)

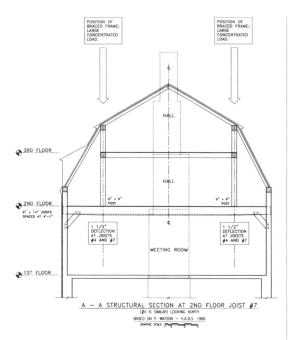

SECTION DRAWING, MEETINGHOUSE
as originally constructed in 1792. The loading
arrangement of the upper levels is unusual in that
the second and third stories are supported by only
two of the ten identical ceiling joists that builder
Moses Johnson used to create a universal meeting
space for Shaker worship on the first floor.

order to create a large, open, flexible worship space. Canterbury's Shaker Meetinghouse
was a radical church form in New Hampshire in 1792, as well as a symbolic and useful
Shaker building.

The New Hampshire Ministry's two elders and two eldresses, appointed by the
Central Ministry in New Lebanon, presided over the communities at Canterbury and
Enfield, New Hampshire. The senior members of the ministry in the founding generation
were known as Father and Mother. The home of the ministry was the meetinghouse, until
1878. Each Shaker family also had two elders and two eldresses, appointed by the ministry,
who lived in separate quarters in the main family dwelling house. The new meetinghouse
on the Canterbury ridge gave the believers a worship space; it provided living quarters
only for the ministry. Many other Shakers were living in temporary quarters at several
farms in the area, mainly those of Whitcher and residents Henry Clough, Joseph Sanborn,
and Chase Wiggin. Without a proper dwelling house, however, the community could not
yet truly live "in order," because the Shaker life of celibacy required a division of members
into brothers', sisters', and children's communal quarters, with at least one large residential
structure to house the adults. Consequently, after the meetinghouse was completed, construction of a dwelling house became a high priority.

Built in 1793, the dwelling house also was in the form of a two-and-a-half-story
gambrel structure of 32 by 42 feet (9.76 × 12.8 m), but it included a basement level for a
communal dining room. Most likely, it was one of the largest new dwellings in central
New Hampshire. The Shakers expanded the building several times in the early nineteenth
century through 1837, when it reached its present form.

The placement of the meetinghouse and the dwelling house was crucial to the
siting of the rest of the buildings and the conceptualization of the Shakers' planned community. The relationship between these early structures at Canterbury demonstrates that
the Shakers built their village on a road running north-south along the ridge, known
today as Shaker Road. We can now determine, by piecing together Shaker tradition and
village building history, the general location and number of pre-Shaker buildings within
the present village.

Most likely, Whitcher converted one or more of his farm buildings into dwellings. In fact, while restoring the present-day syrup shop during the summer of 1992,
restoration carpenters discovered the only possible pre-Shaker building on village property, namely the central portion of the existing syrup shop. Although there is no conclusive documentation that the structure was built by Whitcher, some original features date
to the late eighteenth century, and the distinctive sill construction (of white pine planks)
is not found in any other surviving Canterbury Shaker building. Shaker oral tradition has
identified the shop as a Whitcher building, with some difference of opinion as to whether
it was his house or a granary. Reasonable speculation at this point suggests that it was
most likely his granary, adapted for domestic living in the mid- to late 1780s. The building was moved to its present location about 1841, when it became the distillery for Shaker
medicinal syrups. It was expanded to its present dimensions by additions to the north in
1841 and to the south in 1848. In the twentieth century the syrup shop became the food-
processing center for the village.

Since the area's remaining late-eighteenth-century houses are located along Shaker Road, and since New Hampshire's spring mud is deep and viscous, we can reasonably speculate that Whitcher's farm buildings lay close to Shaker Road, on higher ground, between present-day Asby Road and an old range road just north of the Shaker schoolhouse. This location for Whitcher's buildings can also be inferred from the pattern of laying out the new Shaker community. The Shakers did not have the luxury of clearing the site of all of Whitcher's farm buildings before erecting desperately needed communal structures; they built around them and tore them down as they became obsolete.

Shaker trustee and blacksmith Francis Winkley noted in his journal that the "old [Whitcher] House is puled down" in 1795.[9] The October demolition of the house came only as the new second dwelling house (also a gambrel), set next to the first and also oriented north-south, was completed and occupied. Most likely, the original Whitcher house sat closer to the road than the Shaker dwellings, and the Whitcher farm buildings probably stood to the north and east of the house. Their number and size is unknown, but there is evidence that they housed thirty-five people in 1790 while Whitcher maintained a working farm. In 1803 the Shakers "pulled down the old barns."[10] With documentary evidence of at least two barns, the old house, and the original Whitcher granary, we can conclude that at least four Whitcher buildings were on the farm at the time of its initial occupation by the Shakers.

Architect Penelope Watson deserves credit for the first modern interpretation of a Shaker plan. Her work established the formal, linear aspects of the Shaker village at Canterbury, documenting functional zones, within which the buildings were laid out in rows along a main east-west and secondary north-south axis.[11] The southern village boundary is marked by a ministry row, which includes Meetinghouse Lane, the meetinghouse (set back four hundred feet [122 m] from the road), the ministry shop, and the site of the ministry stable (no longer extant) stretching to the east. Moving north up Shaker Road, next comes an open dooryard, a purposefully designed and protected courtyard separating the ministry buildings from the residential, or dwelling house, row. To the north of the dwelling houses ran a service road effectively dividing the residential section of the village from the industrial and agricultural zones. Two rows of industry buildings were constructed on the north side of the dwelling house row, with another service road to the mills and a row of agricultural buildings to the north. The unique features of the Canterbury plan are the siting of the meetinghouse a considerable distance from the road and the placement of the dwelling house (and the subsequent dwelling houses) at a right angle to the meetinghouse.

Buildings along Shaker Road were designed to accommodate community functions that required interaction with visitors from the outside world. Community members who used these buildings included office deacons or trustees (the brothers who handled the Shakers' commercial transactions), office deaconesses, nurses, patients, teachers, and schoolchildren. Non-Shakers who frequented these structures included individuals who came to the village for business, physicians who treated Shaker patients in the infirmary, and neighborhood children who were educated in the schoolhouse.

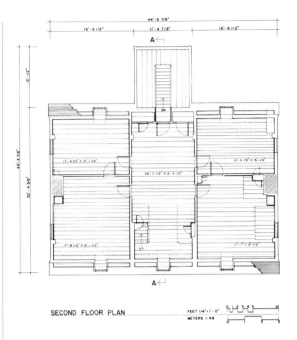

SECOND FLOOR PLAN

MEETINGHOUSE, SECOND-FLOOR PLAN. This drawing shows the modifications of 1815 to the second floor of the meetinghouse, which was occupied by the junior elder and eldress of the New Hampshire Ministry.

VIEW OF THE 1792 MEETINGHOUSE
AND THE 1793 DWELLING HOUSE as
they appear today. The dwelling house has
been greatly altered since 1793.

This year past (1824) we have been tareing down and building almost the whole time. We have built the farmers, Docters, Shoemakers, Wheelers, and John Wadley Shop with a seller all over it, a costly and extradnery building indeed for its use. We have also built a dam to flow the Lake meddow and we have made a Brick yard in said meddow. We have also moved the Shed at the horse barn and built 20 feet on it. . . . We have also built a large wood Shelter at the wood mill and built over the wood mill and its gears and built a [dining] room adjoining said wood mill with a fire place and chimney & Brother John Wadley with other Brethren has this 11 day of Dec dined in it. We have also split and got out a bundance of stone for another building and we are almost tyered.

—FRANCIS WINKLEY DAYBOOK,
December 11, 1824

The industrial element of the village was obviously important for a self-sufficient community; at Canterbury, even before the 1793 dwelling house was erected, a tannery (which no longer survives) was built. In 1794 the Church Family built their first trustees' office, of which we know little, except that it was a 22-by-28-foot (6.71 × 8.54 m) gambrel-roofed adaptation of the basic Shaker architectural template. We know more about the 1810 office (a building now known as the "children's house"), built on a split-level site along Shaker Road. The location helped insulate the village from commercial activity, particularly the exchange of money and daily contact with non-Shaker drovers, drivers, and businessmen. The split-level site also permitted a full-time basement under a Shaker 32-by-40-foot (9.76 × 12.2 m) floor plan, and allowed for a kitchen, dining room, and food storage area to better serve Shaker trustees and their non-Shaker business partners without violating the pattern from the Mount.

By 1818 the most essential buildings for the community were in place. The type and scale of the structures built before 1818 provide insight into the nature of the early Canterbury Shaker community, as well as its planning and building processes. By 1830 the Shaker success in business—in Canterbury and elsewhere—was legendary, and Father Job Bishop finally agreed to allow the Canterbury Shakers to erect a larger trustees' office. The 1810 office was moved to the eastern end of the dwelling-house dooryard, where it was converted to a dormitory for young girls being raised by the Shakers.

The new brick trustees' office along Shaker Road was begun in 1830. In June of that year Elijah Brown, Canterbury's master builder, and tinsmith Thomas Hoit were sent to New Lebanon and Hancock to obtain information on "how to build with stone and brick and tin the ruff" for the proposed 40-by-72-foot (12.2 × 22 m) office. By November 22, 1831, Brown and his crew (which included the first large contingent of non-Shaker day laborers, some ten to fourteen men) were finishing the exterior. Instead of a tin roof, the Canterbury Shakers had decided on another innovation for them—slate—at the hefty cost of four hundred dollars.[12] It was the first structure in the Church Family made entirely of brick, and the first to have a slate roof. When completed in 1833, it was the largest and finest building in the village (and the only completely masonry one) of the Canterbury Church Family.

According to Church Family records, from 1792 to 1833 the Canterbury Shakers built continuously, erecting nearly fifty structures, plus an aqueduct and an extensive system of dams, ponds, and ditches designed to provide water power for a series of mills.

In June 1837, as the United States was experiencing one of the most severe financial panics in its young history, the prospering Canterbury Shakers took on a hired crew of twenty men to assist them with a series of expansions to the first dwelling house. These included moving the "great house porch" from the north to the east side; creating a bakery; enlarging the sisters' living quarters; and raising a large ell on the "great house" to provide a new and larger meeting room (the present-day chapel), chambers for Church Family elders and eldresses, and a finished storage room on the third floor (which contains the finest display of Shaker cabinetry to survive in the village).

Several general principles need to be kept in mind when studying the first group of buildings. First, the Shakers implemented a particular architectural vision from 1792

through 1858. Second, although the New Lebanon Central Ministry generated an ideal building template, it did not determine the specific layout or ordering of the Canterbury Shaker buildings. The Central Ministry did, however, exercise veto power on at least one occasion (it required that the height of the dwelling-house bell tower be reduced by five feet five inches because it was considered excessively vain.)[13] Third, from its earliest conception the village plan was an organic, living one, exemplified by the careful selection of what was to be built, demolished, enlarged, altered, or moved, all with a view to future growth. The Shakers were architecturally responsive to the changing needs of their community, to economic opportunities and necessities, and to technological innovation.

The Shakers built aggressively through the 1850s. By 1858, with the completion of the largest cattle barn in New Hampshire, and after sixty-six years of nearly continuous building, the Canterbury Shaker community was a mature social experiment, with a planned village of several Shaker families, a model farm, and an extensive industrial base.[14]

This first era of building was remarkable considering that during this sixty-six-year period, the number of Shaker men in the Church Family fluctuated, but probably rarely exceeded forty at any one time. The Shaker brothers had many tasks that prevented them from an ongoing, full-time commitment to construction. Eight mills, extensive land, numerous livestock, and a large agricultural enterprise kept every able-bodied Shaker working steadily. Given the multitude of tasks necessary to feed several hundred people and provide income for the community, how did the Shakers manage to build one or two buildings per year?

Although research is only beginning to recover significant information about Shaker builders, several things are clear. Perhaps most important, Moses Johnson did not remain in Canterbury after the completion of the meetinghouse, so he was not the architect of the village development. However, he contributed more to Shaker architecture than the eleven meetinghouses that he would build. Johnson no doubt provided training that enabled the Canterbury Shaker brothers to carry on his design and quality standards. Johnson's vital contributions to Canterbury included his sons. Joseph and James, fortunately for the Canterbury community, did not follow their father on his architectural odyssey, but remained in New Hampshire to build for the Canterbury and Enfield Shakers.

The first generation of Shaker craftsmen was an exceptional group. In addition to Joseph and James Johnson, several other important woodworkers have been identified. Father Job Bishop, the much-beloved spiritual leader and senior elder who presided over the founding of the Canterbury community in 1792 and guided its first forty years of development, was himself a skilled woodworker. Father Job was involved in making crucial decisions concerning design and building processes until his death in 1831. The degree of his involvement in actual construction may never be known, but he was the head planner of both the Canterbury and Enfield (New Hampshire) Shaker villages.

Carpenters at Canterbury, in addition to Joseph and James Johnson (James was also a turner) and Bishop, included James Daniels, Josiah Edgerly, Micajah Tucker, and Ezekiel Stevens Sr. (also a glazier, who supervised early building at Canterbury and, with James Daniels, erected buildings at Enfield and Harvard). Many of these brothers also

assisted with the construction of built-in cabinetry in various buildings. Elijah Brown served as Canterbury's master builder from 1819 through the 1830s. The sheer volume of timber framing, carpentry, and cabinetry suggests that these lead craftsmen had considerable help. Two young Shaker brothers, John Graham and Henry Clay Blinn, arrived during the 1830s. Graham was considered "a nice workman on wood" with great promise as "a leader among the singers" and future elder,[15] but he died at thirty. Blinn lived until 1905, but his many valuable talents—including spiritual leadership, school teaching, dentistry, and printing—took him far beyond carpentry and cabinetmaking. The three sons of Ezekiel Stevens—Moses, Ezekiel, and Levi—were also woodworkers.

Through the 1830s, a core of Shaker brothers worked side by side, erecting the buildings needed by the expanding Shaker community to house new members to support their varied economic enterprises. The quality of workmanship is consistently high throughout this period, with a few notable exceptions in the much-altered dwelling house. Most importantly for the early history of Shaker design, this Shaker crew was the group that from 1792 through the 1830s consistently refined Shaker building and cabinetmaking practices and maintained the original architectural intent.

By the 1840s most of the first generation of Shaker woodworkers had died or were too elderly to do much work. Ezekiel Stevens Sr. passed away in 1830. Micajah Tucker's activity trailed off after 1846, when in his eighties he cut off two fingers on a circular saw; he died in 1848. Elijah Brown and James Daniels both died in 1851. Joseph Johnson died in 1852 (at seventy-one), and James Johnson in 1861 (at eighty-four). By 1841 the Shakers had to hire Lynus Stevens of Claremont to build the north shop and in 1858 John Page of Gilmanton to frame the new two-hundred-foot-long cow barn. The same situation prevailed in the other building trades. Micajah Tucker was also the community's master mason. His chief assistant was Elijah Fletcher, who died in 1836. The blacksmiths were, besides Francis Winkley, Clement Beck and Benjamin Whitcher Jr. Beck defected in 1815; Whitcher died in 1837, Winkley in 1848.

The loss of so many skilled builders and tradesmen in a relatively brief time ended one era of Canterbury Shaker building and most certainly was one factor in the paucity of new construction undertaken after 1858. The second was demographic: even though the Canterbury Shaker community experienced a higher degree of population stability in the second half of the nineteenth century than most Shaker villages, it still declined in total numbers. When construction resumed after 1892, it was clearly work for hire, and supervised by the Shakers.

VICTORIANIZATION: 1859–91

The second major phase of Shaker building history in Canterbury was one of consolidation, maintenance, and selective rebuilding. Fortunately, enough Victorian Shaker photographs and other material culture survive at Canterbury to allow generalizations to be made about building during this time. The most obvious fact is that the Shakers did not need to erect many new buildings and buy or make large quantities of new furnishings in the Victorian era, with declining membership. This was a time of creative male and female

VIEW OF THE CHURCH FAMILY AREA
FROM UNION HILL, looking west, c. 1870.
This is the only known view of the village from
this vantage point.

leadership, in which the Canterbury community declined in number but remained stable and prosperous. The Shaker Victorianization of Canterbury buildings consisted of a veneer of decorative devices, such as the addition of Victorian hoods over exterior doors; the construction of bay windows, dormers, and porches; the change of windows to two-over-two sash with machine-made glass; and the shift to Victorian paint colors. Inside, there were modernizations that included plumbing. All in all, the Canterbury Shakers had little demand for new buildings, but much need for ongoing maintenance. Still, in 1860 a house for hired help was built at the carding mill, and the laundry received a new steam boiler and a tall brick industrial chimney stack.

Landscape architecture began to transform the village plan during this era when trees and flower beds were installed. The Shakers were early and sustained supporters of the rural beautification movement. At Canterbury this started in the late 1850s and continued steadily through the 1870s, when the Canterbury community accepted Victorian floral culture and laid out its first ornamental flower gardens.

MODERNIZATION: 1892–1939

In 1892 the Canterbury Shakers accelerated the task of modernizing their community. A major addition to the infirmary that year provided a modern kitchen, new patient rooms, and live-in quarters for nurses.

Plumbing, telephones, and electricity each influenced architectural modifications. The introduction of automobiles in 1907, for example, led to building a garage/firehouse in 1908, adding a porte-cochere to the trustees' office, creating an engineer's room in the laundry complex, erecting a prefabricated steel garage in 1923, and even moving a small building to provide covered storage for the Shakers' first truck.

These examples of technologically driven architectural change illustrate the flurry of building activity in the village over the first two decades of the twentieth century.

Building activity from 1904 to 1918 reached a level unmatched since the early 1850s. The trustees' office, dwelling house, laundry, horse barn, and cow barn all experienced major remodeling. A new creamery, with a modern hipped roof, was constructed in 1905 to expand capacity for milk processing and butter making. In 1905 the clothier's mill was torn down and a modern pump mill built in its place. The wood mill and sawmill were upgraded. At least six buildings in the village core were moved or torn down, principally to make way for new structures.

Some of these momentous changes were made to adjust to the changing demographics of the Canterbury community. For example, as the number of brothers dwindled through deaths and defections, and the boys' order was closed, the old boys' house was moved to the west side of Shaker Road, near the present horse barn, where it became the hired-men's house.

The demographic impact on community architecture is also illustrated by the need for expanded housing for elderly Shaker sisters coming to Canterbury in the early twentieth century from other communities, particularly Enfield (New Hampshire), as these dwindling communities were closed to Shaker occupancy. The old second dwelling (1794) was in unsuitable condition, so it was dismantled and its remains sold. The brothers' south shop, located next to the second dwelling, was no longer needed, so it was torn down. These two sites were then leveled, and a foundation was laid in 1917 for a new sisters' dwelling house (the present-day Enfield House). Actually, this building was the old Second Family office, built in 1826 and moved from its original location north of the Church Family to the new foundation. Enfield House, first occupied in 1921, was outfitted with new bathrooms and electricity, so it was the most modern living space in the

Right ❖ DOOR LATCH, MEETINGHOUSE, 1792.

Far right ❖ CUPBOARD DOOR "H" HINGES, MEETINGHOUSE, 1792.

ENFIELD HOUSE, hand-tinted color postcard,
c. 1921. The Second Family office was moved to the
Church Family in 1918 and remodeled from 1918 to
1921 to serve as a residence for the Shaker sisters
from Enfield, New Hampshire.

Church Family. These modern practical and sanitary conveniences made it especially suitable as a dormitory for the elderly newcomers from other Shaker villages.

For the Canterbury Shaker building program of the early twentieth century, construction was done exclusively by outside non-Shaker contractors and workmen, and the buildings had little in common with earlier Shaker style and design. In the Shaker spirit of experimentation with new technologies, however, the buildings took advantage of current trends in the building trades—for example, exterior metal siding was installed on the firehouse/garage, powerhouse, and steel garage. In Enfield House, the Shakers took advantage of the new applications for cement. Cement bricks, made on site, were used for the foundation and chimneys, and part of the ground floor was poured cement.[16]

❖

ARCHITECTURAL DESIGN AND AESTHETICS

The Shakers' plan, as it evolved under the succession of early leaders—Mother Ann, Father James Whittaker, Father Joseph Meacham, and Mother Lucy Wright—was a cultural system that challenged nearly all tenets of Western society and advocated new thinking, different behavior, and alternative forms of communication. The Shaker family structure offered new types of family relationships among men, women, and children. The economic system changed associations between producers, products, and consumers. Shaker religion established new relationships between divinity and humanity, introduced fresh forms of worship, and subjected individual desire to community social control through Shaker rule.

In art and architecture the Shakers also broke with tradition. The numerous Shaker villages were physical embodiments of the Shaker concept of community order. Buildings were especially important instruments in the Shaker plan. Traditional New England and New York vernacular dwellings and meetinghouses were not suitable for communal needs, so the Shakers developed a new form for the meetinghouse/dwelling house template and placed the buildings within a village site plan quite different from the traditional town plans in New York and New England.[1]

THE INSPIRED BUILDING

What was the source of the Shaker architectural pattern? The Shakers claimed divine inspiration as the source of their building design as well as their beliefs. Even though there is a general recognition that the Shakers built in the architectural idiom of American Neoclassicism, that style designation does not adequately explain Shaker building design, in fact it is really only appropriate for Shaker architecture of the so-called classic period of Shaker history, from 1815 to 1860.

Recent writers have postulated the origins of the Shaker architectural aesthetic in a wide variety of sources. Architectural historians look for cultural precedents and specific building prototypes. Some suggest a Christian monastic tradition with their cloistered communities, set apart from the world. However, the Shaker goal was not isolation for religious contemplation, but separation in order to regulate Shaker participation in society.

Other writers find a correlation between the Shaker concept of community and the communal dwelling houses of other utopian religious societies, such as the Moravians. The similarities in social organization, and even building types, are quite remarkable, but there is no documented contact between the two groups in the earliest stage of Shaker life. The Shakers did know about these German communitarian societies in the nineteenth century, but the chances of contact prior to the 1785 New Lebanon meetinghouse seem

Opposite ❖ CANTERBURY MEETINGHOUSE, 1792. Brothers' entrance to the left (north) and sisters' entrance to the right (south). The three-story gambrel, 32 × 42 ft. (9.76 × 12.8 m), was the Shaker pattern from the Mount, a unit of the template for first-generation Shaker buildings.

very remote, given language barriers, the fledgling nature of the Shaker movement, its pre-occupation with winning new converts, and the fact that the United States was at war with England until 1781.

A third potential source of architectural ideas is the architecture of American colonial colleges, since they experienced similar requirements to house and feed large numbers. Residence halls at Harvard, Yale, Princeton, and Brown Universities were multi-purpose buildings with dining halls that all predate the 1788 dwelling house at New Lebanon, but there is no direct evidence of Shaker borrowing. An argument for the influence of college architecture might be more easily made for the wave of new Shaker dwelling-house construction in the 1820s and 1830s, particularly in New Hampshire, where architect Ammi Young built a residence hall for Dartmouth College in 1828, then a dwelling house for the Enfield Shakers from 1837 to 1841.

Another theory contends that the Shakers adopted the urban reform mentality of institutions of social control in the early Republic. Useful comparisons can be made between Shaker community buildings and hospitals, asylums, and reform institutions (which establish a controlled environment to reform, heal, and isolate); indeed, many of these institutions also shared a common Quaker lineage. But most of these institutions were developing simultaneously with Shaker villages in the 1790s and early 1800s, and the Shaker pattern had already been established by 1785.

A fifth possible source of inspiration for Shaker architectural ideas lies in the industrial mill villages and workers' boardinghouses of England and America. The visual similarity in the early 1800s between the Shaker villages and New England mill villages must have been as striking to contemporary observers then as it is to scholars today. By the time the Shakers began making maps of their communities in the 1830s and 1840s, the Shaker villages were, in fact, small industrial villages, although they were also agricultural enterprises and religious communities. Again, these do not offer a satisfactory source, since the first Shaker villages predate 1790, the year industrialist Samuel Slater built his modest textile mill in Pawtucket, Rhode Island.

We are forced, then, to return to the idea that, whatever their sources, one or more Shaker leaders connected general architectural ideas with Shaker religious and cultural precepts to form a community plan and unique building types.

The Shakers had begun to develop their primary building type perhaps already in the early 1780s in Ashfield, Massachusetts, where, during a prolonged preaching mission, Mother Ann Lee erected a log meetinghouse with a gambrel roof.[2] Mother Ann and her successor, Father James Whittaker, were surely influential in determining the early Shaker "pattern from the Mount." Although they may have based some of their ideas on English prototypes—perhaps Puritan or Quaker—and applied them to American vernacular buildings, their chief contribution may have been in establishing precedents for the relationships between buildings and people.

Even without conclusive documentation of the specific sources of Shaker architectural ideas, we can safely assume that after Mother Ann's death in 1784, Whittaker, Elder Joseph Meacham, and master builder Moses Johnson were all major figures in the development and dissemination of the architectural pattern from the Mount, which may have served to memorialize the power of Mother Ann's ministry at Ashfield. A fourth leader, Father Job Bishop, was critical to the establishment of this pattern at the two New Hampshire communities, Canterbury and Enfield. Bishop's importance in New Hampshire community development is readily apparent when one compares the known Shaker site plans of Canterbury and Enfield. First, the pattern from the Mount seems to have covered only several core Church Family buildings: the meetinghouse; the first one, two, or three dwelling houses; the office; the ministry shop; and a few support buildings, such as the dwelling-house woodsheds. Second, the pattern did not require a particular site plan. Evidently, each Shaker community was left some discretion regarding orientation of the buildings in relation to each other and to the principal thoroughfare, as long as the meetinghouse and dwelling houses were closely aligned.

We have already seen that in the Canterbury site plan, the meetinghouse is on the southern edge of the village rather than near its center, to leave a substantial open dooryard between the road and its entrances. In addition, a dooryard, rather than a road, separates the meeting and dwelling houses. The original site plan of the Enfield community has been destroyed by modern development, but it has been preserved in an unfinished pencil sketch in the Canterbury archives. The original placement of the meetinghouse matches that of Canterbury in its distance from the road and its orientation to the dwelling-house row. Although the two villages developed differently in terms of the location of later families, the original Church Family site plan of the 1790s at Enfield is identical to Canterbury's core 1790s layout. The hand of Father Job Bishop rested firmly on the two New Hampshire Church Family communities through their respective histories.

The original Canterbury and Enfield site plans are virtually identical, but they are unmatched by any other Shaker communities. The first seven villages reveal the pattern from the Mount in their early core buildings, but display three variations in site plans: Watervliet contributes one variant in community planning, and the New Hampshire communities reveal a second variant of the pattern. In Massachusetts, the villages at Harvard, Shirley, and Hancock appear to approximate the pattern from the Mount more precisely than the two variants.

The explanation for Shaker architectural design probably lies in the Shaker concept of the community as a machine. In this sense, Shaker building can best be understood as a process that required the creation of a basic building template, the adaptation of known building traditions to communal living, and the placement of buildings in an original, intentional community plan.

THE INSPIRATION OF SPACE

The sparseness of the Shakers' exteriors belies the innovative manipulation of their interior spaces. Within their buildings, the Shakers developed an intensive use of all available space, organized it into distinctive Shaker patterns, and differentiated it according to gender and function. The result was a system of Shaker interior design marked by such features as dual entries and staircases, a profusion of storage units, and a repetition of Shaker peg rail. This system, which has no direct vernacular or academic sources, is one of the

SISTERS' ATTIC, the third floor of 1837 addition to the 1793 Church Family dwelling house. The double-walled storage area has seven walk-in closets and fourteen combination cupboards over drawers, containing eighty-four drawers. Other drawers in the attic bring the total to one hundred. The chimneys at the left served stoves in the Church Family ministry apartments on the second floor. The chimneys rest on the floor structure above the large meeting room on the first floor. At the basement level is a large room that was used for cold storage of meats and vegetables.

Opposite ❖ THIRD-FLOOR LANDING, SISTERS' STAIRCASE, DWELLING HOUSE. This staircase, which spans four floors, has an identical counterpart for brothers, on the opposite side of the hall. No wall separates them except on the attic level. The central staircase dates to 1837.

Shakers' most important contributions to the history of design. What most previous writers have failed to appreciate is that Shaker interior design expresses an industrial aesthetic of spare efficiency and potential replication. Shaker interiors are a successful application of industrial ideas to architectural design.

The New Hampshire Shakers were generally at the same level in building technology as their non-Shaker neighbors, although the Shakers were more advanced in the development and use of certain tools and technologies. (They are credited, for example, with the invention of the circular saw.) Their timber frames were assembled with traditional materials, methods, and tools.

The Shaker application of an industrial aesthetic is seen most readily in the organization and design of interior spaces of their core buildings, particularly the meetinghouse and dwelling houses. Anyone in the early nineteenth century who walked into a Shaker building for the first time knew this was a different world. Charles Dickens found Shaker interiors "grim"; other nineteenth-century visitors found them orderly but austere; and twentieth-century observers find them to be strikingly modern and pleasant, a skillful application of the principle "form follows function." In fact, the Shakers of the first generation were inventing new machines for living, working, and worshiping.

This first generation of Shaker interiors, though they were not identical in size or design, shared a number of features. They were uniformly well lit by natural light and highly organized for efficient use, with built-in cabinetry, ample shelving, and cupboards in basements, attics, and even remote attic knee-wall spaces. Rooms on the main floors were appointed with innumerable built-in cabinets and cupboards.

INFIRMARY ATTIC showing 1811 eaves cupboards modified in the late 1840s to incorporate drawers.

Although these numerous built-ins were custom made, they still fit a standardized industrial mold. They are in many cases detachable units, probably produced in a Shaker workshop to individual room specifications. Drawers, doors, and, in many cases, whole units were probably shop-produced, then brought in pieces or as units to their destination, and assembled and installed much like kitchen cabinets and library shelves today. The same principle holds true for Shaker peg rail; it could be made by the running foot, with pegs turned on water-powered lathes, placed into molded rails, and installed between the windows on all four sides of a Shaker room, and in double rows if desired. Such standardization of interiors is consistent with industrial design, and created an atmosphere of a prevailing style throughout the village. Standardization was a necessity if Shaker interiors were to serve the community's need for reinforcing order and facilitating the desired behavior.

Mass production was just as necessary as standardization but for different reasons. Given the enormous building program and the relatively small—and otherwise occupied—number of craftsmen, the Shaker brothers were forced to find more efficient ways to produce buildings and furnishings.

The Shakers' standardization and mass production of interiors in no way diminishes the originality of their interior design or the quality of the work in the years from 1792 to 1858. Surviving cabinetry and architecture from this period attest that Shaker woodworkers varied in skill levels similar to their Yankee neighbors, although the overall level of their workmanship is high. The Shakers rarely had the luxury to spend as much time for a job as it would take to reach true perfection, although in Canterbury there is exceptionally fine woodworking in the meetinghouse frame and interiors, the first dwelling house, and the stair hall and the built-in cabinetry of the dwelling-house addition of 1837. This highest level of achievement is also evident in the trustees' office of 1830–33 and in the 1848 ministry shop.

Substantial variation in Shaker interior work persists until the era of power machinery. It can be seen, for example, in the infinite variety of pegs found on Shaker peg rail throughout Canterbury. The basic concept of Shaker peg rail did not change from 1792 to the 1850s. Thousands of running feet of similar peg rail were made, but the pegs themselves are rarely the same length, diameter, or shape from one room to the next.

STAIR HALL, SCHOOLHOUSE, 1862–63.
The quality of Shaker carpentry generally declined at Canterbury after 1860, but the schoolhouse carpentry is an exception.

Peg rail is a classic example of how the Shakers refined a known architectural concept and adapted it for their particular purposes. The Shakers did not invent peg rail, but they were the first to use it to give a unique Shaker signature to every space. They made it an integral part of their interior aesthetic, and a symbol of Shaker community values such as order and harmony.

The Shakers of the late nineteenth century were restrained interior designers when compared to their middle-class urban counterparts, but they were influenced by Victorian tastes. As the pictures and surviving physical evidence reveal, Shaker interiors of the late nineteenth century were definitely Victorian in style, and looked nothing like the interiors of Shaker museums that follow the modern interpretations of austere Shaker design formulated by Edward Deming Andrews and William Winter in the 1930s.

However, there are Victorian accoutrements that are missing from Shaker interiors. The most obvious of these are textiles. Window draperies appear only in the form of a few white muslin gauze curtains. Upholstered furniture is limited to seat cushions and chair backs, although the Canterbury infirmary nurses had a Victorian daybed. Furniture scarves were used occasionally on lamp tables and case furniture. Woven room carpets are virtually nonexistent, but the Shakers wove some runners and small rugs to adorn offices, sitting rooms, and personal chambers.

The Shakers had practical reasons for their aversion to draperies and carpeting. Although money was probably of some concern, the Shakers were often enthralled with new products and had cash to spend on them when they wished. But draperies blocked light, and carpets and upholstery absorbed unhealthy dust and dirt. Instead of purchasing large quantities of rugs and textiles for their own use, the Shakers focused on manufacturing rug beaters for the people of the outside world, who needed them to keep their rugs decently clean.

Even though the Shakers were governed by an industrial aesthetic, they demonstrated that functional design can also serve the spirit.

THE CHANGING DIMENSIONS OF LIGHT

In New England, where light and warmth are elusive, darkness and cold seem ever present. Winter is always close at hand, in some stage of coming or going. New Englanders learned to adapt their work to take advantage of the sun's precious light. The climate of New England reinforced vernacular building traditions such as the central chimney stack, a southern orientation for building facades, and the minimal use of windows.

The Shakers were in the vanguard of developing new architectural designs and technologies for maximizing light. In an effort to squeeze maximum efficiency from sunlight, the Shakers looked to prototypes in the mills of the burgeoning American metalworking and textile industries. Mill owners sought to maximize the penetration of daylight into their new factories, packing as many windows on outside walls as possible without undermining structural integrity. By emphasizing the southern and northern facades of a relatively narrow building, the industrialists could allow the maximum penetration of light on interior work space all day long, from at least two directions. The east and west walls likewise had many windows and doors, for a long, productive workday was more important than conserving heat for workers.

The Shakers accepted the expense of the added panels of glass as a necessary capital investment. This maximum use of windows was doubly important in the period from 1790 to 1860, for artificial lighting of the era used an open flame. Candles, lanterns, and lamps were highly dangerous, especially in textile mills, where dust explosions were a constant fear.

In addition to maximizing natural light through windows, the Shakers used skylights. These were features of Neoclassical architecture, but the Shakers were among the first to introduce them to vernacular building. Even more innovative was their use of "borrowed light" by penetrating interior walls with "windows" to brighten darker spaces.

Interior windows, or pass-throughs, eventually became fashionable in American housing in the Victorian era, but they were rare prior to the 1840s and 1850s. Among the Shakers, the practice had gained acceptance as early as the 1820s in a few locations, and

Below ❖ SISTERS' SHOP, VIEW LOOKING WEST, 1816. The extensive fenestration maximized the daylight and facilitated the sisters' work.

Overleaf ❖ VIEW FROM THE SOUTH OF CUPOLA AND DORMERS, DWELLING HOUSE. The present gable dormers were added to the roof in the early twentieth century. The building in the foreground is Enfield House, originally constructed in 1824 as the Second Family office and moved to the Church Family in 1918.

LAUNDRY IRONING ROOM WITH
CANTERBURY IRONING TABLE. The ample
daylight is cast into the work area from windows
on three sides.

by the 1830s and 1840s interior windows were used extensively. At Canterbury, many of the finest examples are found in the 1830–33 trustees' office and the 1837 dwelling-house chapel wing.

Nearly every interior space at Canterbury, except for closets and storage rooms, has exposure to natural light on two sides.[3] This attention to exploiting all sources of light is one of the crowning achievements that set Shaker building apart from other contemporary domestic vernacular buildings in rural New England.

At least since the late eighteenth century in Western society, interior fashions have dictated a wide range of window decoration, which seems to have originated in a love of ornamentation, a need for privacy, and the need to reduce the intensity of light on interior surfaces and furnishings.

The use of textile window coverings was never common at Canterbury, even in the twentieth century. Green spring-roller shades were used to control light in the late nineteenth century. Prior to the introduction of roller shades, the Shakers relied on a variety of shutter systems, usually placed on the interiors of buildings. These shutters, most often solid wooden panels, were probably used more to control drafts and retain warmth in winter than to control light. Since the Shakers rose before daybreak and did not retire until well after sunset, they had little need for blocking the sunlight except to cool their retiring rooms on the hottest summer days.

Unlike urban dwellers, the Shakers did not have to consider intrusion into privacy as a disadvantage of street-level windows. Strangers were not permitted in living and work spaces unless invited, and then were always accompanied by members of the community. Uncovered Shaker windows, therefore, permitted two-way visual communication.[4]

Windows were also monitors. With several hundred pairs of Shaker eyes and several hundred of these architectural eyes of glass, the comings and goings of every individual Shaker or hired person were on full view. This all-seeing system fostered familial sentiments and congeniality, but it also could reinforce community standards of propriety and order by virtually eliminating privacy, at least in daylight hours. Windows connected interior and exterior spaces and the people on the inside and outside.[5] The many large, uncovered windows were practical devices for controlling light, an aesthetic expression of Shaker design, and reinforcers of community order.

THE COLOR PALETTE

The colors of building exteriors, interiors, and furnishings were integral parts of the Shaker system. Shaker watercolor maps of their villages and surviving buildings and furnishings reveal that the Shaker palette before 1850 was dominated by shades of white, blue, yellow, red, green, and a few combinations of these basic colors, such as orange. This palette is not uniquely Shaker; from the 1780s, Americans all along the eastern seaboard had equal access to paint color if they could afford it. Paint color is, in its most elemental nature, a combination of pigment, medium, and binding agent. Before 1850 color choice was primarily limited by technology, availability of commercial pigments, and price. After 1850 the increase of commercial paint colors and the decline in the price of paint opened up a new palette to the Victorian world, including the Shakers.[6]

Color is also a cultural phenomenon. The choices of color; its placement on ceilings, walls, floors, woodwork, and furnishings; and the particular harmonic relationships (color to color, painted to unpainted, objects to interiors) express deliberate decisions. The cultural application of color by the Shakers before 1850 was distinctive.

The Shakers color-coded most of their buildings on the exterior and interior—particularly their meetinghouses, dwelling houses, office, and shops. Since they color-coded areas never seen by visitors, this system of color language was clearly designed to speak to the inhabitants of the Shaker communities—children, newcomers, hired help, mature believers. By the 1820s, when the painting of building exteriors was virtually complete, no one in the village could possibly forget the buildings' roles and ranks in the community.

After the 1820s the Shakers began to record their system of color coding in the Millennial Laws. Although these writings described the color system, they did not explain the meaning of the colors assigned to specific areas or classes of objects. It is tempting to ascribe specific symbolisms to blue, white, red, yellow, and green. However, specific designations (white for purity, or yellow for heavenly richness) are speculative, and miss the central meaning of Shaker color coding. The issue is not whether the Shakers used the same colors as the outside world (they did), or borrowed ideas from Neoclassical trends in interior decoration (they did), but how the Shakers creatively applied color

VIEW FROM THE SOUTH OF THE NORTH
SHOP, painted white in the twentieth century, and
the syrup shop, painted with the yellow ocher
siding and dark red trim of the late 1840s. Note the
red painted shingle roof on the entry of the syrup
shop. Red paint was regularly applied to roofs in the
village from 1808 to the 1850s.

choices to create their own cultural color system. Therefore, we should look at the purpose
of the overall Shaker color code rather than for specific meanings of particular colors.[7]

Canterbury Shaker Village's paint history may be divided into four general
periods. In the first period, from 1792 to 1807, in order to conserve time and money, no
buildings were painted except for the meetinghouse, which was painted white in 1794,
with interior woodwork on the upper and lower stories painted a brilliant dark blue. The
meetinghouse floors remained unpainted. In 1807 the first dwelling house was painted
"French yellow," inaugurating a period of painted buildings for the Shakers. The dwelling
houses and trustees' office interiors were yellow with accents of red, and work areas were
mostly red. Floors were unpainted in the meetinghouse, yellow in dwelling houses, and
yellowish orange or orange-red in work areas, if painted at all. According to Henry Clay
Blinn, the decision to paint was reached only after considerable debate within the community and after a visit by the New Hampshire Ministry to New Lebanon for consulta-
tion with the Central Ministry.[8]

Already by the start of the second period of color history at Canterbury, from 1807 to 1860, there must have been some unwritten guidelines for the use of color in village buildings. These color principles were formally codified in 1821 by the Central Ministry as part of the Millennial Laws. By the time of the 1845 expansion of the laws, there were a number of instructions for using color in architectural situations, including:

3. *The meetinghouse should be painted white without, and of a bluish shade within. Houses and shops, should be as near uniform in color, as consistent; but it is advisable to have shops of a little darker shade than dwelling house.*

4. *Floors in dwelling houses, if stained at all, should be a reddish yellow, and shop floors should be a yellowish red.*

5. *It is inadvisable for wooden buildings, fronting the street, to be painted red, brown, or black, but they should be of a lightish hue.*

6. *No buildings may be painted white, save the meetinghouse.*

7. *Barns and back buildings, as wood houses, etc., if painted at all, should be of a dark hue, either red, or brown, lead color, or something of the kind, unless they front the road, or command a sightly aspect, and then they should not be a very light color.*[9]

In general, the Shakers' hierarchical color code accentuated the exterior of the meetinghouse and scaled back the brilliance of the color according to location and building type, so the structures on the edges of the village (barns, warehouses, and mills) were protected with the cheapest pigments in the darkest colors—if they were painted at all. By 1831, when Nathaniel Hawthorne reported on his visit to the village, the exteriors were predominantly yellow, with red roofs. The interior woodwork of these buildings (including door and window surrounds, peg rail, and built-in furniture) was mostly dark yellow, with red baseboards and some orange and yellow paint on floors. Between 1830 and 1860, chrome yellow replaced the somber yellow ocher and a vermilion red appears as an accent on peg rails, stair railings, and some built-in cabinetry in place of the dark red of earlier years. Ceilings and walls remained white throughout the village from 1807 to 1860.

The third color period, from 1860 to 1925, began the year the Central Ministry granted permission for white paint to be used to "lighten the interiors" of their buildings. Many of the existing vibrant but dark interior color schemes were repainted white. New exteriors were generally painted in two-tone color schemes; combinations included a gray body with white trim (east house, 1900; syrup shop, 1903), a dark gray-green body with white trim (schoolhouse, c. 1915), a white body with dark red trim (steel garage, 1923), a red brick and green clapboard body with cream trim (laundry, 1903). In a few cases, pastel shades of green, gray, blue, and tan were incorporated into the two-tone interior color schemes that appear in the 1890–1915 period. White paint again dominates work and residential interiors after 1915.

In the fourth period, from about 1925 through the 1940s, all the buildings within the village—with the exception of the powerhouse, firehouse, steel garage, and agricultural and mill buildings—were eventually painted white. The last building to retain its

Above, left ❖ WOODWORK, THIRD-FLOOR OF 1792 MEETINGHOUSE. This shows the original Prussian blue and orange-red paints. The interior of the cupboard has been protected from more than two hundred years of light damage.

Above, right ❖ WOODWORK, THIRD FLOOR OF 1793 DWELLING HOUSE, with yellow ocher rail and cupboard, and dark red baseboard.

Opposite ❖ SOUTH FACADE OF INFIRMARY, painted in three-tone color scheme, c. 1892. Paint analysis in 1992 revealed that this building had been repainted in 1892 after the addition of a kitchen ell.

pre-1860 colors was the carriage house (called the "yellow house" by the Shakers), which remained yellow through World War II.

Our knowledge of the Shakers' use of color after 1860 is still incomplete. This period, which corresponds to the Victorian era in architectural and interior decoration, has received little attention from Shaker scholars, who have concentrated their efforts mostly on the so-called classic period of 1815 to 1860. Victorian Shaker studies have focused mostly on textiles, fancywork, furniture, and printed ephemera. Even with the scholarly attention given to Victorian-era Shaker furniture in Jean Burks and Tim Rieman's *Complete Book of Shaker Furniture,* interest in these objects by the art and antiques market has been lukewarm.

An assumption of this attitude toward the Shakers of the Victorian era is that the Shaker movement declined significantly in numbers and energy after 1860, and lost its integrity in important ways—in innovation, design, skill levels, and spirituality. Although the Shaker movement entered a period of rapid decline in the 1860s and 1870s and the nature of the Shaker experience changed, the community at Canterbury was still vibrant in the late nineteenth century. Since color is an overt part of the Shaker system of signs, the evolution of the system of interior and exterior color coding is important for identifying and understanding how the community changed over time.

In general, the change in the exterior Shaker color palette is a more controlled version of the patterns of Victorian house painting (dark body, light trim), in which the color is kept to a range of grays and off-whites. Up to 1900, these were sometimes quite intense colors (as in the lavender gray of the infirmary), but after 1900 they settle into a more uniformly light or medium gray with white trim.

BROTHERS' DOOR, 1792 MEETINGHOUSE.
The light blue paint was added in 1878 to replace the
original Prussian blue of the meetinghouse interior.
The room has not been repainted since 1878.

On the interiors, we have already noted the Shaker desire to lighten the interiors of their dwelling houses and some work spaces. In fact, surviving evidence of numerous coats of cream-colored or white paint show that the Shaker trend of the 1860s became the interior norm of the twentieth century. However, the late nineteenth century witnessed two other interior color schemes, which are rarely mentioned in literature about Shaker material culture: two-tone combinations, and the increasing emphasis upon natural wood tones and simulated wood graining. There are several examples of architectural wood graining at Canterbury, mostly on doors.[10]

Numerous interior surfaces at Canterbury still bear their original finish. These include the 1892 infirmary kitchen (new wing), the 1905 creamery (new building), the 1908 laundry (renovation), and the 1917 sisters' comfort room in the dwelling house (renovation), to name the four most prominent examples. These interiors reflect an Arts and Crafts aesthetic as much as a Shaker one, for nearly all display the dark orange tones of hard pine finished with orange shellac. Neither the wood (southern yellow pine) nor the finish reflect a Shaker sensibility except that they are eminently modern, practical, and able to withstand wear and tear, and they required little upkeep from the rapidly diminishing Shaker brotherhood.

DECORATION OF FLOORS AND WALLS

In the Victorian era the Shakers controlled the interior color palette of wall and floor coverings as well as painted surfaces. Their interest in technology is reflected in new materials—most notably in linoleum floor coverings and pressed-tin wall and ceiling panels—and in new colors and their combinations.

Starting in the 1860s and continuing over the next several decades, most high-use areas in Shaker buildings underwent a transformation. Although general Victorian decorative ideas are behind these Shaker renovations, the ideas were put to the service of an unmistakably Shaker style.

The use of wallpaper is a case in point. Its first use at Canterbury is not recorded, but a number of late-nineteenth-century patterns have been found in closets in the children's house, the dwelling house, and the ministry shop, indicating that the use of wallpaper in these buildings was once widespread.[11] Wallpapered rooms survive in other residential areas, such as the trustees' office, Enfield House, and on the second floor of the syrup shop, in a room used as a painting studio for Sister Cora Helena Sarle. Work areas retain their plain white walls.

The Canterbury Shakers found two uses for decorative pressed tin, first for the spot treatment of work areas where the risk of fire was strong—in the laundry engine room, woodworking shop, and the trustees' office kitchen. The use of tin primarily for decoration appears in the trustees' office dining room and in the 1908 addition to the trustees' office that was intended for welcoming visitors and establishing a Shaker gift shop. Generally, the pressed tin in work areas was painted gray. The trustees' office dining room is decorated with elaborate bas-relief tinwork, which is painted several shades of green to accent the wainscoting, walls, and ceiling. The most High Victorian space of all was in the addition to the trustees' office, which has burgundy wainscoting and cream-colored walls, and is further decorated with paintings and prints hung in Victorian fashion by picture wire from the cornice molding.

A transformation in Shaker floor treatments also occurred in the late nineteenth century. Prior to the 1860s the Shakers did not generally use floor coverings, just as they eschewed window hangings. After the 1860s they introduced them sparingly, although they never adopted Victorian carpeting or room rugs, preferring small handwoven Shaker rugs and some early Shaker floorcloths. Examples in either category are now extremely rare because most Shaker-made floor coverings were worn out and discarded. Fragments of both types survive in the Canterbury collections.

About 1880 the Canterbury Shakers began to use commercially produced linoleum, the newest technology in floor coverings. This new wall-to-wall flooring completely supplanted the Shaker-made floorcloths, which were designed for high-traffic areas such as hallways and never completely covered the original wood floors. Small Shaker-made textile rugs continued to be used over linoleum in sleeping chambers and other selected areas. Linoleum was a perfect expression of the late-nineteenth-century Shaker aesthetic, and the Shakers saw no inconsistency in using the material in traditional Shaker settings, such as sleeping chambers and sitting rooms. They also used it freely in work areas and passages for which linoleum was originally intended, and where it was used by most Americans and Europeans before 1915.

Both floorcloths and linoleum were first produced in England and Scotland. Linoleum was patented in 1863 by Frederick Walton, who established his first factory at Staines, near London. By the 1870s there were American factories in New Jersey and New York, with retailers in major East Coast cities. Interest in the products exploded across the country in the 1890s with the development of the Montgomery Ward and Sears, Roebuck mail-order catalogs.

The documentary record of the Shakers' first use of floorcloths and linoleum is sketchy, with almost no sale bills or journal references other than a reference to the installation of new linoleum in the infirmary in 1924 (which is stamped "Staines & Co.") and to the new linoleum in the dwelling-house dining room in 1939.[12] Commercial floor coverings were used in Canterbury from approximately 1880 to 1939; linoleum is documented by late-nineteenth-century photographs of Canterbury and other Shaker villages, including New Lebanon and Enfield (New Hampshire), and many commercial floorcloths and linoleum still survive in Canterbury buildings.

The patterns and colors of linoleum fit the Shakers' aesthetic system. Floorcloths and linoleum were originally created as substitute products for more expensive tile or carpeting, and linoleum patterns ranged from geometric to floral, imitating popular tile and carpet design. From the multitude of patterns, the Shakers consistently chose geometric designs, which imitated the more sober tile and ingrain carpet designs rather than floral carpets or oriental rugs, and which were compatible with the geometry of Shaker interior design. They chose a narrow palette of conservative colors; in the linoleum at Canterbury various shades of green and brown dominate, with accents of black, cream, and occasionally yellow, blue, gray, or pink. Their selectivity is especially apparent when the Shaker

patterns are compared with many pattern and color options illustrated in surviving manu-facturers' trade catalogs and turn-of-the-century mail-order catalogs.

The price of linoleum was directly correlated to quality, and it could differ markedly from the top to the bottom of the manufacturers' lines. On quality, the Shakers were not consistent: they occasionally bought cheap goods, and in a few instances pur-chased high-quality floor coverings. Generally, they were satisfied with middle-grade goods in their color and pattern preferences. A striking feature of Shaker use, however, is the practice of multiple patterns within one building (even though single-pattern installa-tion was more economical, since waste was kept to a minimum). In the dwelling house at Canterbury, for example, each room has a different pattern, with another pattern in hall-ways, still another in the central stair hall. This may simply be the result of piecemeal installation. In Enfield House, which was moved and remodeled in 1917–18 for the elderly sisters from Enfield, the same few linoleum patterns were used throughout the building.

Since the Shakers never adopted the full range of Victorian floor covering op-tions (China matting, mosaic tiles, woven carpets) and since they had made their own floorcloths for years before linoleum was available, they were enthusiastic about the new product. The last Shaker at Canterbury, Sister Ethel Hudson, remembered the relief and joy shared by the sisters when the dwelling-house dining-room floor was finally covered in linoleum, which, compared to the old wooden floors, was so easily cleaned and waxed.

The Shakers had many practical reasons for using linoleum, but their enthusiasm for it went far beyond its durability and easy maintenance. The product appealed to their aesthetic sense, fit into their value system, and reinforced their concept of order.

❖

Opposite ❖ WOODWORK, THIRD-FLOOR SISTERS' RETIRING ROOM in the dwelling house, c. 1900, with two-tone green and white trim, and green and tan linoleum.

WORSHIP AND INDUSTRY

The Shakers established their planned communities, such as Canterbury, for the purpose of accomplishing their twin mandates, "Hands to work, hearts to God." Their material world was self-consciously formed to communicate Shaker beliefs, facilitate community order, and regulate contact between the Shakers and the outside world.

The Shakers departed from many fundamental Protestant beliefs and developed unorthodox practices of worship. Although in the minimalism of their liturgy they had direct antecedents in the Quakers, the Shakers rejected most Quaker religious practice.

DANCING AS WORSHIP

The early hallmark of Shaker worship was religious dance (which they also called "exercises" and "laboring"). Even though group dancing is an ancient form of religious expression and a traditional human bonding ritual,[1] American Protestants were highly suspicious of the practice, as evidenced by the Puritan suppression of maypole dances in seventeenth-century New England and reports on the scandalous Shaker excesses in various eighteenth- and nineteenth-century journal accounts.

FATHER JAMES WHITTAKER'S BIBLE, printed in Edinburgh by Robert Freebairn, 1736. Although the Shakers had many distinctive beliefs, they accepted the Bible as the foundation for Christian belief and practice. This Bible was brought to New Hampshire by Shaker preacher Ebenezer Cooley of New Lebanon, New York.

Right ❖ "THE CONGREGATION OF STRANGERS AFTER LEAVING THE CHURCH, JUNE 30, 1878." Stereoscopic view by Kimball Studio of Concord, New Hampshire.

Opposite ❖ PLEASANT GROVE, detail from map of Canterbury Shaker Village by Henry Clay Blinn, c. 1848. Canterbury's outdoor dance ground was laid out in 1843 one and one-half miles north of the Church Family. The first meeting at Pleasant Grove was held on October 15, 1843, with several spiritual "treasures" received through the Shaker "instruments" or mediums. A one-story structure was built in 1844; the dance ground was enclosed by a fence and fir trees in 1845; and in 1848 an Italian marble slab was carved and installed. The stone, fence, and building (which were all white) were removed in 1861.

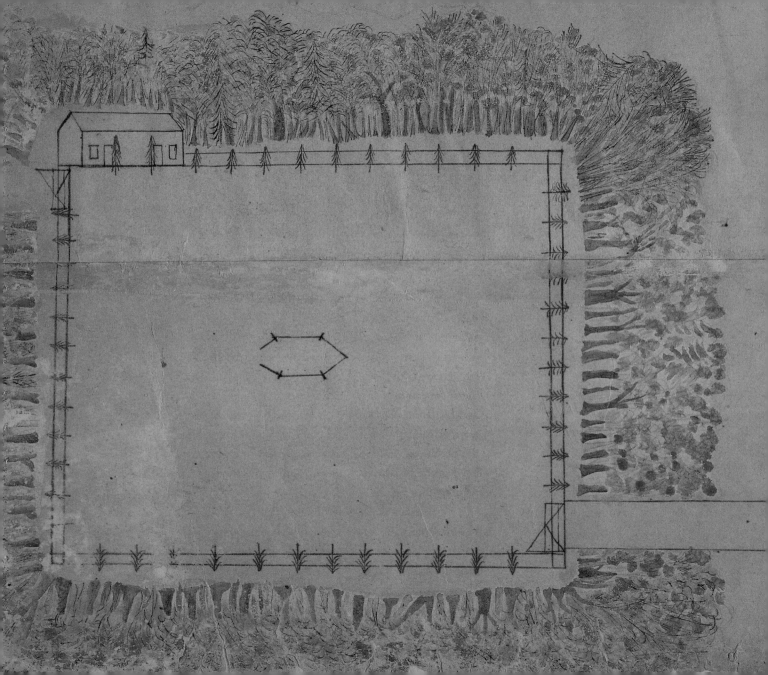

SHAKERS NEAR LEBANON, NEW YORK,
lithograph, c. 1830. Collection of The Winterthur
Library: The Edward Deming Andrews
Memorial Collection.

The evolution of Shaker dance style from its early stages in England to its formalization in marches and "laborings" spans more than fifty years of Shaker history. Early Shaker dance was ecstatic and individualistic, with much whirling, jumping, and falling to the floor, and any believer could spontaneously express himself in dance. Later on, in the early nineteenth century Father Joseph Meacham of New Lebanon, through his writings and verbal instructions, imposed discipline, order, and organization on many aspects of Shaker life, including worship practices. As a result, the most irregular and charismatic aspects of Shaker dance were standardized. Group marches and dances were introduced by the Central Ministry in New Lebanon; these circulated to most of the Shaker communities, and men and women were instructed to dance in orderly, practiced ranks and patterns. Admission to the privilege of worship through dance was also regulated for believers.

Shaker dance was observed by numerous eighteenth- and nineteenth-century visitors from the outside world, but the descriptions are generally very subjective and impressionistic. A few historical prints depicting Shaker dance were circulated in the nineteenth century, but these only hint at the true character of this vital group ritual. Some Shaker written accounts are excellent in revealing changes in community dance practice and in capturing the spiritual intensity of the dancing, especially during the Era of Spirit Manifestations (also referred to by the Shakers as "Mother Ann's Work"). This was a period of intense spiritualistic and revivalist activity from 1837 to 1845, when some young girls became "mediums" to receive "gifts" of new Shaker songs, marches, and dances. Although for the Shakers, dance was generally confined to worship, it did not necessarily take place in the meetinghouse.[2] Documentary references abound for the frequency of religious dance at the Canterbury outdoor dance ground, Pleasant Grove, from 1843 to the mid-1850s.

Dance remained a central component of Shaker worship until the late nineteenth century, when most remaining communities laid aside the gift of dance, probably due to the aging of community members and the decline in the number of brothers.

At Canterbury the waning of dance as worship led to the creation of a remarkable dance manuscript by Sister Julia Briggs (1816–1891) that confirms the vitality of the music and dance traditions at the New Hampshire communities. Briggs, who entered the Canterbury community with her three children in 1852, recorded diagrams and written instructions for twelve group dances and marches, either in the hope of encouraging the younger sisters to continue the practice, or to preserve an important ritual before all memory of it had been eclipsed in the Canterbury community.

The dance manual is the only document of its kind to survive from Canterbury, and it is extremely rare even within the larger Shaker context, because it provides sufficient detail for the dances to be learned. She identifies the origin of each dance by community (all but one are from Enfield and Canterbury), and in one case she documents that the "double square" originated at Canterbury in 1838.[3] This date is important because it coincides with both the completion of the chapel addition to the original dwelling house, and the onset of the Era of Spirit Manifestations within the larger Shaker movement.

In fact, we can date many of the important Shaker dances to the fall of 1837, when the Era of Spirit Manifestations at the New Hampshire communities commenced. Visionary mediums—first among the communities' young women, then their ministries—were inspired to perform new songs and dances, providing for the first time a direct source of new inspiration outside the Central Ministry at New Lebanon. Of the twelve dances diagrammed by Briggs, seven are also mentioned by Henry Clay Blinn as "gift" dances of this first phase of spirit manifestations: the double square, mother's star, cross and diamond, mother's love, Elder Benjamin's cross, finished cross, and square and compass.

DANCE DIAGRAM from Shaker sister Julia Briggs's dance manual.

MEETINGHOUSE FLOOR, showing four examples of permanent dancing cues.

DIAGRAMS OF THE ROWS OF DANCE CUES
(prepared by Richard Conway Meyer, with Dan
Holmes and Jon Norling).

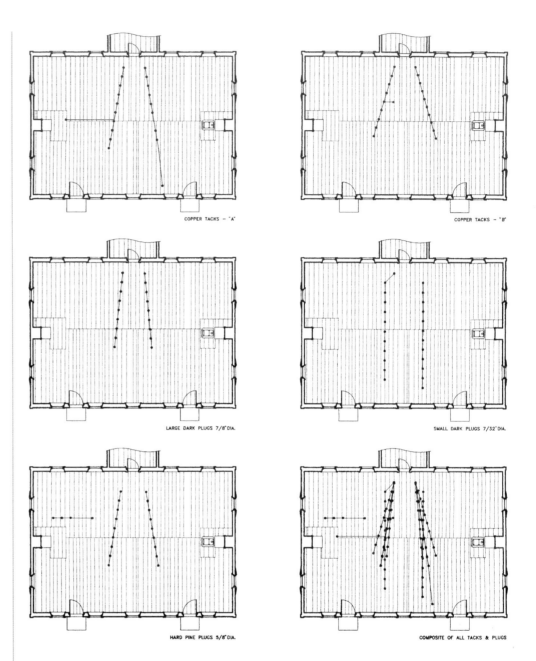

COPPER TACKS – "A"

COPPER TACKS – "B"

LARGE DARK PLUGS 7/8" DIA.

SMALL DARK PLUGS 7/32" DIA.

HARD PINE PLUGS 5/8" DIA.

COMPOSITE OF ALL TACKS & PLUGS

*Almost the first thing I noticed was a line of black
pegs equidistant from each other, and about one foot
apart, made even with the floor, to assist the front
rank in forming a straight line. As the Brethren
entered the room, they removed their hats and coats
and hung them upon wooden pegs which lined the
sides of the room. The Sisters also removed their
bonnets. Then, standing for a moment in perfect
silence, they seated themselves, the Brothers and
Sisters facing each other. . . . Then they arose as by
common consent and stood in silence while the
benches in the center of the room were removed.
The Brethren faced the Sisters, who modestly cast
their eyes to the floor, while one of the Elders from
the center of the group addressed them with a few
words of exhortation. At the conclusion of his remarks,
they bowed their heads for a few moments, when they
commenced the singing of a hymn. . . . This hymn,
of which there were several verses, was sung to an
appropriate tune, without the use of instrumental
music, they all the while keeping time with their feet
and with a rocking movement of the body. Then
after a short interval, one of the Sisters in the front
rank started the words of a hymn, in which they all
joined, marching backward and forward.*

—CHARLES EDSON ROBINSON,
The Shakers and Their Homes, 1893

Blinn also mentions at least six other "gift exercises" from this period that Briggs did not
include, leaving us with at least eighteen recorded dances from the period from 1837 to
1845. Especially after the Era of Spirit Manifestations, the Shakers tolerated new gifts of
dance and tried to channel them into appropriate outlets for group expression.

During this period the Shakers made remarkable developments in their architectural and industrial activities, and they brought similar principles of precision and standardization to their dance. Dances were carefully rehearsed in evening practice sessions in
order to guarantee proper harmony and order in the public worship. At Canterbury a remarkable survival of this precision is still visible in the red pine floor of the meetinghouse.
As dancing developed, and as dance formations became more numerous and intricate, the

Shakers embedded cues in their dance floor. These cues—for example, wooden plugs or copper tacks—form five rows of markers, some in straight lines and some in flaring lines.

Unfortunately, Julia Briggs's manuscript did not inspire the young Canterbury sisters to learn the old Shaker dances. Florence Phelps (who eventually left the Canterbury community) recalled a time in the 1890s when an older Shaker sister came to the young people's meeting to teach a dance. The exercise provoked such hilarity that the sister abandoned her efforts, and Shaker dance remained a quaint relic of a distant past.[4]

Why did the Shakers choose the dance? Dancing as worship immediately brought new believers into the Shaker cultural and religious framework. To dance in a church crossed an unequivocal threshold from mainstream Protestantism to Shakerism: to bring marching, clapping, and whirling into a sacred space and elevate it above the word of God spoken by ordained ministers was simply heretical to most Protestants.

Dance affirmed and celebrated that the believer had a communal—not an individual—relationship with God. Shaker dance was therefore a powerful symbol in the Shaker cultural system.

Music was more problematic in the early history of the Shakers. Since music, unlike dance, was a part of traditional Protestant worship, the Shakers for a time stopped using song lyrics until believers could compose appropriate hymns. In place of words, the Shakers substituted clapping, shouting, stomping, and "solemn songs," which were tunes without words that permitted an individual to insert a "select sentence, as special to themselves."[5]

At first the Shakers borrowed tunes from the repertoire of secular folk songs and ballads (a fact that startled the English traveler James Buckingham when he recognized a Scottish ballad in a Shaker worship). Over time the Shakers composed new music, as well as words, for their hymns. These early hymns were often revival songs written by the western Shakers, particularly by Richard McNemar, of Union Village, Ohio. In 1813 the first Shaker hymnal, *Millennial Praises,* was published in Hancock, Massachusetts.

The importance of Shaker music to Shaker religious life cannot be overstated. The Shakers generally found vocal music to be a rich, expressive, and enduring language. Canterbury was one of the most musically progressive societies, prodding New Lebanon in the 1870s into accepting musical instruments. The Canterbury community published the last Shaker hymnal in 1908.[6]

Shaker dance and song generated group solidarity and provided avenues of inspiration. In worship, Shaker dance and song provided an exhilarating outlet for emotional expression that was rarely encouraged elsewhere in Shaker life.

On the 16th of April 1847, the Church Family marched to the "Pleasant Grove." They left the Family Dwelling at 1 o'clock P.M. and returned at 4-30. The marching was usually accompanied by singing, which was continued a greater part of the way in going and also in returning. This practice of marching and singing while away from the dwellings became quite common.

—HENRY CLAY BLINN,
"A Historical Record of the Society of Believers in Canterbury, New Hampshire," 1892

FIVE HYMNALS AND SONGBOOKS USED BY THE CANTERBURY SHAKERS. The large open songbook, with early "quick" and "walking" songs, contains Shaker letter music notation. The small open music book, with handwritten musical notes, dates to the early twentieth century, but contains songs composed by "DAD" (Dorothy Ann Durgin) in the 1860s.

SHAKER SISTERS in front of the Canterbury meetinghouse, c. 1920. By this time the "old church" was used for worship only in the summer, and all dancing at worship had ceased. Most of the year the Shakers worshiped in the dwelling-house chapel.

DWELLING-HOUSE CHAPEL, c. 1925. In 1929, a used Hook and Hastings pipe organ was installed (upper left). Musical instruments had been introduced at Canterbury in the late 1870s, when music lessons by outside teachers were also introduced, for voice and instrument.

COMMERCE AND INDUSTRY

In the post–Revolutionary War era the centers of wealth and trade in New England were the port cities of the eastern seaboard such as Portsmouth in New Hampshire, and Salem, Newburyport, and Boston in Massachusetts. The Shakers shunned this urban, mercantile America and clustered in rural areas, where farming was the primary economic activity, supported by domestic trades such as blacksmithing, tanning, and weaving. The Shaker message found a favorable reception among small farmers and tradespeople.

In order for the Shakers to implement their ambitious plan to transform religion and society, they had to support themselves. At first, new converts donated land, live-stock, furnishings, and cash to the Shaker cause to launch the building of villages. These same converts continued to farm or practice their trades to generate desperately needed capital, and the newly organized Shaker societies established businesses as quickly as they could. Once a Shaker community had built their meetinghouse and at least one dwelling house, they began building tanneries, blacksmith's shops, and mills to provide for their own needs and stimulate commerce.

In each new Shaker community after New Lebanon's organization in the 1780s, commerce centered on the building trades as the Shakers sought to create adequate phys-ical facilities, and the agricultural trades as they sought to maintain and improve upon the farms donated by early converts. The first cash products were generated by the traditional rural American trades. At Canterbury, for example, these were the products of the tannery (1793) and the blacksmith's shop (1793), which under Francis Winkley, the village black-smith, produced nails and hardware for the aggressive building program and hardware and candlesticks for sale.

In the 1790s the Canterbury Shakers began to manufacture nearly every necessity of life—candlesticks, clothing, hats, bonnets, shoes, harnesses, leather goods, hardware, brass clocks, boxes, pails, sieves, scythes, and shovels. They also produced other necessi-ties, such as garden seeds, medicines, wool cards, spinning wheels, linen and woolen cloth, and brooms.

To manage the business aspect of Shaker life, each Shaker family within the Canterbury society had two office deacons, commonly known as trustees, and two office deaconnesses, usually called office sisters, the community business leaders. Since each family operated autonomously within the larger cooperative framework, each built a sepa-rate office to house the business functions of its trustees. Generally, the trustees lived in the offices, which also housed a dining room and overnight accommodations for hosting business visitors.

The Shakers challenged nearly every tenet of American economic life in the late eighteenth century by organizing into communitarian societies owned by their cove-nanted members. In turning over their personal property to the Shakers and accepting the terms of "joint interest" stated in the Shaker covenant, they eliminated what in their way of thinking was "wage slavery" for daily labor, and worked for the collective good of the community. In turn, individual members were provided with a secure home environment, ample food, adequate clothing, warm shelter, rewarding work, guaranteed health care, and a burial plot. Money became irrelevant to the daily life of the Shaker brothers and

Opposite ❖ CHURCH FAMILY HORSE BARN, on Shaker Road, 1819, restored in 1990. This was one of several buildings, which included barns and a small warehouse, situated on Shaker Road that served the needs of trustees and outside visitors.

TRUSTEES' OFFICE, 1830–33, with early-twentieth-century porches and porte-cochere. Like Shaker dwellings, the original building (42 × 72 ft. [12.8 × 22 m]) was divided in half, with the sisters' quarters and kitchen to the south, and the brothers' section to the north.

sisters, and even the elders and eldresses, except when traveling outside the community. Trustees handled all the commercial and financial transactions of village life, although until the late 1830s Shaker physicians directed the businesses of seeds and medicines.

Even though the Shakers challenged the fortress of emerging capitalism by rejecting individual ownership of property and the profit motive, they were aggressive entrepreneurs. In this respect, they were in the vanguard of modern American corporate life. The Shakers wanted maximum productivity from their workers, and maximum benefit from their labor, but Shaker earnings were invested back into the community enterprises, encouraging still greater growth and productivity.[7]

The Shaker economy can be characterized as entrepreneurial communism because of the aggressive economic behavior of the Shakers. Ralph Waldo Emerson paid numerous visits to Shaker communities, including trips to Canterbury in 1828–29 and 1842. His interpretation of the Shaker economy was that it was a form of "people's capitalism" in which the capitalist never dies and every member has a stake.

Above, left ❖ DAVID PARKER (1807–1867), a Canterbury trustee who managed Shaker businesses, was an effective liaison with all segments of contemporary society outside the Shaker community.

Above, right ❖ PATENT MODEL FOR A COMMERCIAL WASHING MACHINE that trustee David Parker patented on January 26, 1858.

Clearly, whatever the characterization, the Shaker economy was based not on subsistence farming but on the sale of surplus, and the form of economic organization was communistic. Their entrepreneurial attitudes toward work of all kinds led nearly every Shaker community to achieve notable progress in commercial farming—including crop, timber, and livestock production, and the profitable Shaker herb and seed businesses.

The accumulation of capital at Canterbury was impressive by early-nineteenth-century standards. By the 1830s, the Shakers were rich in buildings, land, cash, woodlots, livestock, farm produce, industry, community possessions, and community skills.

The Shakers' work ethic and managerial focus enabled them to outperform most of their neighbors in the towns and villages of New Hampshire and to ride through the economic depressions of the first half of the nineteenth century. With no concern about profit taking, they plowed their early cash surpluses back into more land, additional buildings, new industries, and improved machinery. After the Civil War the national economy overwhelmed them, but for over one hundred years the hardworking Shakers in New Hampshire flourished as farmers, livestock breeders, businesspeople, and industrial workers and managers.

Their balanced agricultural and industrial economy was the envy of their New Hampshire neighbors, as featured in an 1840 article about their achievements published in one of the state's leading newspapers, the *Farmer's Monthly Visitor* of Concord. The editor and publisher of the paper was Isaac Hill, a former New Hampshire governor and United States senator, who had visited the Shakers several times and had even borrowed $6,700 from them to help finance some of his own enterprises. Hill's article was effusive in its praise for Shaker success in agriculture, livestock breeding, and milling, as well as for the Shaker men and women whose enterprise kept them out of debt and profitably employed.[8]

Isaac Hill's Shaker counterpart at Canterbury was Trustee David Parker. Although Parker was credited with great business acumen by Hill, and acknowledged by the Shakers themselves as one of their greatest entrepreneurs, he was only one of many skilled businessmen in the annals of Canterbury Shaker Village. Parker arrived at the Canterbury Shaker community in 1817, a ten-year-old from Boston. By age nineteen he was an assistant trustee under Francis Winkley. By age twenty-nine he was a ministry elder. From 1846 to his death in 1867 Parker served as trustee, guiding Canterbury Shaker Village to increased membership, landholdings, and business enterprise.[9] Parker traveled widely throughout the Northeast on behalf of the Shakers and visited Washington, D.C., during the Civil War, when he successfully petitioned Abraham Lincoln to honor the Shakers' pacifism.

The story of trusteeship at Canterbury from 1792 until the late nineteenth century is one of the most successful in Shaker history. Many other Shaker villages, including Enfield, suffered at one time or another from the failings or sudden death of a powerful trustee. Canterbury experienced a remarkably stable trustee succession from Francis Winkley and Israel Sanborn in the 1790s, to David Parker and James Kaime, then Kaime and Nicholas A. Briggs. Briggs defected in 1894, striking a serious blow to Canterbury's business leadership, but Arthur Bruce capably picked up the business responsibilities for the community.

OFFICE FOR THE LEAD MINISTRY, located in the trustees' office, as left in 1990 at the death of Eldress Bertha Lindsay.

Although our focus is the Canterbury community, Canterbury did not operate in a business vacuum. All Shaker communities were communistic but entrepreneurial, and they were quick to share with one another their business successes, whether achievements in production processes, new technology, labor training, or marketing. Because the villages were widely separated, they rarely intruded on each other's markets. Each village, and even a family within a village, was autonomous in management and operation, but the industries and agricultural enterprises of one potentially benefited all other villages, especially in sharing practical business knowledge and in establishing a national reputation for all Shaker products.

Shaker diversification was remarkable for the early nineteenth century. While most fledgling American industries started by focusing production on a few related products, the Shakers seemed willing to produce anything that could make money for them.

Diversification may well be the central feature of Shaker business enterprise. One benefit of diversification was that the enterprises kept the community busy and took advantage of a wide range of interests and skills within the Shaker labor force. Another benefit was its remarkable ability to insulate the Shakers from the fluctuations of the volatile nineteenth-century American economy. The Shakers were affected, but not paralyzed, by major depressions of nineteenth-century America, such as the panic of 1837.

Shaker economic strength also depended on successful marketing—what we would now call customer service, competitive pricing, and aggressive salesmanship. Surprisingly, it appears that the Shakers quickly learned tactics of survival in the competitive world of American industry. With considerable capital of their own to invest; a flexible, low-cost labor force; and tight management controls, the Shakers, at least for a time, were able to succeed in nearly every business they launched.

Shaker industries in Canterbury started immediately in the 1790s, and they quickly outpaced agriculture in terms of productivity and profitability. This fact is even more

SHAKER BRUSHES of many types were manufactured at Canterbury throughout the nineteenth century, using natural hog bristles and handles produced by Canterbury's turning mill.

Opposite ❖ TURNING MILL, historical photograph, c. 1875.

2½ doz.	mortars	@ 30/	$ 12.50
2 doz.	seives	@ 30/	10.00
6 doz.	candlesticks	@ 30/	30.00
5 doz.	pails	@ 36/	30.00
7 doz.	whips	@ 30/	35.00
6 doz.	lashes	@ 15/	15.00
½ doz.	long lashes	@ 36/	3.00
2 doz.	horn brushes	@ 54/	18.00
3 doz.	pr drawers	@ 90/	45.00
2 doz.	brooms	@ 27/	9.00
3 doz. and 8 par mittens		@ 24/	14.67
16	wool wheels	@ 12/	32.00
20	linen wheels	@ 18/	60.00
240 lbs.	cheese	@ 15/	36.00
100 lbs.	butter	@ 24/	24.00
38 lbs.	shavings-leather	@ 2/	12.66
167 lbs.	medicinal herbs	@	77.06
1 bbl	cider	@ 66/	11.20
7 half bushels		@ 4/	7.67
4 sets measures @ 9/45 pr brushes		@ 3/	8.50
6	calf skins	@ 12/	12.00
16 boxes	garden seeds		140.88
Cash			17.00
D. Howe jr. Note			130.00
Other accounts and notes worth			189.00
and five dollars more in ware			5.12
			$981.62

—HENRY CLAY BLINN,

"A Historical Record of the Society of Believers
in Canterbury, New Hampshire," 1892

exceptional considering that Canterbury lacked a natural source of water power. The Merrimack River, one of the key arteries feeding New England's Industrial Revolution, was only a few miles away, but in the 1790s that distance could be an insurmountable obstacle to industrial success. The early Shaker mills, therefore, had to rely on manpower (as in the case of the blacksmith's shop and tannery) or horsepower (as with the first grist-mill and cider mill).

Product demand—from the Canterbury Shakers' growing community, as well as the surrounding towns of Canterbury and Loudon—led the trustees to a major reassess-ment of the Canterbury Shaker economic situation at the end of the eighteenth century. The Canterbury Shakers saw water power as indispensable to their future, but given their extensive land holdings, relocating the community was unthinkable.

To resolve this dilemma, in 1800 the Canterbury Shakers undertook one of New Hampshire's most improbable hydropower projects. They located a source of water in Lyford Pond, two miles north of the Church Family. Over a period of sixteen years the Shakers embarked on a massive engineering project to bring water to the village, creating an aqueduct called the Long Ditch and a series of eight dams and ponds, upon which they erected their mills. This was a daunting task, considering the fact that Shaker land con-tained only two small, meandering streams and many marshlands and swamps.

By the time of Isaac Hill's visit in 1840, the Long Ditch had been widened and straightened, and the industries of the mills were generating the bulk of Canterbury Shaker revenue. By 1841 the water-powered Shaker mills were primarily devoted to textile operations and the production of wooden wares. The 1832 gristmill, with four runs of millstones (including the finest French buhrstones), was also impressive. It was the largest gristmill in the region, and served non-Shaker farmers as well as the Shakers. The Canter-bury gristmill also contained a sawmill, most likely patterned after the combined grist- and sawmill built at New Lebanon.[10]

Above ❖ Original packing case and paper labels for one dozen bottles of Shaker Syrup of Sarsaparilla.

Below ❖ A bottle of Thomas Corbett's syrup.

At both the New Hampshire communities the Shakers needed trades to generate cash. Equally important to the Shaker leadership was the necessity of keeping their large membership busy in meaningful labor. The choice of trades was probably determined initially more by the skills of new members than by an overall business strategy, but from the outset, the Shaker leadership at New Lebanon set standards of production, even sending samples of their own products to establish a level of quality.

Canterbury and Enfield were receptive to the development of industry, for both had to contend with the rocky, uncompromising soil of New Hampshire, and land consolidation provided great economies of scale in crop farming and the raising and care of livestock. Only a small percentage of the workforce was needed to care for farm operations.

The Shakers were successful in creating a commercial culture that could generate surplus wealth. By the 1830s the accumulated wealth of the Shakers was generating public concern. In 1839 legislation was passed in New York State placing limits on how much land the state's Shakers could acquire. There was talk of land monopoly, and some accused the Shakers of being anti-American. This charge is ironic, for land speculation was a time-honored American practice, even if it was viewed with suspicion by small farmers in the early nineteenth century.

Despite all obstacles, the Shaker industries quietly but efficiently developed new products with improved quality control and more creative marketing. The Shaker name stood for quality and reliability from the 1820s, in large part due to the business acumen of Canterbury trustees Francis Winkley and David Parker.

The Shakers can be credited with establishing the word "Shaker" as one of the first brand names in United States business history. The first products to approach national recognition were Shaker seeds and medicines in the 1820s, 1830s, and 1840s.

Other products soon followed to a national market, and the Canterbury Shakers enjoyed great commercial success through the early 1880s. To be sure, they lost out in many areas to rapid industrialization. The tanning industry's shift from cold processes to hot chemical processes eliminated a highly profitable industry for the Shakers. The same was true for the production of handmade wool cards, when machines eliminated the hand setting of teeth for the wool cards. Each time one of their industries became outmoded, however, the Shaker leadership was able to quickly redirect its skilled and flexible workforce to new enterprises.[11]

By the 1880s the Shakers faced two major problems commercially. They were critically short of male labor, and their management system was breaking under the burden. These pressures became painfully apparent in a rare set of trustee meeting minutes preserved at Canterbury; they are remarkably candid in discussing the principal business issues of the period, and reveal some of the inner tensions of Shaker life in the late nineteenth century.[12]

A CHILD'S DOROTHY CLOAK, sold to
Mrs. C. B. Manning on May 26, 1914, for $6.10
(six dollars for the cloak, ten cents for postage).

At one point the Church Family trustees discussed the possibility of an outside
business partner, for the manufacture of butter boxes, because if they conducted the business themselves, there was the problem of insufficient labor, and the sisters might have to
start working at the turning mill in order to help the Canterbury Shakers "earn their daily
bread." In the end, a decision was made to try the new venture at the turning mill for one
year. Yet there is no record that the Canterbury Shakers ever started the butter box business. However, Eldress Dorothy Durgin and the sisters did start a new business; they
began producing the Dorothy cloak under the brand name Hart and Shepard.

The strains in the Shakers' commercial empire mirrored deeper community tensions. The Church Family sisterhood was as large as it had ever been, and the sisters'
dwelling spaces and work areas were filled to capacity. Meanwhile, both the Second
(Branch) and North families were struggling, and male leadership was in short supply and
aging rapidly.

Fortunately for Canterbury, the sisters' industries continued to be profitable for
many years to come. The last of the sisters' industries—poplarware—closed in 1958.[13]

❖

MIND AND BODY

As the Shakers were millennialists with a firm belief in human perfectibility, they adopted progressive and practical measures to meet the educational and health needs of their communities.

EDUCATION

The educational program at Canterbury began quietly, as a reflection of an early eastern Shaker mistrust of schooling, but it eventually grew to be a highly esteemed system, with some of the most progressive facilities of any school in the region.

Most early eastern Shakers were skeptical of formal education. This was partly due to the pattern established by Mother Ann Lee, who was illiterate herself, and whose "Hands to work, hearts to God" philosophy had no real place for formal education. These attitudes were in sharp contrast to those of the Quakers, or economic reformers such as the industrialist Robert Owen, who established social and economic experiments on both sides of the Atlantic. The early Shakers valued work, and often considered formal education to be an obstacle to Shaker growth, since it taught unnecessary and impractical subjects. Even traditional Protestant religious curriculum generally was not sympathetic to the Shaker way. However, many children had entered Shaker communities with their parents, who expected at least a modicum of schooling.

The eastern Shakers generally did not build schools until the 1820s (Canterbury's was built in 1823), making do with spaces in shops, barns, and dwelling houses for instruction. The western Shakers, however, took a stronger commitment to education, probably due to the strong Presbyterian background of many early Shaker converts in Ohio and Kentucky (for example, Richard McNemar, the founder of Union Village, Ohio, was a former Presbyterian minister).[1]

The Shaker philosophy of education changed greatly with the pioneering role of Seth Wells, a former Albany-area teacher who, after joining the Shakers in the early nineteenth century, began advocating education among the community. Wells was quick to learn from the western Shaker leaders, and was given some leeway by the Central Ministry (which after 1796 was led by Mother Lucy Wright) to institute schools at Watervliet and New Lebanon. He studied and experimented with many progressive educational strategies. At New Lebanon he introduced the reforms developed in the first years of the century by the English Quaker educator Joseph Lancaster.

Lancastrianism spread rapidly among American Quakers and urban education reformers, especially in Philadelphia, New York, and Boston. Wells insightfully saw how Lancastrian ideas fit the Shaker philosophy: the Lancastrian educational system was nonsectarian; held that corporal punishment destroyed a child's educational incentive and potential; and stressed skills of reading, writing, and numbers in order to train workers

Opposite ❖ VIEW OF MIDDLE TERRACE OF THE BOTANICAL GARDEN laid out by Dr. Thomas Corbett c. 1810–16 and restored in 1995–96.

75

and businessmen rather than ministers, lawyers, and gentlemen. Lancastrianism was a humane and practical system of education designed to serve an industrializing order.[2]

In 1821 Mother Lucy officially endorsed Wells's insights and knowledge, naming him general superintendent for believers' literature and freeing him from daily community work. Wells could devote his time to further study and writing about educational theories. In 1823 he traveled throughout the eastern Shaker villages, making many prolonged teaching visits to the Shaker communities, including Canterbury.

Canterbury Shaker boys in the late eighteenth century received only minimal formal schooling. Beginning in 1793, boys would gather in the dwelling house for twenty-minute sessions while the sisters ate their noon meals. The situation in the town of Canterbury was not much better. After an auspicious start in 1794, the town schools fell on difficult times as people balked at the expense of maintaining the buildings and paying teachers. Well-trained teachers were difficult to find, and lengthy vacancies were common. In this lax atmosphere student rebellion—and corporal punishment—were the prevailing order.

In 1809 John Whitcher, a Canterbury Shaker, was sent to New Lebanon to learn the educational ideas of Wells and bring his officially sanctioned theories back to the community. He already had been responsible for a program (in 1806) to educate the Shaker girls and an increasing number of adults. However, Canterbury's school sessions for children were still short and hampered by makeshift facilities and a lack of supplies.

The efforts of Wells and Whitcher were instrumental in the new Shaker attitudes toward education, but it would be misleading to ignore some substantial pressures on the Shakers that came from the outside world. By the early 1820s the Shakers were being criticized for failing to educate their members. The most celebrated instance of this was the legal suit of Mary Dyer, a former Enfield (New Hampshire) Shaker who reported to the local press her sensationalistic accounts of bondage and abuse among the Shakers. Ultimately, Dyer was fighting to retrieve her husband and children from the community, but much of her castigation of the Shakers centered on the lack of available education, which in her mind constituted child abuse. Although Dyer did not prevail in the courts, her stinging criticisms spurred the Shakers to rethink their commitment to education.[3]

Pressure for the Canterbury Shakers to improve their educational standards also came from the town of Canterbury, which in an effort to correct its own educational shortfalls instituted a series of improvements, including an outside committee to oversee the town school districts. Shaker education, in this context, came under town scrutiny.

In 1823 the Canterbury Shakers built their first school. That year they established regulations that committed them to maintaining a legal school district by raising funds from each of the families to support the school and supplies (a total amount of eighty-four dollars per year in 1823 and 1824, ten of which was paid to the town), appointing a three-person committee and a treasurer, and choosing a teacher.[4]

The original 1823 schoolhouse is represented in maps by Henry Clay Blinn (completed about 1848) and Peter Foster (1849) as a one-room, one-story school. Its design was not unlike schools built elsewhere in New Hampshire in the early nineteenth century, except for its separate entries for boys and girls (even though in 1823 they were not schooled simultaneously). The interior was relatively plain, with horizontal wainscoting, Shaker peg rail, "fast-seats" (a built-in bench that lined the perimeter of the room), and a series of raised platforms to support student desks.

Whitcher made it clear in his journal that the location of the new school posed a problem for the Church Family: in the 1790s they had not anticipated the need for a school, and there was no natural place for one in their highly articulated community plan. It was erected, therefore, on the Church Family's northern agricultural fringe. Its place along the cow lane captured, on more than one level, education's status and distance from the core of Shaker life during these early years. That problem was only exacerbated over the decades. The Church Family's massive barn complex was greatly expanded in 1858 to accommodate the village's growing livestock business, making the site even less appropriate for the schoolchildren.

Yet in spite of these physical limitations, the first few decades of the school's history coincided with a flourishing of theory among Shaker educators, and their high standards and progressive ideas were attracting regional attention—and non-Shaker students. Even though the number of entire households converting to the faith was declining at mid-century, the Shakers received dozens of orphans and children from broken and troubled homes, eventually straining the existing facilities and providing incentive for the community to improve the school.

In 1862–63 a new schoolhouse was built; it was relocated several hundred yards south of the original site. Its design reused the original 1823 schoolhouse (with many of its interior features), which formed the second floor and roof structure of the new school. The entire building was reclapboarded, and the two old entries were converted into second-floor closets. A new stair tower was built for second-floor access and to join the school to a small woodshed/privy, which also had been moved from the original location. Since by the 1860s boys were being educated in winter, and girls in summer, a single entrance was deemed adequate for the new building. The restrained Neoclassical exterior trim brought the new two-story, two-room schoolhouse, with its fenced schoolyard, into general conformity with the rest of the Church Family buildings.

Inside, the Shaker school was attractive, well lit, well heated and ventilated (with special double-walled insulation and air pipes), and equipped with the latest in school apparatus such as globes, maps, and books. The new school met the ultimate standards of the day, and for the next sixty years the building functioned as the leading educational institution in the town of Canterbury.

Architecturally, the Canterbury Shakers incorporated the ideas of some of America's most distinguished leaders in education reform, such as Horace Mann and William Alcott of Massachusetts and Henry Barnard of Rhode Island. Alcott and Barnard had published the first treatises on school architecture in 1832 and 1848, respectively; these volumes advocated a school building that would incorporate their overall philosophy of environmentalism, which acknowledged architecture's direct influence in shaping a child's behavior and character.[5]

The Shakers followed nearly all of Barnard's suggestions except one: Barnard recommended two-story schools only for crowded urban settings. Although the Shakers

THE CANTERBURY SCHOOLHOUSE

School House raised, 34 by 24 feet, one story, high posted, in the "North Field," front ranging with south wall of said field, leading from the Cow barn to the highway. (rather close proximity to cow-lane).

In the School room were constructed seats hung with hinges, (each seat for two scholars) raised one row above another by broad stairs. Stationary double desks before the seats with hinged covers, to write on and keep books in. Scholars faced south. Teacher's desk and platform on the south side of the room, facing the scholars.

—JOURNAL OF JOHN WHITCHER, June 7, 1823

SOAPSTONE INKWELL made in Concord, New Hampshire, and purchased by the Shakers for the 1823 schoolhouse. The label "57" refers to the item's number in the historical museum established by Elder Henry Clay Blinn.

CANTERBURY SCHOOLHOUSE, c. 1862–63,
repainted in 1991 to the c. 1890 colors.

built theirs to be two stories in order to recycle their perfectly usable original structure, they used the second floor for a feature that was highly progressive for rural Canterbury in the 1860s—a gymnasium.

The concept of a gymnasium was imported from central Europe and has roots in the Germanic emphasis on physical education. The idea was introduced to New England by Dr. Diocletian Lewis, who opened a school in Boston and a summer training camp for young women in nearby Lexington. Lewis lectured widely in Massachusetts and southern New Hampshire, and in the late 1850s published his influential book *The New Gymnastics for Men, Women, and Children,* which went through at least ten editions into the 1890s.[6] The Shakers were familiar with Lewis's writings by 1862 and wasted no time in implementing them in their new school.[7] Photographic evidence confirms that the Canterbury Shakers purchased the type of exercise equipment recommended by Lewis, including a drum for beating a rhythm for exercises, and several types of exercise aids such as wands and barbells. Rows of metal hooks in walls and ceilings in the upper level of the Canterbury school suggest that the Shakers may once have owned Dr. Lewis's patented Gymnastikon,

a system of rings, ropes, and pulleys for acrobatic exercises—a forerunner of the rings in modern gymnastics.

Throughout the late nineteenth and early twentieth centuries the Shakers enjoyed high-quality instruction in their educational system. The Canterbury School Committee visited annually and regularly praised the teachers and pupils. The curriculum remained nonsectarian and relatively stable, and the students performed admirably. Eventually, however, with no pressure within the community to prepare the students for college education, the school became increasingly outdated, except in instruction of physiology and health, an emphasis unique to the Shakers in rural New Hampshire until the early twentieth century.

In the 1920s the Shaker education system declined for lack of both teachers and a sufficient number of Shaker children. The Canterbury Shakers continued to educate their few young people and some town children until their school closed in 1934. In the 1940s the Canterbury Shaker community made a momentous decision to take no more children into their society.

Above, left ❖ STEREOSCOPIC VIEW OF THE CANTERBURY SCHOOLROOM with Shaker teacher Mary L. Wilson (1858–1939), Kimball Studio, 1875.

Above, right ❖ ORIGINAL WOODEN BLACKBOARD IN AN 1862–63 CLASSROOM. The inscription, copied by Eldress Bertha Lindsay, reads: "Hands to work and hearts to God. Ann Lee."

Right ❖ STEREOSCOPIC VIEW OF SHAKER GIRLS CONDUCTING GYMNASTIC EXERCISES, c. 1875. The use of rings, barbells, rods, and other gymnastic paraphernalia was popularized in the 1860s by Dr. Diocletian Lewis, a German-trained teacher who published widely and operated a gymnasium and school for young women in Boston.

Below ❖ A BOX OF LABELED WOOD SAMPLES prepared by Elder Henry Clay Blinn for instructional purposes. Blinn also established a small arboretum, the first in New Hampshire, to further enhance Shaker education.

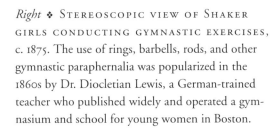

The Shakers engaged in many types of informal education throughout their history. At first, these efforts were directed toward basic skills needed to conduct their business affairs in an orderly manner. From the 1830s on they were also aimed at teaching members about agricultural reform, health issues, and even the economic and political news of the day. The communities received the leading newspapers from nearby cities such as Albany for the New Lebanon and Watervliet societies and Boston for the Harvard, Shirley, and Canterbury communities. These were read regularly by the village trustees, but ordinary members might also hear selected news stories read to large groups in the family dining room.

By midcentury the Shakers as a community were subscribing to important journals such as *Scientific American,* and were building several small, practical libraries for the benefit of community members. By the 1860s the average Shaker at Canterbury had at his or her disposal a library more vast than that available to most rural residents of New Hampshire. The dwelling-house library, for example, included many books on biography, history, science, and natural history. There were additional libraries in the schoolhouse and infirmary.

FOLDING POCKET STEREOSCOPE,
patented in 1872 by Enfield Shaker Nelson Chase.
This example is decorated and packaged for sale
to the outside world, but there is no record of
commercial production of the viewer.

Henry Clay Blinn by midcentury had already established his Shaker museum at Canterbury. Blinn, resident antiquarian and curator, had amassed numerous relics of Shaker history as well as gifts given to the community by well-traveled friends. The museum was housed in his printing office and was used for educating Shaker children and adults.

By the 1870s the Shakers could engage in vicarious travel through the accounts and illustrated travel books in their dwelling-house library. They also began purchasing significant numbers of stereoscopic view cards—nearly six hundred in all—that illustrated local natural and historical sites, foreign views, and popular posed genre scenes. Most likely their knowledge of stereoscopy came through their favorite photographers—the Kimballs of Concord, New Hampshire—or through their own reading.[8] Shaker interest in the development of stereoscopy even led one New Hampshire Shaker, Nelson Chase of Enfield, to invent a folding pocket stereoscope in 1865, which was patented in 1872. While his invention remains in the Canterbury collections, there is no documentation that the Chase stereoscope was ever produced commercially.[9]

The Shakers continued to expand their cultural horizons as new media became available. They obtained wax cylinders for their Edison gramophone and 78 r.p.m. records for the Victrola. By the 1920s they had eagerly welcomed the radio into the Canterbury community, and the television set was accepted just as happily in the second half of the twentieth century.

At the Printing Office . . . we almost fancy that we have struck a department of Barnum's old museum once on Broadway, on the site of the Herald building. Lying all about the room, yet in perfect Shaker order, are old-fashioned curiosities of every name and description—spinning looms, warming pans, clay pipes and smoking tongs; the old iron candlestick of the past and the brass ones of later date, including the veritable old pitch-pine knot, which may have lighted, long ago, some poor old soul in the way of truth and Shakerism.

—CHARLES EDSON ROBINSON,
The Shakers and Their Homes, 1893

HEALING, HEALTH, AND DEATH

The Shakers had one of the most open-minded approaches to healing, health, and death of any community in the nineteenth century. The community at Canterbury practiced a strong program of healthful reforms in diet and the use of tobacco, alcohol, and pork; attention to general cleanliness and personal hygiene, including dentistry; experimentation with herbal remedies; and a trust of the "gift" of spiritual healing. These attitudes helped to lead the Shakers to achieve a level of community health care in rural New Hampshire that for much of the nineteenth century matched the care of the most progressive American towns and cities.[10]

THE GIFT OF HEALING

In the 1780s and 1790s the Shakers had no more faith in institutionalized medicine than they did in formal education. Following the lead of Mother Ann Lee, who had some first-hand experience with the squalid conditions of the Manchester Infirmary in England, the Shakers chose to explore spiritual healing. The gift of healing became one of the most prized of God's gifts in an era when there was little scientific understanding of the causes of illness.

From the beginning, the Shakers subscribed to a dual approach to healing: the power of God delivered through the gift of spiritual healing, and the power of human knowledge as applied through medical practice of the time. This dual system, of spirit and body, inspiration and science, was characterized by an openness to experimentation that was unusual for a religious society. There was no rigid set of doctrines or beliefs that blocked avenues of treatment or learning. Canterbury's first nurse, Sister Elizabeth Avery, served Canterbury from 1792 until 1806 and possessed, by all accounts, the gift of spiritual healing.

The most influential person in Shaker health and medical reforms was Dr. Thomas Corbett, Canterbury's first physician and a Canterbury leader of great stature. Corbett's campaign for good health began with the care of the body as well as the mind. He interpreted his physician's responsibilities broadly and sought to relate his medical knowledge to the development of the Shaker way of daily life.

Corbett took a holistic view of community health care and believed in the power of preventive medical treatment. Nowhere can this be seen more vividly than in his travel to other communities, his correspondence with other Shaker and outside medical practitioners, and his efforts to reform the Shaker diet. The years from the 1820s to the 1850s were ones of great medical experimentation under Corbett, who was highly regarded among the Shakers generally and even by his non-Shaker medical peers. (Corbett became the recording secretary of the New Hampshire Medical Society in the 1820s and was active for some twenty-five years in the development of the New Hampshire medical profession.)

Corbett made important contributions to the Shaker tradition of herbal medicines that was developing in the early nineteenth century. There had been serious experimentation in the realm of herbal medicine at the Shaker communities at New Lebanon (by the work of Eliab Harlow, the first Shaker physician at New Lebanon) and Harvard (by Elisha Myrick). The first medicinal recipe book had been prepared around 1800 by Harlow. A handwritten copy of his book was given to the first Canterbury nurses, Elizabeth Avery and Anna Carr. From approximately 1816, Corbett laid out Canterbury's medicinal botanical garden and developed a packaging system for dried herbs and a distillery for herbal medicines, following the lead of New Lebanon, where botanic medicines were first offered for sale. In 1835 he published Canterbury's first medicinal herb catalog. Corbett created a business enterprise that helped sustain the Canterbury community for the rest of the nineteenth century. By 1837 Canterbury's medically related enterprises—bottled medicines, dried herbs, and manufactured medical devices—were reaching annual sales exceeding one thousand dollars.[11]

Many buildings at Canterbury in the nineteenth century were at least partially devoted to the herb industry. There were numerous rooms and attics for drying herbs,

A temperance wave seems to have passed over the Society this year [1828] which must have made a deep impression on the minds of all who were accustomed to the use of alcoholic drink or of cider. It had been a universal custom for all who chose so to do, to take a glass of spirits every morning before breakfast, as an appetiser, and then more or less through the day as circumstances favored. Even with this freedom, a genial care was exercised in the use of liquors. The spiritual growth of the people, however, had reached the place where an additional self-denial should be practiced in this respect, and the Society of New Lebanon had already set the example. It was published as the death of "Old Alcohol."

—HENRY CLAY BLINN,
"A Historical Record of the Society of Believers in Canterbury, New Hampshire," 1892

mill operations for pulverizing herbs, stripping rooms, packing areas, warehouses, and an extensive distillery operation in the syrup shop.

  Although Shaker medicine was grounded in spiritual healing, with a strong emphasis upon herbal medicine, the Shakers still kept in touch with physicians of the outside world, and called upon them as needed, especially for surgery. As new medical treatments were introduced in nineteenth-century America, the Shakers read about them and at times experimented within their own communities.

  Consequently, the Shakers were open to medical knowledge from the traditional European herbal therapies as well as from the practices of Native Americans. They reserved their greatest skepticism, in fact, for the prevailing methods of treatment of academic medicine. Early on, for example, Corbett rejected the practices of leeching and bleeding in favor of such gentler means of treatment as herbal remedies. The scarifier, a nineteenth-century bleeding device, was not discarded but was, however, placed into Henry Clay Blinn's museum as an object lesson.

SYRUP SHOP ATTIC, in continuous use since Corbett's era for drying herbs.

Believers had lived plainly as a whole, but were consumers of a great deal of beef and swine's flesh. . . . Br. Garrett Lawrence of New Lebanon had corresponded with Thomas Corbett on the subject, and a number of the Brethren & Sisters were interested to adopt the new system, then called the "Graham System."

It was a vegetable diet & required the abstinence of condiments and stimulants. It was to be a great and radical change for those who had been accustomed to meat & butter, more or less, three times each day, and to tea and coffee and tobacco to leave all these and live as simple as their formula now stated. They were to have water for drink, were to abstain from tobacco and were advised to take frequent or daily ablution in pure water.

—HENRY CLAY BLINN, "A Historical Record of the Society of Believers in Canterbury, New Hampshire," 1892

BRASS MOLD FOR CLAY PIPE, WITH A PIPE BOWL MARKED "#11," from Henry Clay Blinn's museum. The Canterbury Shakers had a small clay pipe manufactory at the Second Family's blacksmith's shop.

On November 27, 1835, Brother Garret Lawrence of New Lebanon wrote to Corbett, "It is remarkably healthy here at this time," and in another letter reports that "animal food is eaten more sparingly by nearly all."[12] Dr. Corbett was ever alert for dietary improvements. On January 22, 1836, he forwarded copies of Brother Garret's letter to Enfield, New Hampshire, and Alfred, Maine, noting that it had had wide circulation at Canterbury "with good effect."

More controversial and more difficult to implement were the other reforms brought on by the advent of the Era of Spirit Manifestations in 1837, namely abstinence from foreign tea and coffee, and the eating of "swine flesh." Shakers over fifty were allowed "free will" in the matter. Younger members were strongly advised against the use of China tea, and were encouraged to drink substitutes of home manufacture from native plants.

Corbett was not alone in his campaign for health reform. Evidently the Order of Physicians at all Shaker communities shared in a regular exchange of information. Successful experimentation in one village was quickly and directly transmitted to another—a networking system that was faster and more direct than what was possible in the world of academic medicine, with its network of medical societies, journals, and schools.

The Shakers did not concern themselves with the major medical issues of finding the causes and cures for disease. They left that research and the exceptional cases to the outside world's physicians, hence Shaker acceptance of smallpox inoculation and calls to the outside for surgery. The Shaker interest was in promoting the general health and well-being of the entire Shaker community. The goal was to keep members healthy, productive, and content with community life by preventing disease, if possible, and curing their patients.

The Shaker leaders did not want to risk party division over sumptuary matters. They preferred to educate about an evil, experiment with its control or temperate use, and hope that the sense of community would prevail. Deviant behavior could be tolerated in matters of dietary rules, though not in cardinal Shaker principles such as pacifism and celibacy.

Tobacco was another target of the Shaker physicians; physical evidence corroborates that the Shakers struggled with this Shaker persuasion to reform. For example, a brass pipe mold and white clay pipe survive from Blinn's museum. In a summer 1996 archaeological excavation at Canterbury Shaker Village's Second Family blacksmith's shop, David Starbuck and coworkers found striking evidence of an early clay pipe manufactory in the shop in the form of wasters (manufacturing rejects). The quantity of pipe bowl wasters reveals substantial production of pipes in the early to mid-nineteenth century, perhaps for outside sale as well as for use by the Shakers.

Although by the 1830s preventive medicine and dietary reform were an integral part of the Shaker health system, the Shakers were only marginally ahead of their non-Shaker neighbors in most matters of life and death. The general conditions of the time, such as the lack of medical knowledge and the toll of daily hard work, imperiled Shaker brothers as much as any man. Nevertheless, many Shaker workers, especially the sisters, lived into their seventies and beyond. Shaker longevity was most likely due to their consistently good diet, sanitary living and work conditions, the availability of prompt medical care, and community sanitation efforts to prevent epidemics. The Shaker women were spared the greatest threat to women in the nineteenth century—complications in childbirth. However, Shaker women were susceptible to death by tuberculosis because they worked long hours indoors in groups.[13] Canterbury had a reputation among Shaker communities for its relatively successful treatment of the disease.

With a progressive approach to community health care, supported by modern facilities and equipment, the Canterbury Shakers could provide medical care superior to that available to the average rural New Englander. Although this alone was not incentive enough for many to join the community, as Canterbury Shaker Village's history demonstrates, it was a benefit of daily life that could not be had by ordinary farm people in the outside world.

Treatment of the injured or ill required skilled, compassionate care and appropriate facilities for treatment. Early in the history of each Shaker community the appointment of the Order of Physicians and Nurses was quickly followed by the creation of a "nurse shop," or infirmary.

At Canterbury, the first infirmary was a section of the second dwelling house. By the late 1840s a new infirmary had been created out of the 1811 visitors' house. There was a growing need for an expanded infirmary. In 1842 the village experienced a frightening outbreak of measles; this was at a time when the rising number of elderly called for a much

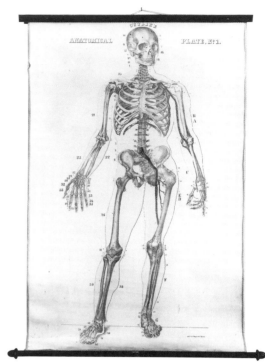

ANATOMICAL CHART FOR THE INFIRMARY, mid-nineteenth century.

PHARMACY ROOM, INFIRMARY, showing Shaker medicines and the counter (c. 1850) for the preparation of medicines. The medicine bottles were purchased from Massachusetts and New Hampshire glassworks; the Shakers printed their own labels.

larger and more modern medical facility. With renovation and new furnishings in 1849, the expanded infirmary opened to serve the demanding health needs of the Shaker community.

The infirmary of 1849 was thus a two-and-a-half story facility, with a 32-by-40-foot (9.76 × 12.2 m) plan and a full basement. Medicine storage and a kitchen occupied the basement; the attic was used for storing undertaking apparatus, bed linens, crutches, and other medical equipment. The first floor contained an office/library/sitting room for infirmary nurses, a pharmacy room for mixing and storing medicines in use, and two patient rooms. The second floor contained more patient rooms. Physicians and nurses, other than those providing attending services, were located in another building until 1892, when a kitchen wing was added and attending nurses moved into the infirmary to live.

By the middle of the nineteenth century the infirmary was probably the most modern facility in the village. Water lines were installed throughout the village by 1849. The patients in the infirmary were the first Shakers at Canterbury to have access to an up-to-date water closet, built in the upstairs hall in 1852. By 1854 the infirmary had its own kitchen, in the basement. Modern plumbing and water closets were first installed in the infirmary in 1886, even before such luxuries entered the trustees' office, ministry, and dwelling house. After the 1892 renovations, which saw new hospital furnishings such as

Opposite ❖ INFIRMARY SOUTH FACADE, originally built in 1811 as a visitor's house. In 1849 it was converted into an infirmary, then enlarged and renovated in 1892. The infirmary has been restored to the color scheme of the 1890s.

PHARMACY ROOM, INFIRMARY, where dentistry was practiced in the early twentieth century. Henry Clay Blinn was Canterbury's dentist in the 1890s and saw patients in the ministry shop. Visiting dentists from Concord would use the infirmary in the twentieth century.

ATTIC CLOSET, INFIRMARY, where biers and undertaking equipment were kept until the 1960s, when most of the equipment was discarded by the Shakers.

metal beds, the Shaker patients had running water in each room and a full bathroom with tub on the first floor.

In spite of their seriousness about health care and cleanliness, the Shakers occasionally encountered a situation beyond their control. Tuberculosis was one of the most dramatic of these situations, as was mental illness. Instead of immediately institutionalizing their problem patients, the Shakers' first approach was to provide compassionate care within the community. This at times led the Shakers to create separate quarters for a tubercular patient, or to allocate a small building exclusively for the use of a mentally disturbed member. In an extreme case Sally Miller, a Shaker sister, suffered from pyromania, putting the whole community at risk. She was eventually admitted to the new state hospital in Concord.

In general, the Shakers were remarkably lenient and tolerant of people with mental and personality disorders and eccentricities. In fact, there is reason to believe that over time the Shakers may have attracted more than their fair share of troubled, socially dysfunctional people, partly because society offered few refuges and little sympathy. Some of these people joined the movement and stayed. More were sheltered for a time and then moved on. One believer, Bradbury Merrill, had only been with the Shakers a few weeks before he had to be admitted to an asylum; shortly after his release he left the community.[14]

PATIENT ROOM set up to the period of the late 1840s, when the Shakers converted their dwelling house for visitors into a medical facility. The furnishings in this room have been supplied from several different eastern Shaker communities.

DEATH

The Shakers faced death with great composure, partly because they believed life was in the spirit, which was immortal. The Shakers viewed death as a passage from one phase of life to another that freed oneself of mortal flesh. Since the Shakers, unlike most other Protestants, did not believe in bodily resurrection, they had little use for most of the funerary customs of nineteenth-century Americans.

Shaker customs seem almost irreverent in their austerity. The bodies of the deceased were laid out on a plank as soon as possible after death, then wrapped in a "winding sheet," rather than good clothes. Sisters had a cap, cape, and collar added to their sheets. After 1861 at Canterbury, Henry Clay Blinn noted, sisters were dressed in white robes. The funeral was generally short and interment was in no particular order.

The Shakers followed the Quakers most closely in burial practice, giving each deceased believer a grave marker of equal size, in a modest burial ground. In fact, in most Shaker cemeteries men and women were not segregated, and the Shakers permitted the burial of non-Shakers in certain situations. The great urban cemetery parks of the 1830s and 1840s shocked the Shakers and led a Sabbathday Lake elder, Otis Sawyer, to write in the Shaker Manifesto in June 1872: "Such 'cities' of the dead as New Auburn and Greenwood are fashionable institutions of idol worshippers. Money is lavishly, wickedly spent there, while the living poor have not where to lay their heads, or wherewith to appease their hunger."[15]

A Shaker's grief centered on the loss of a beloved friend, not on death, for the Shakers did not believe the separation was long lasting. Their belief in the world of the spirit, and their ability to communicate with that world, enabled the Shakers to rejoice that a friend had moved from one community to another. The Shaker funeral was a ritual act of community mourning that also served to bond those who remained.

An essential part of the bonding process was the memorializing of the dead through a recognition of their contribution to the community. In these spoken speeches and testimonials, in written verse, and through objects, the Shakers added the memory of each passing Shaker to the community's memory, whether in the funeral service itself or in other ways, especially through poetry, oral history, and photography.

The most official memorial was the community's Obituary Journal, a book kept by the Canterbury Shaker nurses. The Canterbury Church Family entered the name of every covenanted Shaker brother and sister into the journal, along with the date of birth, date and cause of death, and a memorial tribute, often in the form of a poem or short sentiment such as the following tribute to Mary Maria Basford, who died of pneumonia in 1929 at eighty-seven: "We cannot think of her as gone/Faith does not part with those we love."[16]

A rather startling glimpse into Shaker attitudes toward death can be gained by examining an unusual death ritual enacted by the Shakers in New York in 1835. Concerned that the graves of their founding father and mother were being forgotten, the Shakers decided to exhume Mother Ann Lee, Father William Lee, and Mother Lucy Wright, and rebury them in a row in the Watervliet burial ground. When their bodies were recovered, a Shaker observer noted that their coffins were badly rotted but their bones were remarkably intact, even fingers and toes. While new coffins were being constructed, the community of

Lizzie Flagg of Lawrence came here to search of a home, but should have gone to the poor house of that city. Her babe of 3 mo. died on the 24th, and was buried in our cemetery. The little girls conducted the funeral with aid from an older sister. . . .

George W. Webster was stopping for a few days at our north family. He was 46 yrs old and an ordained minister. Being tired of life he committed suicide by hanging himself from a beam in the horse barn. He was not found till life had passed from him.

—HENRY CLAY BLINN,
"Church Record," c. 1895

SHAKER CEMETERY WITH IRON FENCE
AND SINGLE MARKER, early twentieth century.
A wealthy Boston friend of the Shakers paid for the
marker, the fence, and fifty hydrangea shrubs to be
planted inside the stone walls.

Opposite ❖ HEADSTONES of individual graves
were removed from the Shaker cemetery in the
early twentieth century and recycled throughout the
village. These stones line the drip course of a new
porch installed on the south side of the dwelling
house in the early twentieth century. Because they
believed that neither the body nor the spirit of the
deceased was present at the grave site, the Shakers
were unceremonious about individual graves.

Shakers was encouraged to view the bones of their beloved founders, inspiring a time
of renewal with their spirits. One Shaker observer was moved by the cracked skulls of
Mother Ann and Father William, and reminded of the beatings and mob violence they
had endured.[17] Some scholars believe this event was instrumental in eventually sparking
the period of spiritual gifts of the late 1830s, known as the Era of Spirit Manifestations.

The Shakers revered the relics of the past, especially of their most important
leaders. Blinn's museum was the repository for some of the most important of these
memorial objects, which included textile fragments reportedly from garments worn by
Mother Ann Lee, Father Job Bishop's leather coin purse, a sander used by Mother Lucy
Wright, and William Lee's Bible, given by Father James Whittaker to the first Shaker missionaries to New England.

❖

DAILY LIFE AND WORK

The Shakers developed a concept of home distinctive from that of most Americans in the eighteenth and nineteenth centuries. Their home was their village, which they rarely left and where they spent their time living and working in communal order with fellow Shakers. The rituals of daily life and work were predictable, and the necessities of life were reasonably secure, as long as the high standards of the community were upheld.

South facade, dwelling house, seen from the fenced enclosure of the meetinghouse. The dwelling house was expanded to its current size with five additions built between 1793 and 1837. There is no known Shaker drawing of the original 1793 dwelling house.

DAILY LIFE

The dwelling house was the center of Shaker daily life. It was the bell house—the source of daily communications—and the gathering place daily for group activity in the form of meals and meetings. It was the largest residential space within a Shaker village, and the most functionally diverse of Shaker structures. By the 1840s, each of the Shaker dwelling houses was home to sixty or more adult believers.[1]

Within the Shaker Church Family order, the Shakers built at least two dwelling houses in the eighteenth century for every one meetinghouse. Where are the twenty or more eighteenth-century Shaker dwelling houses? The only eighteenth-century one in a Shaker museum is Canterbury's 1793 dwelling house, which is now encased in a much larger structure that has been modified five times since it was built for the Church Family. At Canterbury many features of the 1793 dwelling house have been obliterated or covered by later alterations. Its timber frame is intact, and several rooms on the third

Opposite ❖ Dwelling house, attic landing, with brothers' and sisters' staircases to storage attics and retiring rooms on the third floor. Originally the partition wall had no door.

DWELLING HOUSE, ENFIELD, CONNECTICUT. This dwelling house has been misidentified as a meetinghouse by earlier authors. In fact, this may be the only photograph of the original gambrel-roofed 1792 Shaker dwelling. The end-wall fenestration provides a clue as to how intensively the Shakers used space to provide cooking, storage, dining, sleeping, and meeting space for over forty men and women in one building. The 1876 dwelling house in the background shows the evolution of the Shaker dwelling-house form.

Opposite ❖ CHURCH FAMILY BUILDINGS, VEGETABLE GARDEN, AND THOMAS CORBETT'S BOTANICAL GARDEN, detail from map of Canterbury Shaker Village by Henry Clay Blinn, c. 1848.

floor retain their original architectural features. A 1794 Church Family dwelling house exists at Harvard, and is now a private residence. Its eighteenth-century exterior was modified from a gambrel to a gable roof by the Shakers in the nineteenth century; on the interior many eighteenth-century details are visible.

The best place to locate these original eighteenth-century Shaker dwelling houses is on the Shakers' nineteenth-century community maps. Unfortunately, by the time the first Canterbury map was completed in 1848, the Canterbury 1793 dwelling had already been altered five times, and none of the eighteenth-century dwelling houses at Canterbury retained their original gambrel roofs. On the Harvard map, three gambrel-roofed dwelling houses are visible. These same three Harvard Church Family dwellings are visible on a late-nineteenth-century photograph of the Harvard Church Family, although by that time all three had gable roofs.

To support Shaker order, the dwelling house needed to communicate gender separation and community harmony, and provide for the practical daily needs of at least several dozen residents. This meant large food preparation spaces, a communal dining area, common space for meetings, storage areas for bedding and clothing, and sleeping chambers. In thinking through the building's functions and its future inhabitants' needs, the community's leaders needed to plan carefully. New converts were arriving steadily, and buildings and furnishings took time to build. The Shakers could ill afford to make mistakes.

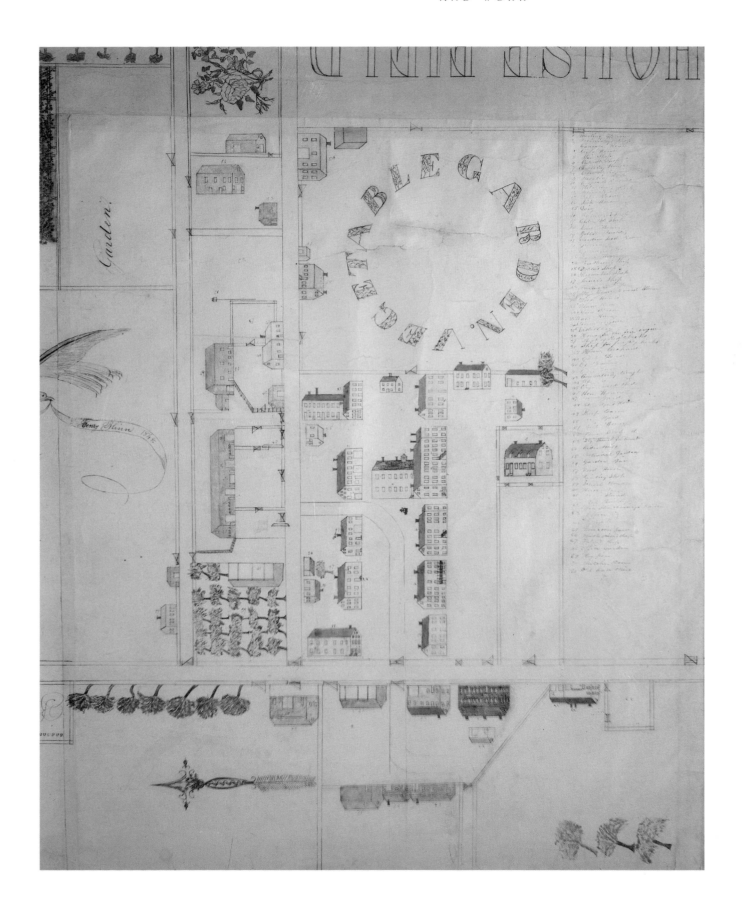

Under pressure, the Shakers built quickly but well in that first generation, at least at Canterbury. In recent years scholars have unearthed scathing criticisms of early New Lebanon buildings, especially dwelling houses, by Elder Isaac N. Youngs of New Lebanon, who disliked the small, crowded first-generation buildings, with their steep stairs and inadequate hall spaces. They have used his remarks and the evidence of replacement buildings to judge first-generation Shaker dwelling houses as inferior structures, contributing little either to Shaker order or to the Shakers' reputation as builders. Physical evidence at Canterbury shows that both the meetinghouse and dwelling house were buildings of excellent workmanship. They may have quickly become crowded, and bear characteristics of eighteenth-century construction (steep stairs, small halls), but these features do not suggest poor construction.[2]

At Canterbury, the gambrel roof design was difficult to expand and enlarge to accommodate the population that increased within a decade of its completion. The only solutions to growth pressures were to keep on building duplicates, as was done in most Shaker villages, where the Church Family built two, and even three, identical dwelling houses in a row, creating an architectural "peg rail" of Shaker residences. However, when even these were no longer adequate to house all the Shaker converts, the Shakers began to alter the first-generation dwellings, often at the expense of the structural integrity of the original. After twenty to forty years of this retrofitting, it is not surprising that the communities would need to design new dwelling houses that could house more people and might later be expanded in any direction. Consequently, the Shakers altered their eighteenth-century template in the 1820s and 1830s, and then adapted it again in the late nineteenth century for the last generation of Shaker dwelling houses at New Lebanon (1876), Enfield, Connecticut (1876), and Sabbathday Lake (1883).

Canterbury was one of the few eastern Shaker communities to not build a new Church Family dwelling house in the 1820s or 1830s. The reason was not a lack of funds, for the Canterbury community was thriving in the 1830s; nor was it a lack of demand. Canterbury was growing so rapidly in the 1830s that the Church Family undertook a major dwelling house expansion in 1837, and added a central ell to the existing dwelling house, complete with a new vegetable and meat cellar, a chapel, ministry apartments, and a sisters' storage attic for seasonal bedding and clothing.

The New Hampshire Ministry, which had to approve the new ell at Canterbury, also approved a massive new dwelling house at Enfield, called the Great Stone Dwelling (1837–41). More expensive than the Canterbury project, its masonry work was so challenging that the Shakers called in Ammi Young, the architect of a college dormitory at Dartmouth College, Wentworth Hall (1828), in nearby Hanover, New Hampshire.[3]

Why did one New Hampshire Shaker community expand its eighteenth-century dwelling whereas the other erected an entirely new building? Given the same ministry, the same general need, and the financial stability of both communities, then either the Canterbury Church Family did not want a new dwelling house built outside their dwelling house south row, or else they did not want to tear down the old dwelling to make way for a new one at the center of the Church Family.

Left ❖ "DWELLING HOUSE, EAST CANTERBURY, NEW HAMPSHIRE," Kimball Studio, c. 1880. This photograph was carefully composed for external appeal, but the well-dressed Shaker sisters and girls are headed for the brothers' entrance!

Below ❖ SECTION DRAWING, DWELLING HOUSE (prepared by Richard M. Monahon and Donald R. Watson, 1980s). This drawing is generally accurate for the building after its expansion in 1837.

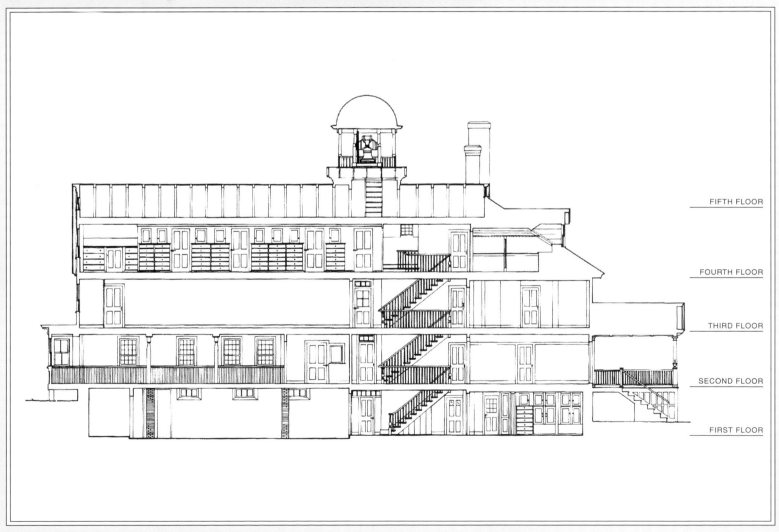

FIFTH FLOOR

FOURTH FLOOR

THIRD FLOOR

SECOND FLOOR

FIRST FLOOR

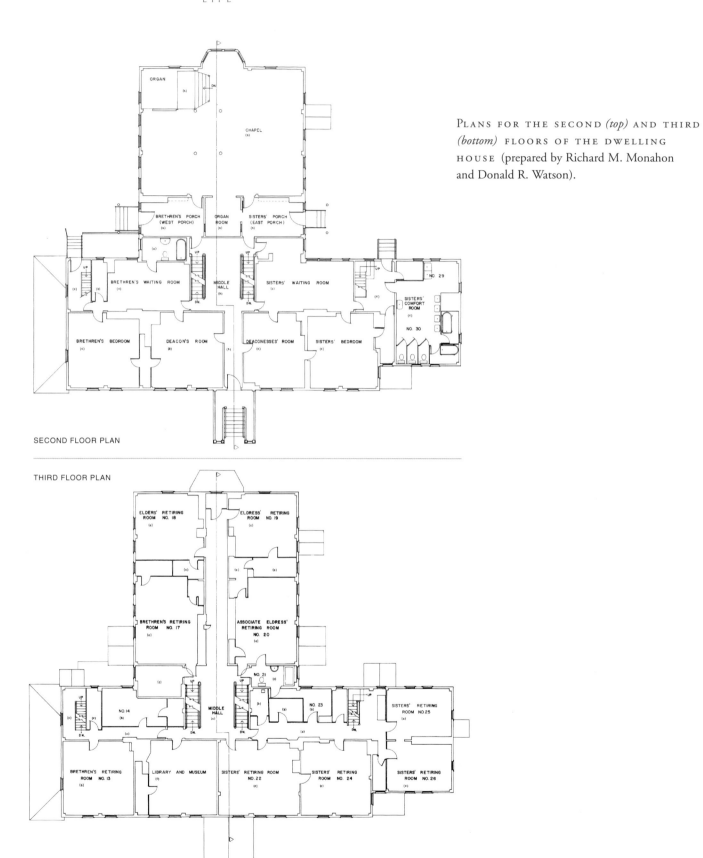

PLANS FOR THE SECOND *(top)* AND THIRD *(bottom)* FLOORS OF THE DWELLING HOUSE (prepared by Richard M. Monahon and Donald R. Watson).

SECOND FLOOR PLAN

THIRD FLOOR PLAN

GREAT STONE DWELLING, Enfield,
New Hampshire, 1837–41.

The choice of an architect for the Great Stone Dwelling at Enfield is significant in Shaker architectural history, for it is one of the earliest known occasions on which the Shakers turned to the outside world for such professional assistance. The use of an outside architect was unusual, but Young was the best person in the region for the task at hand, because of his experience in building mass housing (for unmarried students) and in masonry construction.

All students of Shaker architecture have missed the central fact about eastern Shaker dwelling houses, namely that there is a deeply rooted pattern to them that does not change from the 1780s to the 1880s. Over time there is an evolutionary development, and the dwelling houses change significantly in size, floor plan, building materials, and interior appointments, but the basic concepts remain constant.

Shaker dwelling houses are inherently more complex than meetinghouses, which were designed for very specific purposes of public worship and ministry occupation. Dwelling houses had to serve multiple purposes, both practical (cooking, eating, and sleeping) and symbolic (central hearth, communication center, meeting place). Their design was particularly important, for the concept of gospel order might fail in daily life if these structures did not do their job. In the larger scheme of village architecture, with a community of believers functioning as a "living building," the dwelling contains the physical and psychological "carriers" of the living, or spiritual building. (A carrier, in architectural terms, is the largest beam on each level of a timber-frame building, spanning the center and tying the sides to each other.)

The prototypical eighteenth-century Shaker dwelling-house plan was organized around a centrally located space or core, which was based on the manipulation of square dimensions.[4] On the ground level this was the community dining room, approximately square in dimension. This space, symbolically divided into two parts (a brothers' side and a sisters' side), had separate entrances for men and women. There was no physical barrier in the dining room. Kitchens and pantries flanked the dining room on one side, with a ministry dining room and pantry on the other side. A central entryway and double staircase provided vertical and horizontal transition spaces for the dwelling.

On the second floor of these early dwelling houses, the Shakers built another central space: the meeting room. A double square, it sat directly above the dining room, and was accessed by another entryway/stair hall. The flanking wings on this floor were separated by gender, with waiting rooms for sisters and brothers on the opposite sides of the building, adjoining the stair hall.

The central space on this second floor had to be treated differently than the dining room, since the meeting room needed to serve multiple purposes. This was done in the manner of the earliest 1780s Shaker homes, by means of a movable partition, a practical device that was also common in American and English Quaker meetinghouses, and in New England taverns. Most of the Shaker examples have long since been re-moved, but at Canterbury three sections of these eighteenth-century partitions survive in cut down, reused form. Evidence of similar partitions survives in later dwelling houses at New Lebanon's South Family and Hancock's Church Family, to mention only two examples.[5]

THE EARLY SHAKER DWELLING HOUSE

It now became necessary to provide buildings for the accommodation of the large family, which numbered some sixty persons. A building 34 x 44 ft. and two stories high was planned for a Community dwelling and finished before the close of the season (1794, Enfield, NH). It contained the cook room and dining room in the basement and on the first floor above ground, a meeting room extending the whole length of the house. Three partitions running across the room were folded back in times of religious service and gave the family a room of convenient size. When these partitions were closed, four rooms were formed, two for the use of the Brethren and two for the Sisters. Several rooms were also finished for the accommodation of the Brethren and Sisters on the second loft.

—HENRY CLAY BLINN, "Historical Notes Having Reference to the Believers in Enfield, New Hampshire," n.d.

The first-generation dwelling houses of the 1790s were clever and successful patent models of gospel order. They proved to be inadequate because they simply became too small for the explosive growth of the early Shaker communities. At fault was the stricture that no other core building could greatly exceed the 32-by-42-foot (9.76 × 12.8 m) size of the meetinghouse. The early leaders clearly envisioned multiple dwelling houses and a domestic scale for their villages, and sought to maintain a distinctive Shaker site plan and architectural look. The 32-by-42-foot gambrel-roofed buildings, with or without base-ment, with or without dance floor, could be replicated endlessly, at least in theory. But as the Shakers built the second and third dwelling houses, with no end in sight, they were forced to revise their plan.

The Shaker fathers and mothers of the eastern communities resisted allowing alterations, building larger buildings, and giving up their prototypical structure. At New Lebanon, Mother Lucy Wright simply ignored all entreaties and all evidence of over-crowding in her refusal to build a new meetinghouse. Upon her death in 1821 the New Lebanon ministry launched a building program that led to a massive new meetinghouse in 1824 and a series of new and larger dwelling houses. In New Hampshire, the Shakers had to wait until Job Bishop's death in 1831 to add a major wing to the Canterbury dwelling house and to plan for the Great Stone Dwelling in Enfield. Once the limitations of the pattern from the Mount were demonstrated, and Shaker fathers and mothers had died, the succeeding leaders were quite capable of building to their needs and planning for growth. The second-generation dwelling houses of the 1820s and 1830s were designed and built well, and most served their respective communities through the high population levels of the mid-nineteenth century.

Numerous writers have assumed that these second-generation dwellings are new building types that reflect the true genius of Shaker architecture. This is correct in terms of overall size, and in the expansion of space and light within them, but these dwellings are not really new forms. They are improved buildings, with more spacious hallways and staircases, larger windows, and important refinements for daily living, but their basic form and underlying proxemic pattern is the same as the first-generation dwelling houses based on the pattern from the Mount.

The 1820s South Family dwelling at New Lebanon survives essentially intact as built. Although twice as long as the first-generation dwellings, and with a gable roof, the building still retains the same distribution of space as the eighteenth-century originals. The kitchen and dining room are on the ground floor, with the meeting room directly above the dining room. Even the stair hall mirrors the early dwelling houses, although the staircases are open and more spacious. The 1830s Hancock Church Family dwelling has a radically different floor plan than the first-generation buildings, but all the same functions are present. In this case, the dining room has been moved from the first floor to the second floor, allowing more room for food storage and preparation in the basement. The two principal group spaces are no longer stacked in the center of the structure, but are spread to the ends of the second floor and linked by a massive central hallway and double staircase in the center of the building. The 1837 Canterbury renovation reveals yet another variation on the same proxemic pattern. The meeting room is still on the second floor, but has been moved to the new ell. Nevertheless, all traditional dwelling-house functions—food preparation, dining, meeting, waiting, sleeping, and storage—are included. The 1837–41 Great Stone Dwelling in Enfield represents yet another variation on the same pattern. The dining room is located in the center, with the meeting room stacked on top of it, but the stair halls are split to the far ends of the building.

In 1876, as the Shakers built the third generation of dwelling houses, the fundamental proxemic pattern persisted. These buildings are even larger than their second-generation predecessors, made so chiefly by adding a multistoried ell, as at Canterbury.

THE SHAKER MINISTRY

The highest order among them is called the "Ministry," or "Holy Anointed of God on Earth," consisting of two males and two females. Their Bishopric extends over the two societies of Enfield and Canterbury. The Ministry reside in the chambers over the church; four chambers in the second story. There are two doors, one stairway and a hall; the males occupy one end, the females the other. They have another building, called their workshop, where they work days. Evenings, nights, and Sundays, they stay in their chambers. Nobody but Elders are allowed to go there, and they only on business.

The government was a veritable theocracy. The Ministry were "The Holy Anointed." They were in a way aloof from the people. They lived in a house by themselves alone. They ate in a room by themselves and their food was cooked by a sister in a kitchen provided for the Ministry only. If a member had a grievance against an Elder and desired to appeal to the Ministry, permission to see the Ministry must first be obtained from the Elder.

—NICHOLAS A. BRIGGS,
"Forty Years a Shaker," 1921

The most interesting feature of this innovation is that the last Shaker dwelling houses return to the purity of the original patterns in the most essential placement of the meeting room directly over the dining room in the center of the building, although in an ell. The double staircases are returned to the center of these third-generation buildings at New Lebanon, Enfield (Connecticut), and Sabbathday Lake.

In nearly one hundred years of dwelling-house construction, the Shakers experimented with the pattern from the Mount, stretched its boundaries, and changed its external shell dramatically over time, but retained its central meaning and use.

Housing for the ministry was incorporated into the meetinghouse. The original New Lebanon design, replicated ten times by Moses Johnson, provided rooms in the upper two lofts, or levels, of each meetinghouse, to be used by the presiding elders and eldresses.

The ministry provided spiritual leadership for all families of the New Hampshire bishopric (comprising Canterbury and Enfield). Because of this importance, the Shakers believed that the ministry needed to live in separate quarters in order to preserve their spiritual purity, free them from the overwhelming trivia of daily communal life, and maintain their impartiality for their problem solving and leadership among the communities. They maintained living and work spaces in both Canterbury and Enfield, and divided their time equally between the two communities.

Actually, the New Hampshire Ministry rarely mingled with the larger body of Shakers in the early decades of the settlement. The meetinghouse had no separate kitchen, so in the early years the ministry had their food brought to their living quarters. Their daily work was carried out in a separate one-story workshop. In 1848 a larger ministry shop was built directly behind the meetinghouse, but oriented north and south facing the Church Family dwelling house. This new facility contained a workshop for elders on the first floor (with an entry on the north), and for eldresses on the second floor (with an entry on the south). Each group had a separate granite walk leading to their respective ministry shop entrances.[6]

In 1878 the New Hampshire Ministry abandoned the meetinghouse living quarters and moved permanently into the ministry shop, a combined residence and workshop. They took their meals in a small private dining room, with its own pantry and its own exterior entrance, in the dwelling house. The ministry's dining room could not be seen from the main dining room, but a built-in wall pass-through allowed servers to transfer food without intruding.

The ministry was not the only group to receive special attention. The Church Family had a significant number of children from 1792 through the 1930s, children of adult converts, but also children from broken and economically distressed non-Shaker families. These young believers were treated well in order to develop the next generation of workers and leaders. As with the larger society, boys and girls were segregated, but instead of being housed in one large building, they were reared in separate buildings under the tutelage of specially appointed live-in brothers and sisters. At Canterbury a girls' house was designated as early as 1830, when the second trustees' office (1810) was moved to a prime site fronting the dwelling house dooryard to the east.

Opposite ❖ RETIRING ROOM OF ELDER HENRY CLAY BLINN on the first floor of the ministry shop, built 1848. The portrait of Blinn is a museum addition.

VIEW FROM THE SOUTH, SHOWING THE
RELATIONSHIP OF THE MEETINGHOUSE
TO THE 1848 MINISTRY SHOP, the first
building at Canterbury to have a tin roof. Several
Canterbury Shakers saw such a roof first in 1834 on
the United States Arsenal, near Utica, while on a
trip through the Erie Canal. The New York Shakers
were the first to experiment with tin roofs.

CHILDREN'S HOUSE (FOREGROUND),
SISTERS' SHOP (BACKGROUND).
The children's house was built in 1810 as
the Church Family office and moved to
its present location c. 1830.

After the mid-nineteenth century, the decline in the number of brothers created a labor shortage. Brothers first were needed to fill positions as trustees, ministry elders, and family elders, so the Canterbury Shakers hired outside men to keep their vast enterprise functioning. Many of the workers resided in the Shaker community because they were needed for daily chores such as farming in the summer and filling woodboxes in the winter. Housing was modest; until 1905 they lived in a separate building in the brothers' section of the village, then to the west of Shaker Road, behind the trustees' office, horse shed, and horse barn.

DAILY ROUTINE

From 1793 to the building of the chapel wing in 1837, Shaker home life was quite austere. Even though food and clothing were ample except in a few brief hardship years, the community kept focused on work and worship.

A typical day in the life of a nineteenth-century Shaker brother or sister began before dawn—at 4:30 A.M. in summer and 5:00 A.M. in winter in the first part of the century, and half an hour later in the second part of the century. Since it was common to have two to six brothers or sisters sharing a dwelling-house retiring room, everyone rose at the sound of the bell, and had one hour to dress, strip bedclothes, and do morning chores before another bell called them to breakfast.

The brothers and sisters, ranked from the oldest to the youngest, filed silently down their respective staircases to the communal dining room. The two ranks entered the dining room simultaneously, but through different doorways; they proceeded to designated tables, knelt in silent prayer, and consumed a hearty breakfast without conversation. Sister Ethel Hudson, when asked what she remembered most about the Shaker system of dining, said, "Pie, and the simultaneous scraping of chairs on the floor," as everyone knelt for prayer, then stood, then took their seats for dinner. Food was served in Shaker style, that is, "foursquare," with each group of four place settings serving as a dining unit, having its own serving dishes, beverages, and condiments. At the end of the meal the silent prayer was repeated, and all filed out in ranks (only in reverse order, with the youngest leading the processions) and dispersed immediately to their assigned work.

They would begin work as daylight was breaking upon the village. At 11:30 the bell summoned the community from the fields, mills, and shops (the brothers in the distant mills ate the noon meal in their mills or adjoining quarters). Precisely at noon the process of seating and dining was repeated, and the main meal of the day was served. Work resumed from 12:30 to 5:30; the evening meal was served promptly at 6:00. The evenings might be spent in group singing meetings; "union" meetings, in which men and women conversed with one another in a carefully controlled group setting; or, if no meetings were planned, individuals could read, write, or study until the community bedtime, usually between 9:00 and 10:00.

On Saturday evening there was usually a service of preparation for the Sabbath, which technically extended from sundown on Saturday to sundown on Sunday (allowing for some necessary chores to be performed late on Sunday). Sunday, of course, was devoted to worship rather than work, with services typically on Sunday afternoon early in the nineteenth century, and on Sunday morning in the late nineteenth and twentieth centuries.

STEREOSCOPIC VIEW OF THE CHURCH FAMILY DINING ROOM, set for sixty people and decorated for the Christmas holidays. By Kimball Studio, c. 1880.

ELDRESS BERTHA LINDSAY cooking in the trustees' office kitchen, 1977.

Opposite, top ❖ HAYING IN THE NORTH FIELD. These hired men were supervised by Brother Irving Greenwood, who took their picture about 1920. According to Sister Bertha Lindsay, the wagons were overloaded at Brother Irving's insistence, for the purpose of making a dramatic photograph: "After Irving took the photograph, the men could not fit the wagon through the barn door, as the load of hay was too wide. It sat outside overnight and 'exploded' the next morning."

Opposite, bottom ❖ CANTERBURY SHAKERS' COW BARN seen in an historical photograph. It had three extensions to the south and was 250 feet (76.3 m) long, making it the largest barn in New Hampshire when completed in 1858. A similar barn had been built at Enfield, New Hampshire, in 1854.

DAILY WORK

The Shaker expression "Hands to work, hearts to God" summarizes how daily work was central to their spirituality.

Work was a badge of Shaker faithfulness; it was worship. Manual labor was not only a religious duty (as it was with other Protestant groups), it was a religious ritual. Labor was as much a religious "gift" as the Shaker gifts of healing and song. Departed Shaker friends were lauded and remembered for their utility in the community. Josiah Corbett (1758–1833), father of Dr. Thomas Corbett, was remembered as "a very industrious man [who] improved every moment in doing something useful."[7]

The Shaker work ethic was imparted to Shaker children by the example and encouragement of older members. In a 1908 letter to young Edith Green, an older sister praised the girl's work habits and cheerfulness as evidence of the proper correspondence of works and faith, as well as hands and heart. Sister Amanda passed to Edith advice she had received as a young Shaker: "I was told when young if I did not sweep out the corners of a room when cleaning it, that was the way the corners of my heart looked. I have never forgotten the lesson."[8] No person, whether a presiding elder or a young child, was exempt from the expectation that he or she provide useful manual labor for the good of the community. The nature and intensity of the workload was modulated according to age and ability, but essential to the Shaker way was the assumption that all but the most infirm could continue to be of use to the community. Even as late as the summer of 1990, a few months before her death, Canterbury's blind, ninety-three-year-old eldress Bertha Lindsay insisted on greeting visitors for short periods of time as her health permitted. When she could no longer greet visitors, she asked to help strip mint, share her memories, or do anything she could to contribute to the well-being of her friends and the village.

For the most part, the Shakers maintained strict boundaries between the work of men and women. The gender division of work closely paralleled that of the outside world. Shaker women handled domestic concerns such as cooking, cleaning, gardening, spinning, sewing, and the packaging of products for sale. Shaker men ran the mills, the farm, the sugar camp, woodlots, and certain industries. At Canterbury, the brothers developed in the early nineteenth century the trades of tanning, hatting, tailoring, shoemaking, blacksmithing, tinsmithing, carpentry, wood turning, stonecutting, and coopering; and making shingles, cabinets, clocks, wheels, pipes, brushes, brooms, and sieves. The brothers also made axes, hoes, shovels, scythes, whips, wool cards, and specialty items for the sisters. The sisters produced few products for sale until the 1820s, but were actively spinning and weaving from the earliest years of the community, making yarn, hosiery, and mittens, as well as butter, cheese, and applesauce. Although the print shop was run by Henry Clay Blinn, the typesetting was generally done by the sisters, at least in the second half of the nineteenth century.

Since the Shakers believed in labor rotation to sustain high worker motivation, teach respect for all types of labor, and promote work equity, the range of business enterprises and daily community tasks was an essential ingredient of internal harmony, and must have diminished the feeling of drudgery often expressed in contemporary non-Shaker diaries and journals about repetitive farm work, housework, and textile factory

Above ❖ Shaker brother at the sugar camp, stereoscopic viewcard, Kimball Studio, c. 1870.

Right ❖ Interior, Canterbury's cow barn, as it appeared c. 1910. The woodwork is made of American chestnut.

Opposite ❖ View of brothers' workshops, looking east. The small building in the center is the carpenter's shop, built in 1806 as a visitors' house. To the right is the brothers' north shop, built in 1824.

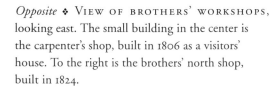

labor. The range of trades practiced represents the spectrum that would have been found in most American rural communities in the same period, but the Shakers specialized in them to a degree normally found only in a fairly large town.

The sisters developed several industries that lasted throughout the nineteenth century and helped support Canterbury financially as the brothers' industries faded in the years after 1875. These included canning vegetables and fruits; producing fruit and honey; and making candy, applesauce, butter, brushes, whips, palm leaf and straw bonnets, baskets, and poplar fancywork. In addition, other daily work was required for the community: vegetable gardening; laundering, ironing, and mending clothing; and record keeping. As with the brothers' trades, the sisters' work paralleled that of other farm women in northern New England, but the scale of their work quickly became commercial rather than household, and often required a specialization of labor rarely found in the ordinary farm household. This was especially true of food preparation and laundry, where some sisters would for a time be assigned to only kitchen work, other sisters just laundry tasks.

Shaker perfectionism is often touted as the basis for the quality of Shaker products. Edward Deming Andrews has argued that Shaker religion created such a "spirit of fine workmanship" that "nothing but faultless craftsmanship was tolerated." Andrews's source for this idea of perfection comes from the Shakers themselves.[9] As Henry Clay Blinn once stated: "Faithfulness in the manufacture of articles that were for sale was strictly enjoined. They were to be substantially made but without ornamentation. The Trustees were counseled not to sell any article unless it was free from blemish. The defective ones might be reserved for home use, or given to the poor."[10]

Above ❖ SISTERS' DOORYARD on the east side of the dwelling house, showing the sisters' entrances, from left to right, the sisters' shop, the dwelling house, and the laundry. The corresponding brothers' dooryard to the west was destroyed in 1905, when buildings were removed to prepare the way for the new creamery.

Opposite, top ❖ SISTER REBECCA HATHAWAY standing at the cooking arches in the syrup shop, where she supervised food processing and canning, c. 1960.

Opposite, bottom ❖ WORKROOM ON THE SECOND FLOOR OF THE LAUNDRY, set up to illustrate Canterbury's candy-making industry.

In fact, Shaker workmanship varied greatly within a given community, from village to village, and from time to time. The physical evidence seems to support the view that the highest standards of work were enforced within the various church families, and especially in objects made for use by the ministry, and a slightly lesser standard for items made for sale. This pattern seems to hold true for Shaker buildings, furniture, and household furnishings of all sorts. At other levels of Shaker community life, standards varied greatly and practicality seems to have been the operative principle.

Perfectionism may have been the rule, but examples of poor construction can be found in surviving Shaker buildings, furniture, and objects. In products made for the world, the Shakers were remarkably consistent for their day in the quality of consumer goods, earning the respect of consumers and strong sales of most Shaker products. The Shakers had learned how to use several of the most important ingredients of modern mass manufacturing and marketing: a stable, disciplined workforce; product standardization (workmanship of certainty); economies of scale; quality control; customer satisfaction; and brand-name marketing. The source of this customer orientation lay in Shaker religion and communitarianism rather than in the capitalist drive of the outside world, which emphasized high volume, low cost, and profitability.

In the period from 1790 to 1860, when the American economy was transformed from an agrarian base to an industrial one, even farming became connected to a market economy. Home-based trades shifted to a "putting out" system (an early stage of industrial development in which items such as shoes, knit hosiery, and palm leaf hats, tablemats, and fans were produced). Manufacturing became the new driving force. The American economy shifted from subsistence agriculture to cash-based industries. To prosper, people needed to generate both capital and cash.

The Shakers, as we have seen, supported this transformation with ardor, proving to be highly successful at generating capital and cash. However, the Shaker goal was for the individual to be freed from the insecurities of wage slavery and competition but also enjoy the benefits of a successful economy. This attitude set the Shakers apart from many utopian thinkers, as well as scientific socialists such as Karl Marx, who railed against the rise of the industrial order and cities, and attacked capitalism and its leaders as the enemies of mankind.

BROTHERS' MAPLE AND CHESTNUT
WORKBENCH, second half of the
nineteenth century.

SISTERS' TAILORING COUNTER, first floor of
the sisters' shop northwest workroom (33¾ ×
94½ × 36 in. [85.7 × 240 × 91.4 cm]). This was
the sisters' equivalent of the brothers' workbench.
Natural light from two sides of the room was
supplemented by electricity in the 1910–13 period.

In their daily work, the Shakers also participated in another economic trend in nineteenth-century life—that of the mechanization of the household and the transformation of domestic work. The cult of domesticity for American women meant that affluent women were to be freed from the drudgeries of housework through prosperity (enabling them to hire servants), new labor-saving devices, and changing definitions of a woman's role in the family. Women were transformed from laborers to household managers.

Scholars debate the extent and meaning of this revolution, but they agree that its effects were profound for the definition of women's roles in society and their relationship to men and power. Many women's studies scholars see the cult of domesticity as a male tactic of social control over women, and see the transformation as a net loss of women's rights, rights that had to be reasserted in the early twentieth century.[11]

The Shakers never endorsed the ideas of the cult of domesticity. Shaker women were always set apart from the experiences of the average American woman, largely due to the fact that they were not mothers, though Shaker communities valued children and some sisters and brothers assumed parental responsibilities over the children. Most Shaker sisters interpreted their childless situation as freedom to enjoy the benefits of

VIEW OF THE KNITTING ROOM IN THE LAUNDRY. The second floor of the laundry included a small knitting factory for manufacturing sweaters that were sold under the label of "Hart and Shepard."

sisterhood; a Shaker woman was not isolated from her female companions, like so many rural housewives bound to their farm chores and families and urban housewives in their domestic cocoons. In this way the Shaker women had more in common with their non-Shaker "mill girl" counterparts, who in this era enjoyed the company of their large sisterhood of workers.[12]

The Shaker sisterhood grew in strength from the late nineteenth to the twentieth century. The Shaker women had to assume nearly all community functions, including many leadership and business roles formerly reserved for the brothers. The feminization of Shaker life and work became a dominant characteristic of this era in every Shaker community.

LEISURE

The Shaker way of life makes no provision for recreation, and the prodigious achievements of the relatively few Shakers and the rigorous schedule of Shaker daily life left the Shakers with minimal leisure time. The rarity of known Shaker toys for children and a long-standing tradition prohibiting novels and pets also reinforce the concept that work and worship prevailed at all times.

Above, left ❖ LAUNDRY DRYING RACKS.

Above, right ❖ LAUNDRY ROOM ELEVATOR for carrying wet wash to the second-floor steam drying room. This elevator dates to 1908, when the laundry room was extensively renovated and new non-Shaker washing machines were installed.

Opposite ❖ VIEW OF LAUNDRY FROM THE EAST, showing, left to right, the original spin shop, the central laundry additions of 1816 and 1844, and the 1852 dry house, which was connected to the main laundry in the early twentieth century.

Against this all-work-and-no-play image, one needs to juxtapose the known facts of Shaker life at Canterbury in the late nineteenth and early twentieth centuries. The oral histories of the last generation of Shaker women are replete with tales of picnics, parlor games, popcorn parties, music, dramatic skits, winter coasting, and many other childhood and adult pastimes. As new technology entered their lives, the Shakers added bicycle riding, stereograph viewing, photography, phonograph listening, nighttime reading by electric lights, and evening radio listening.

Photographs of the village in the early twentieth century document some of the daily pleasures of Shaker life.[13] The candid photos taken by Shaker brothers and sisters also reveal their fondness for their animals and demonstrate that at least by the twentieth century, they did have beloved pets. Brother Irving Greenwood's dog Dewey, captured in photographs performing a variety of tricks, is only the prime example of a twentieth-century menagerie at Canterbury that included dogs, horses, cows, cats, and parakeets.

The abundance of well-worn books in several Canterbury Shaker libraries illustrates the fact that the Shakers had time to read, were encouraged to do so, and in fact read a wide range of fiction and nonfiction. The Church Family's dwelling-house library, for example, has holdings in history, natural history, religion, science, travel, and literature. Many are illustrated books on butterflies, flowers, foreign lands, and other subjects. A generous number of biographies of famous men and women line the shelves, along with extensive bound runs of *Scientific American* and *Century* magazine. Among later magazines, *Life* and *National Geographic* predominate. The number of novels, however, is probably the most surprising fact of this extensive library. Of the several thousand volumes, the novels represent a significant section—several hundred books. Eldress Dorothy Durgin was probably most responsible for relaxing the earlier Shaker prohibition of novels. This change seems to have come in the last quarter of the nineteenth century, since the dates of the novels in the dwelling-house library fall mostly in the period 1880–1930.

Recreational reading on any subject is an intriguing Shaker leisure activity because it appears to be antithetical to the basic Shaker tenets of communal life. Individual Shakers were rarely alone until late in the history of the village, for private activity was circumscribed by rules and the watchful eyes of the Shaker ministry. Weekly confession, potentially one of the most individualistic of Shaker religious practices, was made directly to an elder or eldress, rather than to God, in order to bare the most private, individual thoughts and practices to ministerial scrutiny. Reading was one of the most individualistic of Shaker acts. A Shaker could choose what to read—within the boundaries set by the library—and read it at his or her own pace and with his or her own thoughts, even though the individual read in a shared chamber or common living space.

The Shakers sought purpose in recreation, and in every era of Shaker history the leadership controlled types of activity and regulated its practice to serve the social ends of the group. Group dancing, union meetings for conversation between men and women, group singing, and group sewing are examples of regularly scheduled early-nineteenth-century Shaker social activity sanctioned by the ministry. Picnics, staged dramas or skits, games (such as croquet), and group reading were added in the late nineteenth century.

SISTER ETHEL HUDSON with a new pet, December 25, 1941.

Opposite ❖ PICNIC TRUNK purchased from Winship and Co., Boston, c. 1875. The porcelain-covered metal dishes and cups in the trunk were made in Sweden. The picnic was a Victorian leisure activity that the Shakers enjoyed.

"ENTERTAINMENTS"

An activity which afforded much pleasure, was the writing, staging and acting of entertainments, by the young people. Leader in this activity was Sister Josephine Wilson, who staged large Bible Scenes, with many actors. At Christmas, Easter and mid-summer, these entertainments of drama or comedy continued. Later the direction was under the leadership of Sister Aida Elam until about 1936. Once we staged a pageant of 103 characters, with only 30 actors taking part. Of course quick changes of costume made this possible, and it was fun to work out the plan.

—SISTERS MIRIAM WALL AND AIDA ELAM, *History of the Shakers: Education and Recreation*

ORIGINAL SHAKER ORCHESTRA, seen here in the music room of the sisters' shop, consisted of two violins, a cornet, a bass-viol, and a piano. A later orchestra included saxophones, drums, cymbals, and a pipe-organ. The orchestras performed concerts on holidays such as Easter and Christmas.

In the twentieth century groups of Shakers gathered in the chapel to sing, listen to the radio and the Victrola, and worship.

Although the restrictions of Shaker belief and communal practice appear harsh compared to American life today, which values individual choice, a powerful current of celebration flowed through Shaker recreation. In spite of restrictions such as celibacy and the Millennial Laws, the Shakers were radically exuberant in their celebration of life through music and dance, although the main goal of these activities was worship.

As the community matured, and as the nature of Shaker worship became more generically Protestant, dance as a form of worship declined. The Canterbury Shakers stopped dancing in worship about 1890. Recreational dancing, however, continued well into the twentieth century.

With the introduction of musical instruments into the community in the 1870s, worship and recreation changed, and congregational singing took a more prominent role. Groups of singers and instrumentalists formed for religious and social purposes, and gave performances for the Canterbury Shakers and for other religious and community organizations. Among these musical groups were the Que Vive Quartette; the Que Vive Trio; the Que Vive Quintette (with four sisters and Elder Arthur Bruce); and various instrumental groups such as the Spiritoso Orchestra with violins, cello, saxophones, and cornet. These groups traveled extensively in New Hampshire, providing special music for religious services, public library dedications, and Old Home celebrations. The longest trip of the Que Vive was in 1904, when they performed for the Shakers in Enfield, Connecticut; Hancock, Massachusetts; and Mount Lebanon and Watervliet, New York. The Shaker children also had special music ensembles.

One of the most prolific and interesting of the group recreations of the Canterbury Shakers is the form they called "entertainments," performances of dramas or skits, which the Shakers began to write and produce in the late 1870s. The content was often less important than the process of writing, staging, and performing the entertainment. Tremendous amounts of time must have been consumed in these activities, but they were wholesome outlets for creative expression, and everyone could participate at some level. The entertainments were central to the social life of the Canterbury Shakers for more than forty years.[14]

Some of the entertainments were partly or wholly original, but the majority were borrowed or adapted from a vast body of non-Shaker literature available from the 1870s through the 1920s. This genre of literature was created for the rapidly expanding Protestant Sunday school movement and for public schools, which staged pageants to promote patriotism and to demonstrate student achievement. The Shakers carefully screened their selections and occasionally edited dialogue in order to maintain Shaker propriety. One example of this material is Mayme Riddle Bitney's volume *Humorous Dialogues,* published in 1906 in Chicago. Two of the monologues are checked in pencil. In one, "An Aspiring Dishwasher," the setting is a country kitchen, and a young woman washing dishes talks to herself, dreams of the future. For their entertainment based on this piece, the Shakers eliminated the young woman's expletive "Oh, my gracious"; altered her wish for a "pale blue silk dress with low neck and short sleeves" into one for simply a "pale blue silk dress";

and substituted a Longfellow sonnet for a Shakespearean one. The original—unacceptable—poem reads:

> *Tying her bonnet under her chin,*
> *She tied her raven ringlets in.*
> *But not alone in the silken snare*
> *Did she catch her lovely, floating hair,*
> *For, tying her bonnet under her chin,*
> *She tied a young man's heart within.*

EASTER 1932. A Canterbury Shaker religious pageant performed in the Village chapel and featuring sister Marguerite Frost (center) as Jesus.

One of the longest original Shaker pageants was the Wonder Ball, compiled by Eldress Emma B. King from the events of the year 1929 and performed on Christmas Eve of that year. The pageant portrayed the year in the village in fifty-nine parts recited by village residents. Perhaps the most creative of the pageants is a historic play with an introduction titled "An Evening with the Revideo." The revideo is a device with a dial that enables the viewer to recapture the past. There is no date on this pageant, but it predates television, since the presentation of Canterbury entertainments ceased in 1936.

The Shaker entertainments were created originally for the Shaker community, but they grew so proficient at these performances that non-Shakers attended as well. Using a road sign to attract travelers, the Shakers offered dinner to visitors and their horses (fifty cents each) as well as wholesome entertainment, creating one of New England's earliest dinner theaters.

Most of the entertainments were presented in the chapel of the Church Family dwelling house. A stage curtain and sets were placed in the rear of the chapel, with access to the stage from the dwelling house. Scenery was painted on sheets by sisters Cora Helena Sarle, Bertha Lindsay, and others, and elaborate costumes were created by the skillful Shaker seamstresses. Sound effects included thunder rumbling from a log rolled down the hallway above the chapel, and a crash of lightning snapping from a tin sheet. The entire chapel was decoratively transformed, often using green or dried flower garlands. On at least one occasion, for the performance of Longfellow's "Song of Hiawatha," the meetinghouse became the scene of an elaborate drama. Rocks, tree branches, and green ferns provided the forest setting.

The Shaker ministry was deeply involved in the planning and execution of the entertainments. Shakers Jessie Evans, Josephine Wilson, Emma B. King, Lillian Phelps, Marguerite Frost, and Bertha Lindsay—who all eventually became eldresses—each participated in the pageantry, whether religious or secular.

❖

COMMUNITY ORDER

REGULATING EVERYDAY LIFE

For many Shakers, the communal life of order and rule was liberating. Their discipline in the community led to rewarding collective achievements in the affairs of life and meaningful fusion with fellow believers and God in the spiritual realm. Although many Shakers chafed under the burden of discipline, and ultimately more people left or were dismissed than stayed, the testimonies of fulfilled Shakers abound.

Over time, outside observers of Shaker life noticed the inherent tensions between individualism and community, and freedom and structure, within Shakerism. Nathaniel Hawthorne adeptly exploited the tension between individual will and community order in his short stories, and expressed a strong but polite skepticism of the Shaker way in "The Canterbury Pilgrims." He unequivocally sides with the story's two young lovers, Josiah and Miriam, who are fleeing the Canterbury community and represent the future of young America for Hawthorne. The discouraged and trouble-ridden refuge seekers on their way to the Shakers are the broken victims of life, opting for the security of the past, like "that other refuge of the world's weary outcasts, the grave."

To understand the Shaker concept of order, one must know how it worked for members of the community. The Canterbury Shakers developed a set of physical and intellectual boundaries, signs, and systems to reinforce gospel order. The common belief is that this concept of Shaker order is delineated best in the Millennial Laws of 1821 and 1845. This set of laws can be read as, variously, the bible of daily Shaker living, proof of social control in the extreme, or an attempt to deal practically with the growth strains of

Pages 122–23 ❖ VIEW SOUTH FROM THE DWELLING-HOUSE BELL TOWER, showing the paths and the 1830s picket fence surrounding the meetinghouse.

Opposite ❖ SPIRIT DRAWING OF "THE HOLY CITY," with twelve exterior gates and twelve interior gates. This pen-and-watercolor drawing (31 × 24¾ in. [78.7 × 62.9 cm]) was produced on March 16, 1843, at New Lebanon, New York. An inscription reads "Sacred Sheet From Mt. Lebanon." The drawing came to Canterbury after the closing of the New Lebanon community in 1947, and was subsequently sold to Mr. and Mrs. Julius Ziegat. Collection of the Philadelphia Museum of Art.

Left ❖ PAINTED INSTRUCTIONS like "Shut this door," on the carriage house doors, were a regular part of Shaker organization techniques, which left very little to chance or individual discretion.

a particularly turbulent era of Shaker history. In truth, the Shakers in Canterbury were guided in life not so much by a rule book as by operating systems of signs and symbols that provided a framework for harmonious living and group regulation.

The goal of Shaker community living was to free the individual from worldly concerns and the minutiae of daily decision making. This freedom, the Shakers believed, would improve production, diminish human frictions, and liberate the spirit for pure thought and dedicated worship. The less thought invested in decisions like when to get up, what to wear, what work to do, what to eat, how to make a living, and how to behave, the more productive and spiritual one could be.

The Shakers developed a range of physical and intellectual boundaries and systems designed to reinforce their concept of gospel order. Collective conceptions of comfort and convenience were often shaped by knowledge of technological innovations gleaned from the Shakers' reading. Always on the cutting edge of technology, the Shakers incorporated up-to-date labor-saving devices (which by increasing efficiency, they believed, helped to provide more time for singing meetings and worship), adopted modern conveniences and systems well in advance of their local and regional neighbors, and experimented liberally with new labor-saving devices such as sewing and knitting machines.

Systems of circulation, numbering, storage, communication, water and sanitation, heating, fire protection, and light control were designed to serve community goals. These physical systems were reinforced by patterns of oral and written communication that formed the mortar of Shaker society.

THE PROPER PATH

Most world religions share the concept of a spiritual journey or pilgrimage with the goal of arriving at a sacred place in order to achieve forgiveness, healing, and growth. The physical path has a distinct identity, with zones, boundaries, landmarks, and focal points, all of which provide a clear sense of direction toward a sacred center. The more clearly a religious community expresses belief systems through architectural and spatial patterns, the more successfully the community's members will be able to follow the intended spiritual path.[1]

The most obvious vehicles for expressing religious belief are sacred places—churches, temples, shrines, and the spaces around them. Unlike many religions, however, Shakerism did not have an exclusive sacred space—Shakers believed divine presence resided in people, not in a particular building, such as their meetinghouse; religious expression could occur in any number of places and settings. The entire village formed a spiritual entity, and the paths, dooryards, work spaces, and dancing ground would direct each believer through work and worship.

But just as architecture is more than physical form, the sacred place is more than a building. It encompasses not only the site but also the the approach to that site, the patterns of access and circulation, the flow of voids and solids, and the experience of the participant's dynamic interaction with it. A sacred place is meant to be experienced totally, with all senses active as the participant moves toward and through it. Assuming that paths and sacred spaces are just as key elements of architectural composition as buildings and

Opposite ❖ GRANITE WALK TO THE MEETINGHOUSE, from the entrance to the dwelling-house kitchen.

their purposeful stairways and rooms, one can examine the details of the village layout at Canterbury to better understand Shaker belief and practice.

As we have seen, the pattern of Canterbury Shaker Village was determined as early as 1793 by the relationship between its two most important buildings: the meeting-house and the dwelling house. An elaborate system of circulation devices was installed and increasingly refined and routinized until the first era of new construction in Church Family architecture ended in the 1850s.

Circulation through the village was controlled by solid devices such as granite walks, steps with iron railings, wooden fences, and stone walls, all of which reinforce the geometric order of the village architecture and strictly regulate the passage of people from one place to another. But there are also guiding paths, entrances, hallways, stair-cases, and doorlocks. In addition, movement through the village is enhanced by comple-mentary views from within the buildings, outside vistas, and by the interplay of solids and voids within the overall architectural and landscape compositions. In this sense one could see a parallel between the regimented choreography of Shaker dance and the daily ritual of life.

Opposite ❖ MEETINGHOUSE with 1815 porch addition and double entrances leading to the single staircase used by elders and eldresses of the New Hampshire Ministry.

Below ❖ GRANITE WALK INTERSECTION at the west end of the dwelling house, showing one of the only two Shaker-made diagonal paths in the village. Both diagonal paths lead away from the dwelling-house kitchen door.

Stereoscopic view of Kimball Studio, c. 1870. This shows the dwelling-house row (what the Shakers called "south row") with granite walk built by Micajah Tucker in 1835.

Right ❖ Box, cupboard, and door keys, mid- to late nineteenth century, from the Canterbury Shaker Village collections.

Below ❖ Wooden box lock, chestnut, c. 1800. The lock was part of Henry Clay Blinn's museum at Canterbury.

Neither outsiders nor members of the Shaker community could circulate freely between buildings. A person in an inappropriate place would be noticed quickly. Many interior and nearly all exterior doors had locks, restricting free movement. Access to many buildings, rooms, closets, and chests was restricted to those who were given the right to be there. The survival of an impressive range of keys at Canterbury testifies to the fact that although village security was surely a major concern, control of unwanted access from within the community may have been just as important as the fear of theft. To us, the existence of circulation controls at the village might be seen as excessively manipulative, but it is perhaps best understood as part of the symbolism of the overall order of Shaker life.

The purposeful circulation pattern insulated each Shaker at several levels. It isolated non-Shakers from the Shaker community; separated the Shakers by gender;

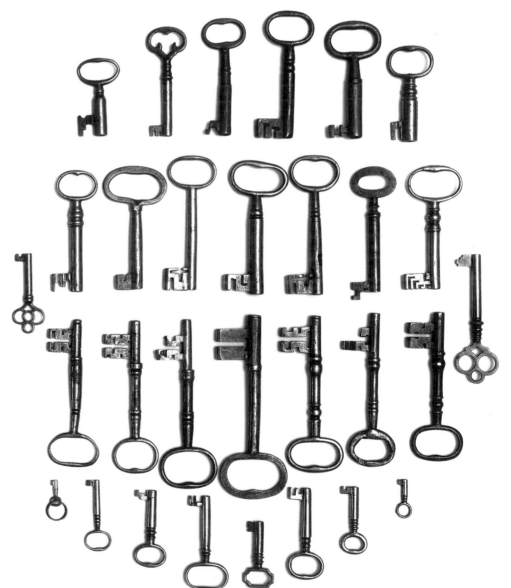

segregated the ministry from the brothers and sisters; and guarded against unintentional encounters by business visitors and hired men with Shaker children and members of the community.

The Shakers were not deliberately trying to be secretive or mysterious. In the Church Family plan, the visible pattern of solids (roads, paths, buildings) and voids (dooryards, gardens) was overlaid with an invisible pattern of implied boundaries that were observed through knowledge and discipline. These symbolic boundaries were hardly cloistered walls with locked gates; rather they were subtle—and often invisible—reminders of internal discipline. The Shakers, as we have seen, were spiritualists at heart, accepting communication with both the physical and the spirit world. So, too, in matters of the passages around their village and community, they were fluent in thinking of both the visible and the invisible worlds.

GROUND-FLOOR DWELLING-HOUSE LANDING, showing the double entry that leads into the dining room and the twin staircases.

LETTERS AND NUMBERS

In addition to the control of circulation, the Shakers regulated their lives through an extensive classification system of numbers and letters. This is usually interpreted today as charming evidence of the Shakers' adherence to the dictum "a place for everything and everything in its place." The process of numbering was a way of ensuring that everyone would contribute to community neatness and order and would know exactly where the things assigned to them should be kept. All buildings were assigned letter designations, such as "D" for dwelling house. In common usage, the Shaker records generally refer to buildings by their letter. For example, "House E" was the east house and "House I" was the infirmary. Metal plates with these letters were mounted above the front doors of buildings throughout the village.

Within buildings, most rooms and many closets were numbered; "D19," for example, was a chamber in the dwelling house. In certain cases, the system of letters and numbers was extended to drawers and cupboards, so that it would be possible for someone to be sent to drawer 96 in the new sisters' attic in order to store a blanket for the summer.

Shakers were obsessed with classification through numbering and labeling. One can imagine that gospel order could have been maintained with fewer numbers. The

BANK OF DRAWERS AND CUPBOARDS flanking a large walk-in closet in the new sisters' attic of the 1837 dwelling house. Each separate storage system (closets, cupboards, and drawers) has its own numbering sequence.

numbering at Canterbury takes on added significance, however, when it is seen as a system of signs within a larger communication system of architectural composition.[2]

Numbers communicated several important ideas, and their visibility served as regular visual reminders of those ideas. The numbers and letters were symbols of the underlying moral and spiritual order of the Shaker community. They were also a device to facilitate assignment, by deacons and deaconesses, so that there would be no reason for internal bickering or sloppiness. By eliminating choice by the rank and file, and ensuring equality, the Shakers hoped to undercut the basis for rivalry concerning the size or location of spaces for work or daily living.[3]

LAUNDRY BASKETS IN THE IRONING ROOM. Each basket sits in a designated space. Newly ironed clothing would be placed in the appropriate basket ready for delivery to the appropriate buildings and rooms.

A PLACE FOR EVERYTHING

The Shakers elevated storage to an art form. Their attention to detail in the amount of time devoted to planning and building storage units, and the level of finish accorded them, is astonishing compared to the relative lack of attention to storage in the outside world.[4]

In the 1790s built-in closets and cupboards were sparse in New England houses—as they were in the first generation of Shaker buildings at Canterbury, from 1792 to approximately 1815. After that first wave of building the Shakers began expanding storage capacity with a vengeance, providing much-needed space for the products of their burgeoning industries as well as space for supplies and goods used by the community.

The attention to storage units, both freestanding furniture as well as built-in cupboards, closets, and cases of drawers, was in direct response to the growing population and prosperity of the Canterbury Shakers. The seemingly endless flow of storage chests, built-in and freestanding cupboards, and closets made from 1820 to 1845 is ample testimony to the Shakers' rapidly expanding capital around the middle of the nineteenth century. The apogee of this storage boom is especially evident in the building of the trustees' office (1830–33) and the new sister's attic in the dwelling house (1837), and in the erection of the north shop (1841), a three-story industrial building with considerable storage space:

Below, left ❖ Third-floor storage cupboard with access ladder, trustees' office.

Below, right ❖ Dwelling-house basement food storage, showing the hanging rack for dressing meat and various food storage cabinets.

Opposite ❖ First floor of sisters' shop, showing floor-to-ceiling built-in cupboards, peg rail for chair storage, wood box, and tinder box.

Right ❖ THIRD-FLOOR CLOSET, MINISTRY SHOP, with double rows of pegs. Note the initials "EMH," for Eldress Emmeline Hart. The peg rack dates to 1848, the year the ministry shop was built.

Above ❖ INTERIOR OF ONE OF THE STORAGE CLOSETS, third floor of the 1831–33 trustees' office. An unseen transom window admits natural light into this closet; the light then travels through the interior window shown, transmitting "borrowed light" into an adjacent knee wall closet. The baskets are a mixture of utilitarian and fancy baskets, some made by the Shakers and others purchased for use in the community.

the lower floor held wood and dry goods; a second floor had closets or built-in cupboards in every room; and a double loft served general storage.

The attention to detail in designing efficient storage is seen in the fine workmanship invested in all these buildings. The most accomplished Shaker woodworkers in the 1830s spent an inordinate amount of time in village attics, lavishing their skills on the moldings of units serving seemingly mundane purposes, located in spaces seen only by the Shakers. This dedication to the service areas within the village was scarcely matched by their worldly counterparts—few of whom could afford, or saw the need, to spend as much of their hard-earned money on their attics as on their parlors. But for the Shakers, the woodworkers' extra effort paid out in the preservation of valuable textiles and clothing. The investment in quality storage served their commitment to order and their desire to meticulously protect their household goods from light, air, dust, and insects. This attention to storage was not a luxury, rather what modern scholars would consider an anthropological necessity. It helped to ensure the long-term care of valuable textiles and clothing and the efficiency of industrial enterprises. Their system of storage reflected the Shaker belief in a life of rule and gospel order.

COMMUNICATION

Communication was essential to the Shakers' interaction with the outside and further ritualized their own lives. Since travel to and from New Lebanon and other villages, and letter writing, consumed so much ministerial time, early on the Shakers developed printed works to transmit their beliefs to the widely scattered communities and the outside world. These books encouraged inquiry and were used to defend the Shakers against derision and persecution. Throughout the nineteenth century Canterbury became an increasingly important center for Shaker printing, especially after 1850 under the leadership of Henry Clay Blinn.

Internal communication was particularly important because of the Shaker need to ritualize and coordinate the daily schedules of the entire community. This concept is as central to successful communal living as time management was to early industrial capitalism. As with most monastic and communal societies in history, the Shakers exercised strict control over their seasonal calendar and daily schedule in order to fulfill their mandate of gospel order.

From 1792 at Canterbury the official communicator, or regulator, was a large shell, which was blown as a signal for rising before dawn, for mealtimes, and to end the workday.[5] This device was replaced first by a tin horn, then by the dwelling-house bell, cast for the Shakers in 1832 by Paul Revere and Sons of Boston. The bell tower at Canterbury was greatly enlarged in 1837, when the new wing was added to the dwelling house, and the bell presided over the community until the death of the last Canterbury Shaker in 1992, when it tolled the passing of Sister Ethel Hudson.

Nov 3, 1900—today a bell, formerly the one used to call sisters to the barn for milking is put up on the school house to be rung at school time to prevent tardiness among the boys especially, although the sound is heard distinctly throughout the village. (rung first time Nov 5.)

—DIARY OF SISTER JESSIE EVANS

DWELLING-HOUSE BELL TOWER with "Revere Boston" bell, c. 1837.

*Dec 24, 1862 Br David Parker makes the present of a
watch to the Elders for the use of the family. It has
been some twenty years since watches were generally
used. This is called an army watch and has a German
silver case. Cost $20.00 No one except Trustees has
carried a watch since they were discontinued. It was
by the urgent request of the Brethren in the several
Societies that they were again admitted. No watch
was used by the Ministry during several years.*

—HENRY CLAY BLINN,
"Church Record," c. 1895

BATTERY-POWERED TELEPHONE on the first
floor of the old spin shop in the laundry. This system
of magneto telephones is still in operating condition,
for internal communication only, courtesy of the
New Hampshire Telephone Pioneers.

The dwelling-house bell tolled five times a day, regulating the general daily rituals of the Canterbury Shakers. In 1900 it was supplemented by the schoolhouse bell,
which regulated the children's days when school was in session.[6]

The Shakers were quick to adopt other regulatory devices. From the beginning,
with no town or mill clocks or bells in proximity, the Canterbury Shakers began making
their own clocks. The first clockmaker, John Winkley, was a founding member of the
Canterbury community. Some time after his departure in 1795, the Shakers' skilled young
physician and mechanic, Thomas Corbett, became the village clockmaker. In time, the
Shakers abandoned the clock industry altogether, purchasing clocks from the highly tal-
ented clockmakers of Concord—Levi and Abel Hutchins and Timothy Chandler. Tall
case clocks by the Concord makers were installed in the 1793 dwelling house, the 1811 visitor's house, and the 1830–33 trustee's office. Numerous wall and shelf clocks from the
nineteenth century also would have been scattered throughout work areas and common
living rooms, but many of these were sold or collected from the village, leaving only their
dust shadows on the walls of Canterbury's buildings.

The intensive use of timepieces served both the industrial and spiritual needs of
the Canterbury Shakers. This practice set them apart from the Shakers' farming neighbors, many of whom could not afford clocks in the 1790s and would have preferred anyway
to live by the sunrise and sunset of the prevailing season. The acquisition of such fine
timepieces was never questioned by the Shakers, who saw time precision as a necessity of
gospel order and industrial efficiency. However, in their early years the Shakers drew the
line at the possession of pocket watches, for personal timepieces were deemed unacceptable

in a communal society. After December 24, 1862, however, the Canterbury Shakers tolerated the possession of individual timepieces; pocket watches and shelf clocks soon proliferated, especially among the ministry. The growing acceptance of clocks and watches reflected the Shakers' endorsement of change and technological innovation.

In methods of communication, as in other aspects of their daily lives, the Shakers often adopted those modernizations before their rural neighbors in New Hampshire. For example, there is evidence in the dwelling house of an early hand-pulled bell system, similar to the type found in wealthy British and American homes of the late eighteenth and early nineteenth centuries. The dwelling house also retains parts of a set of signal chimes, an early-twentieth-century magneto telephone system, and a 1930s system for radio reception. At one time, the village maintained its own switchboard in the trustee's office to serve an extensive network of magneto telephones throughout the village. (Today, Canterbury Shaker Village has the only working magneto telephone system in New Hampshire, with an internal system connecting seven museum buildings.) The infirmary was one of the first buildings to be connected to the village telephone system. This supplemented the infirmary's internal call bells, which had been installed in 1892. The signal box hung in the nurse's sitting room and library, with call bells in each patient room. The system, made in Concord by F. W. Landon, was similar to those used in Victorian homes to call domestic servants.

These many communications systems at Canterbury were used not just to keep people in line. They were necessary for sustaining teamwork and maintaining the pace of community life.

CLEANLINESS

Given the number of Shakers at Canterbury and the lack of a major river or lake, the reliable supply of clean water was a major community concern, and over the years it consumed much energy and capital. Fortunately, good wells were plentiful, and rainfall and snow accumulation provided ample water for cisterns. Nevertheless, by the late 1840s the village was faced with the need to create a small municipal water system. The seriousness of the water issue, and the Shaker determination to keep improving their system, can be seen in Peter Foster's 1849 map, which documents the Canterbury water lines.

Once water could be directed to individual buildings, the Canterbury Shakers could plan for running water and internal water closets. The first indoor commode was installed in the infirmary's second-floor hall in 1852. No detailed information survives on the nature of this system, but it was almost certainly an earth closet. Full indoor plumbing was not available in the village until the early 1880s, and once again the infirmary was the first building to have true water closets and wash basins. Plumbed bathtubs soon followed, and by the late 1880s full baths with running water and water closets could be found in the trustee's office, the ministry shop, and the dwelling house at the Church Family, as well as the infirmary.

Until the 1880s toilet apparatus consisted of chamberpots, closestools, privies, and outhouses. Today at Canterbury Shaker Village, only one of many outhouses survives,

TALL CLOCK, Concord, New Hampshire, T. Chandler, c. 1815. This clock, signed by one of Concord's premier clockmakers, stands in the second-floor stair hall of the dwelling house.

a small separate structure, formerly attached to the ministry stable, that was reserved for the elders and eldresses. Two indoor privies remain: one is in the 1825 carriage house, where it served the community physicians until the 1850s; the other is the schoolhouse privy, attached to an older woodshed.

Internally before the 1880s, various types of closestools were available. These ranged from small wooden closestools, to Shaker potty chairs, to a wide variety of chamberpots—from plain English ironstone pots to English Staffordshire pots—many of which have been found recently in the attics of the infirmary and dwelling house.

As time passed, the Shakers introduced the improvements available to most middle-class urban Americans of the late nineteenth and early twentieth centuries, including copper hot water tanks heated from wood-fired cookstoves and porcelain bathtubs and bathroom fixtures. Many of these systems from the period from 1890 to 1920 remain intact in the village today and display the evolution of plumbing technology in the twentieth century.

The village continued to develop its water supply and storage capabilities. The 1849 water system supplied a rapidly growing community, and one that was changing its

Opposite ❖ DRY SINK in one of the second-floor ministry retiring rooms in the 1792 meetinghouse, c. 1840. The sink connected to a lead drainpipe that was encased in an exterior wooden downspout.

Below ❖ TIN BEDPAN made by Canterbury tinsmith Thomas Hoit, c. 1840.

Bottom ❖ VIEW OF A TWO-BAY MINISTRY PRIVY, looking south, built in the early nineteenth century as an addition to the 1794 ministry horse stable.

SHAKER POTTY CHAIR, c. 1840, with
Staffordshire chamberpot, in one of the infirmary
first-floor patient rooms. The chamberpot is one
of several imported ceramic pots found in the
infirmary attic during restoration in 1991.

THE SHIRLEY MEETINGHOUSE

*There are two Stoves inserted into the two chimnies
at the end of the Building, but they are not in the
middle, but so placed as to unite with the sides of the
passage which lead into the chambers, with which
there is a communication from the sides of the
building without, near the front corners.*

—REV. WILLIAM BENTLEY, 1795

sanitation habits to include the more frequent laundering of clothing and the introduction
of personal bathing. By the 1880s, with a proliferation of bathrooms through the village,
reliance upon only one well was becoming increasingly risky. In 1900 the Church Family
erected a windmill to pump well water into a large water tower, which would gravity-feed
the village's water distribution system. The tower and tank were a landmark at Canterbury for over forty years.[7]

HEATING

In New England heat is a precious commodity, and traditionally its supply has been a year-
round obsession. For centuries, wood has been the principal fuel. To ensure an adequate
supply of seasoned wood for home cooking, heating, and tasks such as maple sugaring required a substantial wood lot, careful planning for more than one season, and year-round
hard work—cutting, logging, preparing cordwood, and stacking it near its intended places
of consumption.[8]

Domestic heating for most New Englanders from 1620 to 1860 was by means of
the traditional English fireplace. All of the Canterbury Shakers' heated buildings from
1792 to 1810 contained fireplaces. However, extant buildings from 1810 (the old office,
now the children's house) and 1811 (the old visitors' house, now the infirmary) were erected
without fireplaces. Canterbury Shaker Village records reveal that at least by 1815 the
Shakers were tearing out fireplaces in the 1792 meetinghouse and reworking chimneys to
accommodate iron stoves.

The concept of radiating heat has a distinguished history, from the Roman hypo-
caust, which heated their floors, to the tile and metal stoves of central and northern
Europe. The English, however, long resisted the heating stove and developed entrenched
architectural traditions that enshrined the inefficient fireplace in its elaborately carved and
paneled chimney breasts and mantelpieces. The radiating iron stove was used mostly in
the homes of the Germans of Pennsylvania, New York, Maryland, North Carolina, and
Virginia, and the Dutch of New Jersey and New York. It was also used on sailing vessels,
especially in the cabins of ship captains. Otherwise, iron stoves were rare in the colonies.

No one has yet adequately explained the transmission of the Continental stove
into Shaker use, especially since they did build fireplaces into their earliest structures. The
Shakers at Shirley may have been the first in New England to use stoves;[9] the New Lebanon community may well have adopted the Dutch tradition of stoves, although the early
Shaker examples relate more closely in form to the box stoves of ships than to the large
heating stoves of the Dutch or German Americans. The Canterbury Shakers incorporated
both Franklin stoves and box stoves into their buildings, and by 1812 they may have been
capable of manufacturing their own stoves. Henry Blinn provided an account of the shift
from fireplaces to stoves in Shaker buildings:

> *The work of raising new buildings and of remodeling those already made seems to
> be one of the heavy burdens of the Society. It has now been decided to make some
> alterations on the "Meeting House." The stairs at the ends of the building are to*

Left ❖ EAST WOODSHED, 1861. This building was one of a matching pair of woodsheds located in the agricultural zone of the village.

Above ❖ CANTERBURY SHAKER BOX STOVE, c. 1820. In the late nineteenth and early twentieth centuries the Shakers purchased decorative tin heat shields to protect their floors.

be taken away and a flight built on the east side, in an addition attached to the building for the purpose. The chimneys are to be rebuilt, but the fire places will not be made again. For some few years past stoves have been gradually introduced into the Society and they will now be placed in all the rooms. Those first introduced were called Franklin Stove[s]. The next were so arranged that the front could be opened and exposed the fire, and have something the form of a fireplace. A room heated by a stove, however, was very disagreeable to Father Job. The heat was oppressive and often induced the headache.[10]

Whatever the reason for abandoning fireplaces, the adoption of stove technology was swift. By 1815 most buildings in the eastern Shaker communities were equipped with Shaker-made iron box stoves. Very few Shaker communities had their own foundries where they could cast their own stoves, but most communities were close to non-Shaker foundries that manufactured stoves to Shaker specifications. Not content to copy worldly examples, the Shakers improved the box stove's efficiency by reducing the number of parts—from the five to ten plates of the German-American stoves to the Shakers' two-piece stove with a single cast-iron box and separate iron bottom plate. By reducing air penetration significantly, the Shakers could generate maximum heat from a much smaller stove than did their Dutch- and German-American counterparts. The iron box stoves were also much cheaper to install than a fireplace, so they could equip a multitude of domestic and industrial spaces with stoves; once installed, they were also much less expensive to operate than fireplaces.

The Shakers experimented with their iron stoves and eventually produced a range of sizes and types. By the late 1840s two factors determined the demise of the Shaker-made stoves. First, as the Shakers were no longer able to compete with much larger and better-equipped foundries in the outside world, the villages began to close down their

Above ❖ BUILT-IN STOVE, by Ford & Co., Concord, New Hampshire, in one of the sisters' workrooms on the second floor of the 1841 north shop.

Right ❖ CANTERBURY'S WOOD MILL (seen in an historical photograph, c. 1915), to the left. The stone pump mill, with its waterwheel, provided water for brick-lined cisterns and, ultimately, the cow barn complex.

Above ❖ SMALL WOOD BOX, with compartments for sawdust, kindling, and stove wood, c. 1840. Yellow paint on the lid interior suggests the original color of this box and its probable original location in a dwelling house.

Opposite ❖ WOOD STORAGE BOX in the second-floor stair hall of the dwelling house.

foundries. Second, a widespread American craze for the stove was in full gear. By the 1850s, the Albany-Troy area of New York State was producing stoves for the nation's growing cities and towns. In Concord, New Hampshire, the leading foundry was Ford & Co.—so it was also the logical choice of the New Hampshire Shakers. From the 1840s through the 1860s, Ford & Co. produced hundreds of stoves to custom specifications for the Canterbury and Enfield communities.

The Canterbury Shakers never abandoned wood as their principal fuel, probably due to the fact that there was no acceptable alternative in rural Canterbury until after World War II. As late as 1900 the Shakers were still cleaning and repairing up to four hundred stoves annually in the Church Family alone, and burning up to four hundred cords of wood each year.[11]

Burning wood on this scale required extensive community planning and hired labor for cutting, chopping, and hauling. The Shakers were aided by an extensive system of water-powered mills, and after 1845, by steam-powered splitters. However, there was no escaping the hand labor of the final tasks of storage and daily supply to several dozen buildings.

Wood burning required indoor storage to ensure a large supply of dry, seasoned wood. Nearly all Shaker villages had wood mills and woodsheds for cutting and storage; Canterbury's were extensive. Canterbury's wood mill is now gone, but two of the woodsheds survive. The east woodshed is one of a pair that bordered the barn complex. The north shop, erected in 1841, provided dry wood storage for the dwelling house on the ground level.

The Shaker system of heating was based on simple technology and hand labor. Many of the Shakers' nineteenth-century land purchases were wood lots for fuel supply. The flow of wood from forest to stove was steady and smooth. Firewood logs were first cut

Above ❖ Exterior door to the infirmary wood bin, a small room off the 1892 kitchen.

Right ❖ Box stove, Ford & Co., c. 1850, installed in a sisters' retiring room in the dwelling house. Kindling was kept in a Shaker work basket—lined with leather, canvas, or bed ticking—that was kept in a small storage cupboard near the stove.

Ash bucket, Thomas Hoit, 1843 (h: 10½ in. [26.7 cm]; d: 10 in. [25.4 cm]). Collection of the Philadelphia Museum of Art.

into cordwood and then into stove-length sections. After splitting, the wood was stacked in covered woodsheds, then eventually carried to woodbins in the various buildings. The woodbins were usually accessed through small doors high on an exterior wall, thus protecting the stacks of wood from the elements. From these ground-floor storage bins wood was carried to smaller bins on each floor, and from there to smaller woodboxes in each room, which was equipped with its own stove, implements, kindling, sawdust, and wood. This efficient relay of firewood ensured that the community of several hundred individuals never had to worry about running out of heating fuel.

FIRE PROTECTION

With so many fires burning daily in the winter months at Canterbury, it comes as no surprise that the Shakers practiced zealous fire prevention. They suffered accidents, of course, but these were remarkably infrequent compared to those in the outside world, and they were less destructive than other rural farm fires or the devastating urban fires of the late eighteenth and early nineteenth centuries.

In most American rural communities, a single family could not fight a raging fire. Rallying sufficient help was difficult, and often too late. In towns and villages, buckets and brigades were more successful. In cities there were organized fire companies, but an urban blaze among wooden buildings could quickly exceed the capabilities of horse-drawn equipment, hand pumpers, and inadequate water supply and pressure.

With a cautious fear of the ravages of fire, the Shakers worked assiduously to train their communities to prevent and extinguish them. They had a greater chance of controlling and quenching fires than their neighbors because they had a large and ready labor force, an adequate water supply, excellent training, and good equipment.

But even such a disciplined community workforce might not be quick enough to save a wooden building from ravenous flames. In 1800 the Canterbury Church Family experienced its first sobering confrontation with the dangers of fire, when someone discarded pipe ashes in a wooden "spit box" containing sawdust. The ensuing blaze threatened to destroy the entire cooper's shop, but a community bucket brigade was able to prevent more extensive damage.[12] The warning for the New York Shaker communities followed in 1820, in the form of a savage fire in Troy.

At Canterbury in 1822 the enterprising Dr. Thomas Corbett interrupted his medical practice, herb business, gardening, syrup production, and clockmaking long enough to build the only Canterbury Shaker fire engine, a hand pumper that remained on active duty in the community until the late nineteenth century, although it was rarely called into service. (Today the pumper is in the Shaker Museum in Old Chatham, New York.) Yet in a rural village of wood-frame buildings, even a hand pumper and an adequate water supply were only as good as the firefighters themselves. The Shakers had, on site at

1822 FIRE ENGINE

The building of a fire engine was among the important events of the present year. Thomas Corbett was the director and did much of the work. It required the aid of twenty four men to operate it. This number would send a half inch stream some sixty feet. With much less help, in the year 1838 it threw a stream over the belfry of the dwelling. Since that date a suction hose has been attached. In 1860 hemp hose was purchased which is still with the engine. At the present date (1891) neither engine nor hose are of use, as they have not been out for trial for many years.

—HENRY CLAY BLINN,
"A Historical Record of the Society of Believers in Canterbury, New Hampshire," 1892

CANTERBURY'S CARRIAGE AND HAND PUMPER on parade in Concord, New Hampshire, c. 1900, seen in an historical photograph.

FIREHOUSE AND GARAGE, C. 1910, in an historical photograph.

the Church Family, many dozens of people, accustomed to working together, who could respond to a fire alarm within minutes.

Since the threat of fire was a menace to all Shaker communities, they also developed a series of preventive measures that in 1821 were published as part of their Millennial Laws. The section called "Orders on Prudence, Especially to Avoid Fires" lists rules prohibiting candles, lanterns, tobacco pipes, open stove doors, and hot ashes near such combustibles as sawdust, unspun wool, and textiles. These regulations were further refined in the 1845 Millennial Laws, which gave even more specific restrictions on pipe smoking. The fire prevention rules seem to have inspired caution and discipline among the Canterbury Shakers, for they experienced very few fires in the nineteenth century, and most of these were quickly contained.

In one instance in January 1852, failure to extinguish an oil lamp in the dwelling-house kitchen led to an early-morning smoldering fire discovered by an elderly sister who happened to be up and saw the flames. (The physical evidence of this 1852 fire was found in 1996 during the restoration of the dwelling house.) Another incident occurred in 1870 at the Canterbury Second Family, but the cause of that was faulty chimney construction.[13]

Throughout the nineteenth century new technology generally served the cause of fire prevention. The shift from open fireplaces to box stoves wrought a revolution in heating but also greatly reduced the dangers of fireplace sparking. The replacement of candles with kerosene lighting greatly increased nighttime visibility, and it somewhat reduced the risk of fire because of the lanterns' glass globes. Nevertheless, a kerosene accident could create a burst of flame far more dangerous than a candle, so when kerosene lanterns were introduced to the village in January 1862, they were forbidden in the Shaker barns.[14]

In the twentieth century the Shakers continued to adopt new techniques of fire prevention. When the windmill and water tower were built in 1900, the Church Family installed fire hydrants. This feature was not available to the Canterbury North and Second families, who consequently suffered several major fires from the 1890s through the 1940s. In the early twentieth century the Shakers installed chimney flue liners, added lightning rods to their tallest buildings, built "fireproof" buildings such as the garage/firehouse (1908), and lined some interiors with decorative tin. Yet in spite of these measures, as time passed, the Shakers became even more vulnerable to the ravages of fire. They lost their key resource—a large, readily available fire-fighting force—and had to depend, as did everyone else in the town of Canterbury, on a scattered town volunteer fire company.

1908 FIREHOUSE TOWER for hanging and drying fire hose. The wood-framed building is clad in tin siding, which the Shakers then assumed to be fireproof.

Arsonist enemies of the Shakers were the cause of the most tragic fires throughout the nineteenth century in all Shaker communities. A series of suspicious fires (some started accidentally by careless hired men) destroyed important buildings at each of the last three Canterbury families. The last, and largest, of these destroyed the Church Family cow barn complex on a scorching day in August 1974. This blaze (in which arson was suspected, but no one was convicted) marked the low point in Canterbury Shaker history. The loss of New Hampshire's largest barn was a disaster for the state as well as the Shakers. However, the great fire rallied neighbors, friends, the new nonprofit board of trustees, and the State Historic Preservation Office into action that ultimately led to the preservation of Canterbury Shaker Village.

LIGHT CONTROL

We have already seen that as the Shakers began to build their material representation of gospel order, they opened up their buildings to provide maximum exposure to natural light.

In addition to maximizing natural light through innovative architectural techniques, the Shakers were keen followers of technological innovations in light control and artificial lighting.

One of the earliest and most profitable Canterbury Shaker industries was the manufacture of iron candlesticks by Francis Winkley, who with Clement Beck produced over two thousand candlesticks per year for sale, in addition to supplying Canterbury's needs. A measure of individual production can be seen in the drop in annual output of candlesticks (from 2,119 to 1,263) when Brother Clement left the Shakers in March 1815. Although the Shakers at Canterbury surely used Winkley's candlesticks, and profited from

Below, left ❖ AN OIL LAMP AND TWO LIGHTBULBS, part of a collection of artificial lighting in the Henry Clay Blinn museum in the dwelling house. This collection also included early pine knots and Shaker-made candlesticks.

Below, right ❖ EARLY-TWENTIETH-CENTURY ELECTRIC LIGHT FIXTURE in the dwelling house. The surface wire molding has a double channel, which provided insulation.

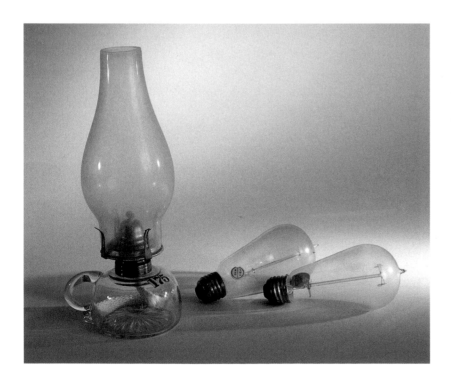

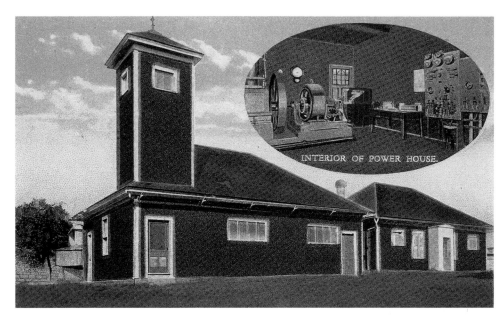

INTERIOR OF POWER HOUSE.

Left ❖ THE 1908 FIREHOUSE AND
GARAGE AND THE 1910 POWERHOUSE,
with its interior electrical panel and generator,
postcard, c. 1915.

their sale, early scares with potentially disastrous fires quickly turned the Shakers against open flames. Since the Shakers typically replaced technologies, once outmoded, lighting devices were rarely retained. Consequently, only a few candlesticks survive in Shaker museums, and none have been found in the numerous archaeological excavations at Canterbury. Enclosed lanterns were introduced throughout living quarters and work areas around 1810.

Little is known of the lighting practices of the Shakers in the early nineteenth century, but the choices were limited and there was probably very little difference between the devices owned by the Shakers and those of their neighbors. As new forms of fuel such as whale oil and kerosene were discovered, the Shakers were quick to adopt them. By 1862 kerosene was the lighting fuel of choice among the Canterbury Shakers. The dwelling house, where the most lighting fuel was used, eventually had its own underground iron tank for storing up to 250 gallons. The supply line was fed through the foundation wall of the food storage cellar under the chapel to an indoor gauge and valve, where lamps could be refilled safely.

The use of oil lamps can be confirmed by photographic evidence. Since the Shakers in New Hampshire never had their own glass factory, they purchased their lamps from the outside world. Only a few oil lamps remain in the Canterbury Shaker Village collection, although a few bases and fragments have been found in recent archaeological excavations. The only distinguishing features of Shaker lamps are that their bases and globes are generally free of etching and molded decoration, and they tend to have circular wicks to increase the light output. Kerosene lamps required regular trimming to reduce odor and smoke, but even with careful maintenance there was inevitably oil residue on interior windows, ceilings, and furniture. To compensate, the Shaker tinsmiths created homemade "chimneys," with vent pipes connected to existing stove pipes and flues. These funnels floated directly above the glass chimneys of the oil lamps and effectively eliminated smoke and soot. One intriguing chapter of the history of artificial light that seems

Above ❖ EARLY-TWENTIETH-CENTURY
PORTABLE ELECTRIC LIGHT, in the sisters'
attic storage closet, in the dwelling house.

to have escaped Shaker tinkering is gas lighting, since there is no evidence that the Canterbury Shakers purchased or installed a gas plant. Electricity, however, took the Canterbury Shakers by storm.

Electricity, like gas, was an urban lighting phenomenon in the early twentieth century. Knowledge of the technology of direct current was accessible to the Shakers through journals and publications, and by 1900 electricity was relatively common in the larger New Hampshire towns. The Shakers at Canterbury installed a direct-current generating plant in 1910, building a modern power plant to house the generator and to store voltage in a room filled with DC glass batteries. The supervision of electrical installation fell to Brother Irving Greenwood, one of the few Shaker brothers remaining at Canterbury in 1910. Brother Irving's installation journal survives, revealing the design and installation of the village's entire electrical system.[15] Even more remarkable is the survival of most of the system, except for the DC generator and batteries that were discarded or sold when the Shakers shifted to alternating current. Because the 1910–13 system still worked, it was not arbitrarily upgraded in the post–World War II era. The 1910 powerhouse remains intact, with part of its original electrical control panels; throughout most of the twenty-five extant buildings of the Church Family, the period surface molding and insulated wires still feed period lighting devices. This early-twentieth-century system has been restored to operating condition.

The Shakers remained eminently practical with their lighting. They did not follow fashion trends to eliminate ceiling lights in favor of decorative table and floor lamps; instead, Sister Cora Helena Sarle decorated a number of glass ceiling fixtures. The progressive attitude of the Shakers toward artificial lighting is consistent with their overall philosophy of modernization.

RECORD KEEPING, DOCUMENTATION, AND MEMORY

Like most things Shaker, the community's system of record keeping is deceptively simple and richly textured in meaning. For good reason, the Shakers are often regarded as a folk community, having strong oral traditions; the first published testimonies of the Shakers did not appear until 1813. The origin of the Shakers' meticulous record keeping could be attributed to their fear of legal action by disgruntled former adherents or antagonistic neighbors, which was a concern especially in the era from 1820 to 1850, at the height of anti-Shaker passions.

Throughout their history, all Shaker communities kept alive their oral history, songs, and dances, transmitting them between villages and from elderly Shakers to the young. Eldress Bertha Lindsay, who died in 1990, felt keenly the responsibility of passing the knowledge of her eighty-six years at Canterbury to others through taped interviews. Equally essential are community documents, which serve to balance the vagaries of personal memory and oral tradition. One of these records was the covenant that each Shaker signed upon entering the community.

Official Shaker records include covenants; membership records; cemetery maps and records; and a plethora of journals, registers, and notebooks kept by the ministry, trustees, and deacons. These included financial transactions with the outside world and between Shaker families; ministerial records on relations with the Central Ministry and between villages; visitor registers; and community management records such as kitchen journals, infirmary journals, building notebooks, and farm diaries. An individual Shaker's death or departure is noted on the covenant document that he or she signed upon entry into the community, but the Canterbury Shakers also kept a separate Obituary Journal, which is one of the most unusual records at the community.[16] Another valuable document is the daybook of Francis Winkley, a longtime Shaker trustee, who recorded community events from Canterbury's founding in 1792 to his death in 1848.

Record keeping was central to the Shaker concept of community order. The Shakers needed to record every aspect of their activity to monitor operations and measure success. They clearly kept an eye on the hostile world they had rejected, but their first concern was the spiritual and financial health of the community. Their assiduous record keeping is matched by other religious societies, such as the German-based Moravian Brethren, who had communal settlements in the eastern United States, or the Quakers.

IRVING GREENWOOD, CHURCH FAMILY BUILDING JOURNAL, which contains an alphabetical listing of buildings and their improvements from 1792 to the 1930s.

LATE-NINETEENTH-CENTURY PHOTOGRAPH ALBUMS, including one pocket-size album with a pullout series of stereoscopic views of Canterbury Shaker Village.

PAGE FROM HENRY CLAY BLINN'S
PHOTOGRAPH ALBUM, C. 1880.

The Shaker passion for record keeping extended to individual brothers and sisters as well as to community leaders. We have strong documentary evidence that all members of the community, even children, were encouraged to keep personal journals. If this practice was officially sanctioned, then why do so few of these personal journals survive at Canterbury and other Shaker villages? Thousands of Moravian and Quaker autobiographies survive today—and they include documents from farmers and tradespeople as well as religious leaders, women as well as men. The paucity of extant Shaker journals seems disproportionate to the number of believers, and this disparity is not due to illiteracy. The most prevalent theory regarding such personal accounts and records is that at some point the Shaker ministry systematically destroyed them. While the evidence of this is mostly hearsay, it is not without foundation: destruction of personal journals would be consistent with Shaker efforts to deindividualize the community.

Whatever the case, modern analysts of the Shakers are left mostly with official records and the personal accounts of village leaders. At Canterbury the most revealing of these are the early journals of John Whitcher and Francis Winkley; the journals and histories of Henry Clay Blinn; the autobiography of Nicholas A. Briggs; and, for the twentieth century, the diaries of Jessie Evans and Irving Greenwood. Against these can be balanced the extensive body of anti-Shaker literature, exemplified by the court records of former Shaker Mary Dyer, who severely criticized her former Enfield (New Hampshire) community, and by the many accounts—sympathetic, neutral, and hostile—of non-Shaker travelers and neighbors.

There were also important visual records of community growth and order; Robert Emlen has thoroughly documented Shaker maps in his excellent *Shaker Village Views*. Canterbury's Blinn was the premier Shaker mapmaker, and there is also an exceptional 1849 map by Peter Foster of the Canterbury Church Family. The map of Canterbury by David Parker is one of the largest and most remarkable survey maps of any Shaker community.

After the middle of the nineteenth century, photography became the most important form of visual record keeping. Although the Shakers usually did not think of photographs as part of an official community record, they came to assume great personal importance as the Shakers allowed brothers and sisters to keep individual photo albums—which, in fact, probably helped to displace the earlier Shaker tradition of written diaries.

As one might expect, there is a great difference between surviving images from the nineteenth century and the vast body of spontaneous images from the twentieth century (predominantly from 1910 to 1940). The official and controlled imagery from 1875 to 1910 is limited by technology, the reliance upon non-Shaker photographers, and available products. The surviving nineteenth-century photographs include studio portraits, stereographic views of village scenes, and village postcards, nearly all produced by professional photographers.

Most of the photographs in the Canterbury Shaker Village archives are from the twentieth century. They are informal pictures, recording daily life and work, special occasions, and, above all, the Shakers in community order and among their friends. These spontaneous, direct, and fresh images clearly were not made to fulfill an elder's mandates to document events, but to preserve a joyous spirit of friendship and precious memories. They also graphically reveal the vitality of the increasingly feminized Shaker community at Canterbury.

The most important collection of photographs belonged to Eldress Bertha Lindsay. In the 1920s, as a young woman, she enthusiastically photographed her Shaker community, providing numerous pictures for the albums of other Canterbury sisters. She also assembled many albums of her own, and, late in life, even a few albums for selected non-Shaker friends.

Artifacts are another important source for sustaining community memory. At Canterbury, Blinn institutionalized Shaker memory by creating his museum, which was located in the village print shop until his death in 1905, then moved to the dwelling house, where it was maintained by the Shaker sisters. Blinn's museum contained far-ranging antiquarian material, including memorabilia collected from other Shaker communities. Although much of Blinn's museum has been dispersed, several hundred items are still preserved, many with Blinn's original acquisition numbers, in the Canterbury Shaker Village collection.

The oral accounts and written records bonded believers and confirmed the unity of their history. Like the other Shaker systems described in this section—such as communication, storage, and cleanliness—methods of record keeping were maintained and updated as modernizations became available. But just as a Shaker's circulation around the village had its physical and invisible paths and boundaries, so did these documentary aspects of Shaker life contribute, to a more literal or spiritual degree, to the Shakers' overall life in community order.

"HITCHING RING taken from elm tree at Shirley, where Mother Ann and the Elders hitched their horses. Probably about 1780." The number "2" found on this tree fragment indicates that it was one of the earliest objects placed in Blinn's museum.

SHAKER STYLE

CLASSIC DESIGNS

Although the Shakers prided themselves on being outside the changing fashions of American society, they have greatly influenced twentieth-century style. Based on traditional art-historical approaches, the style of an object can be shaped by issues of ethnicity, class, religion, and other forces, but is governed by aesthetic considerations. For practical and commercial items, style is generally an aesthetic packaging of economic and cultural factors such as time, materials, tools, skill, form, ornament, and function; then the product—such as furniture, textile, or woodenware—is given style by the maker and put up for sale. In time the maker begins anew, perhaps with some modifications in style in response to market conditions.

The overall process of creating a "Shaker style" is clear to us only in fragmentary evidence. We know that a Shaker pattern of community planning and architecture evolved in the early 1780s and was implemented in the eastern communities between 1785 and 1795 as the gambrel-roofed meetinghouses and dwelling houses were built repeatedly. Nevertheless, the Shaker style of architecture was malleable within certain limits, and was modified over time. The building of separate communal societies set the Shakers apart from the world so they could implement other changes. By laying out their villages in one of several Shaker patterns, and by building distinctive-looking core buildings and painting them in coded colors, the Shakers created a Shaker architectural style that could be adapted to different objects.[1]

We have already seen how the Shakers' technical innovations were central to the efficient, simplified aspect of their style. Their communal philosophy dominated design and process in material culture and religion, with three primary results. First, the Shakers developed a collective design aesthetic that provided them with a badge of identity. A classic example of this is the Shaker peg rail, an identifiable design feature that could immediately "Shakerize" any interior space. Second, the Shakers developed a durable, high-quality product whose minimalist appearance has imparted an enduring aesthetic appeal. The Shaker oval box is a prime example of an object with a "Shaker" style achieved by reducing or eliminating ornamentation. Third, by promoting technological innovation rather than resisting it, the Shakers were able to modernize production with no displacement of workers. By substituting machine "workmanship of certainty" for the old hand-craft "workmanship of risk," the Shakers made tremendous gains in precision, uniformity, efficiency, replication, and refinement with no compromise to their universal designs.

The Shakers did not find it necessary to "Shakerize" everything. Products intended for sale to the world might at first be identical to those manufactured elsewhere. There was a consumer market for a familiar kind of iron candlestick, nail, wagon, scythe, or wool wheel, and the Shakers complied. However, as the Shaker enterprises gained outside recognition, they were able to outsell their competitors through better prices or superior quality. In their own communities, the Shakers had a flexible approach to design. They rejected certain aspects of worldly goods completely, tolerated others (such as the furniture

SISTER ETHEL HUDSON, seated at her kitchen table in the dwelling house, c. 1977. Sister Ethel and her pet cats were the only residents of the communal dwelling from 1977 to her death in 1992.

Pages 156–57 ❖ DETAIL OF DOUBLE CUPBOARD over double case of drawers, Canterbury, 1841 (see page 172).

Opposite ❖ SHAKER BASKETS in the Canterbury Shaker Village collection. The Shakers made work and fancy baskets of all sizes; many of the fancy baskets were probably sold outside the community.

SISTER ETHEL HUDSON'S CHAMBER in
the dwelling house, shortly after her death in 1992.
This room is in the original 1793 section of the
building. This picture shows the overlapping layers
of time and styles from 1793 to 1992, as well as
some of Sister Ethel's personal belongings, ranging
from the Native American slipper moccasins to
the computer-generated personal portrait above
her bed.

of new converts) until they could provide substitutes, and accepted others (such as tools) with little or no modification. But in general, they substituted new forms for old ones to be able to shape the behavior of the believers.

The following sections—on furniture; woodenware and baskets; clothing, textiles, and fancywork; maps, paintings, and drawings; and stonework—illustrate the many dimensions of Shaker community style.

FURNITURE

The development of a distinctive Shaker style of furniture in Canterbury took approximately thirty years, until at least 1815. Until that time the Shakers used furniture brought into the community by converts, and built cupboards and closets that mirrored those found in contemporary vernacular buildings. Even though Shaker cabinetmaking had no equivalent of the master builder Moses Johnson to transmit the furniture patterns from the Mount, we can be sure that original furniture designs from New Lebanon and Watervliet were known in Canterbury.

The path to nearly any topic on the Shakers bears the footprints of Edward Deming Andrews, who was the most important early dealer and collector of Shaker furniture. His books stimulated widespread interest in the subject, and with his wife, Faith, he published *Shaker Furniture: The Craftsmanship of an American Communal Sect* in 1937 and *Religion in Wood* in 1966. Andrews believed that among the Shaker craftsmen, religious ideals pervaded the workshop and were expressed in furniture of the highest quality, in a uniform Shaker style. The Shaker style was transmitted from New Lebanon to other

Opposite ❖ ELDERS' ENTRANCE TO THE
MEETINGHOUSE STAIR HALL, 1815. The door,
with its lock, latch, and strap hinges, is believed to
date to 1792, when it served as an entrance to an
original staircase to ministry rooms.

communities by sharing knowledge, craftsmen, and examples of products. In Canterbury's case, Mother Hannah Goodrich (1763–1823) and Father Job Bishop (1760–1831) were often the channels for specific designs: "We often received specimens of the various kinds of manufacture as samples, made in the most substantial and perfect manner, such as leather, sieves, clothing, boots, shoes, pails, small oval boxes, hoes, nails, and other articles."[2] In the face of this strong documentation about community style, Andrews still asserted that

The Shaker joiner was a free and self-reliant craftsman . . . responsible for each project's skillful and early completion. Profit considerations did not condition the work of the wood turners' shop, and the principles of division of labor and scientific cooperation on which most Shaker industries depended for their success play a minor role. Cabinetmaking was thus a less standardized occupation, and one allowing of the expression of some personality.[3]

Andrews's vision of such a master artisan, with all the time and skills required to achieve sublime perfection, must be viewed as misguided. The Shaker woodworkers at each community were not motivated by profit, but they were production driven in the early years, for some were carpenters or turners as well as cabinetmakers, and all had other tasks assigned to them. They were under no less control than other Shaker workers, nor any less open to technological innovation than their counterparts in other Shaker trades. The fact of life was that in the late eighteenth and early nineteenth centuries, woodworkers were often the machinists of their communities. These Shaker woodworkers not only built structures and supplied them with furniture, they most likely helped make and repair the predominately wooden tools and machines used by many other brothers and sisters. Andrews's argument is flawed in another way. His theory could not explain why Shaker furniture varied widely in quality within a single time period, then changed stylistically over time and among communities. The inevitable conclusion to his premise is that a diminishing of religious fervor and loss of central control brought about the Victorianizing, or decline, of Shaker furniture.

More recent publications by Jerry Grant, Douglas Allen, Charles Muller, Tim Rieman, Jean Burks, and most recently John Kirk have finally moved beyond Andrews's pioneering but flawed work and advanced the understanding of Shaker furniture making.[4] We now know that many of the identifiable woodworkers of the Shaker communities were spiritual leaders as well. At Canterbury, Job Bishop, Benjamin Smith, and Henry Clay Blinn were all ministry elders for extended periods of time, and the last two made what might now be regarded as Victorian Shaker furniture. We also know that each community produced furniture for its own use that differed markedly from that of other Shaker communities, though maintaining some regional identity. And, in fact, the Shakers were aware of and did borrow ideas from the outside world, occasionally applying these ideas in very original ways to create new forms. Although much has been written about Shaker furniture, there is still much more to learn, which this study of Canterbury can only begin to facilitate.

Nearly all surviving, identifiable Shaker furniture falls within a recognizable universal pattern, even though there are differences in its form, construction, materials, or finish. Among domestic woodworking trades in northern New England, three predominated: carpentry, cabinetmaking, and turning. The cabinetmaker required specialized tools for dovetailing and other joinery work, and the ability to frame a case and construct doors and drawers for it. The skills of the carpenter and turner were generally not interchangeable with those of the cabinetmaker, although the distinctions between trades in New England were not as rigidly drawn as they were, for example, in Europe. At Canterbury, there were several men with multiple woodworking skills.

Previous Shaker furniture studies have demonstrated that Shaker furniture design, like their architecture, is a vernacular interpretation of the prevailing Neoclassical style. Unlike most American cabinetmakers, who had to respond to fashion, the Shaker artisans were problem solvers for their communities, charged with inventing new forms, refining them over time, and fitting them to special needs. Most Shaker communities did not produce furniture for the market, and did not need to meet consumer demand.

Nineteenth-century cabinetmakers were of necessity moving toward factory production and away from custom furniture making and traditional handcraftsmanship. The Shakers likewise, as we have seen, eagerly adopted new machinery and were sympathetic to principles of industrial design and precision, but they were not subject to the same pressures for industrialization in furniture making as non-Shaker artisans. Consequently, they maintained custom furniture production even as they moved away from using hand tools. As the century progressed, the Shakers needed relatively small quantities of new furniture, and there was only minimal new building construction in most Shaker communities. The relatively few Shaker woodworkers were also relieved of certain responsibilities as the Shakers began hiring outside contractors and buying furniture.

Evidence is accumulating, however, that whoever the artisans were, the distinctive design of Shaker furniture began with the ministry. There is no doubt that living conditions and necessity required that new converts' existing furnishings be used throughout the various Shaker communities. But the ministry furnishings, particularly beds, were supposed to be "newly" made. This can be interpreted as newly built and never used; "new" can also mean "of new design"—just as we have seen Shaker inventions in forms of architecture, dance, music, and theology, new furniture design may have been required for the ministry. Once approved for their use, adaptations could be made for the rest of the community. My contention is that many distinctive Shaker furniture forms and designs were made first for the ministry.

A test case for this theory at Canterbury is the tailoring counter made for Mother Hannah Goodrich's chamber in the upper loft of the meetinghouse (now on display at the Shaker Museum and Library, Old Chatham, New York). There is no documentable Canterbury Shaker freestanding case furniture predating this tailoring counter, although several blanket chests and freestanding cupboards may be as early in date. It was fastened in place against the existing east wall of the south chamber on the third floor. The entire third floor was repainted in Prussian blue. The work counter, made of white pine, was

I will sketch an account of the Meeting House and the order that lived in it: The lower part is a large room where the families meet on the Sabbath for worship. The second loft is divided into rooms and four beds: these were said to be two of them for their waiters, a man and woman: the other two were called spare beds, for those of the ministry that should come on a visit. In the third loft was two rooms, which were called Father's and Mother's sleeping rooms: in each was a bed common for bigness. Those beds were made of new feathers which had never been slept on because otherwise they were polluted and would defile Father and Mother. All the bedding and furniture must also be that which had never been used, because otherwise it would be unclean and pollute the Sanctuary. When we entered the chamber at the head of the stairs was a large trap door, the bigness of the stairway. It was hinged with large iron hinges, and a large iron hasp to hasp it down which they said was to keep the devil out.

—MARY DYER
"Account of Sister Alice Beck" from
A Portraiture of Shakerism, 1822

MODERN REPRODUCTION OF THE
TAILORING COUNTER from the third floor of
the meetinghouse, built by Anna Mazetti-Nissen
and Inger Bergstrom (104⅞ × 39 × 25⅝ in.
[266.3 × 99.1 × 65.1 cm]). The original, purchased
by John Williams in 1955, is now in the Shaker
Museum and Library in Old Chatham, New York.
The original counter has a Prussian blue base with
a dark orange top and dark orange interior shelves.
It has no back and was built into the east wall of
Mother Hannah's room, as seen here, in 1815.

painted the same blue, with a dark orange top and interior to match the interiors of original built-in cupboards in the chamber.

As additional Shaker furniture from Canterbury comes to light, we can begin to
trace a pattern begun by Mother Hannah's counter that may apply to more than furniture,
and to other Shaker societies. A sizable body of ministerial furniture from all communities survives, largely due to the practice of handing down prized objects from elders and
eldresses. Until the last generation of sisters at Canterbury, most of these items were
retained for ministry use, and thus fit the pattern of segregation that characterized the
ministry's living and dining arrangements. Although the body of ministry furniture at
Canterbury is relatively small, several items have strong histories. Each one is notable
either in form, quality of construction, or types of woods used. For example, ministry
tables from Canterbury are more likely to be of bird's-eye or curly maple than tables made
for general Shaker use.

Using Mother Hannah's tailoring counter as the pattern, one can trace the development of this furniture form throughout the village. The sisters' shop was built in 1816
to advance the sisters' textile industries. Three large tailoring counters survive in situ, two

TAILORING COUNTER, first floor, sisters' shop, c. 1816–40 (33¼ × 109 × 36 in. [84.5 × 276.9 × 91.4 cm]). This cupboard was custom-made for the location, which is lit by a window on the right side.

downstairs and one upstairs. All three are too large to remove from their respective rooms without dismantling them, and there is no obvious way to safely disassemble them. They are similar in construction details and woods, although not identical in size, drawer and door placement, or construction details. All three most likely were built and installed as the shop was constructed in 1816, or were assembled in their respective spaces shortly after 1816 and never moved. All three bear molding profiles of the 1815–45 period. Other tailoring counters dating from this same period or slightly later survive at Canterbury, and more reside in public and private collections. One of the largest examples outside of Canterbury is now on display in the Hancock dwelling house, where it has been restored to its original yellow color.

There is a definite pattern to the entire body of Canterbury tailoring counters, although no two are exactly alike. Mother Hannah's work counter was fixed in place against a wall and lit from a window to the right. It is asymmetrical, in that its left side features a cupboard, and is configured, left to right, as: cupboard, bank of drawers, bank of drawers. The ends are plain, with no panels, doors, or drawers. Two of the sisters'-shop work counters are placed in a corner against the wall in their respective rooms, with a window

Above, top ❖ TAILORING COUNTER, second floor, sisters' shop, side 1, 1845. This work counter (12 × 4 ft. [367 × 122 cm]) is the largest in the Canterbury Shaker Village collection.

Above, bottom ❖ TAILORING COUNTER, second floor, sisters' shop, side 2.

to the right casting light across the work surface—an advantage for right-handed workers. They too, like Mother Hannah's counter, have a cupboard door to the left next to a bank of drawers. Each counter is deeper than Mother Hannah's model, and each has a few details that make it a singular piece of furniture within a common style.

The third sisters'-shop counter is on the second floor, where it dominates an entire workspace. The counter is twelve feet long and four feet wide (3.7 × 1.2 m), double the depth of Mother Hannah's counter, and is finished on both sides. One facade is divided into four units, beginning on the left with the traditional cupboard, bank of drawers, and bank of drawers, and adding a second cupboard. Unlike all other large counters at Canterbury, this giant counter was meant to be situated in the middle of its room, where it could be accessed from all four directions. Therefore, this counter has a second facade, also divided into four units; left to right they are: cupboard, bank of drawers, bank of drawers, and—surprisingly—a double bank of little drawers. This magnificent work counter is truly a custom-built machine—a Cadillac of its type—yet it retains the proxemic patterns of its fellow work counters and remains within the style of the Canterbury Shakers.

The pattern continues to appear in work counters from the 1820–50 period. Most of these are smaller versions of the large counters in the sisters' shop, which simply remove a bank of drawers, and so are configured with a cupboard on the left and bank of

Left ❖ Tailoring counter, Canterbury, c. 1820–40 (36¼ × 59 [100 extended] × 26¾ in. [92.1 × 149.9 (254 extended) × 68 cm]). This counter is typical of Canterbury's many tailoring counters, in that it can be moved easily to the center of a room for work. The original drop-leaf extensions to the top provide additional work surface; the rear drop-leaf extension is a later addition. The surface retains evidence of yellow on the base and red on the countertop.

Below ❖ Tailoring counter, Canterbury, c. 1840.

TAILORING COUNTER, Canterbury, built in the deaconesses' storeroom on the second floor of the north shop, 1841. Brass tacks line the front edge of the top to facilitate measurement of cloth.

drawers on the right. The variations are numerous, although still within the accepted community style, and a few examples may have been made for left-handed workers.

Unfortunately, it is difficult to trace the development of most other Canterbury furniture forms with such precision. Jean Burks has described the evolution of the Shaker sewing desk, a later and miniaturized incarnation of the tailoring counter, designed to accommodate one or two sisters. The first of these desks were most likely built for the eldresses, and patterned on the Federal ladies' desks popular in Boston, New York, Philadelphia, and Baltimore. The Shaker sewing desks were not designed to replace the great work counters, but they could complement them in the communal work spaces. By the late nineteenth century, the sewing desks were also being located in spaces such as retiring rooms, away from communal work spaces.[5]

The only other furniture form whose evolution can be suggested at Canterbury is the cupboard over chest of drawers. This form is a universal one among the Shakers, but it takes on distinctive characteristics at each community. At Canterbury the classic form is tall (essentially floor to ceiling), with either one or two cupboard doors over a case of drawers, which range in number from five to nine. At Canterbury the narrow cases have drawers that contain one large central pull. As with the work counters, these standing cupboards were constructed within an established community vocabulary, but no two are exactly alike. Remaining pieces at Canterbury allow us to trace the beginning of this form to 1814–15. The story, however, begins with the dwelling house, so it might at first seem to call into question the ministry origin of new furniture forms.

Most of the original 1793 interior of the dwelling house has been lost to numerous later alterations. Surviving built-in cupboards date to every period of change. By following the changes in construction and molding profiles, and matching them to original doors in both the meetinghouse and dwelling house, it is possible to follow the development of the distinctive Canterbury standing cupboard over drawers.

The earliest built-ins in the Canterbury dwelling house date to the substantial renovations of 1814, when the building was expanded eighteen feet (5.5 m) on both the east (sisters') and the west (brothers') ends. They are four similar built-in cases of drawers, one each on two floors on the sisters' side of the building and one each on two floors on the brothers' side. The cases have no visible cupboard above them, only a plastered wall. In fact, there is a cupboard above each case of drawers—but it faces the opposite direction from the drawers, and opens into a different room! From the cupboard side, the back of the case of drawers is covered by a plaster wall under the cupboard.

The dwelling-house cases of drawers have no meetinghouse precedent, but the raised panel doors to the 1814 cupboards are similar in molding profile to the original 1792 and 1793 interior entry doors and small cupboard doors in both the meetinghouse and the dwelling house. From all indications, the built-in cases of drawers and built-in cupboards are two separate items.

The first instances of the combination of a built-in cupboard and a built-in case of drawers are found in the 1814 ministry dining room and in the Church Family elders' and eldresses' apartments in the dwelling house. Two standing cupboards in the brothers' apartments in the dwelling house relate closely to the ministry dining room's built-in. These are full-fledged cupboards over drawers, constructed as one piece of case furniture, with raised panel doors and molded lip drawers. These two cupboards were fabricated as freestanding units and then lightly built into preexisting spaces, probably in 1814. They vary in the number of drawers, the size of the cupboard above, and construction details. These dwelling-house examples relate closely to a standing cupboard over drawers on the second floor of the meetinghouse, which most likely dates from the building's renovations of 1815.

After 1815 molding profiles changed throughout the village, and raised-panel door construction was discontinued, except for exterior doors. The tall, narrow, standing cupboard over case of drawers proliferated as the dwelling house expanded to the east, west, and north, and the roof was raised. The molding profiles on the cupboards date them to the 1815–40 period.

SEWING DESK, Canterbury, 1861 (38½ × 27¾ × 23 in. [97.8 × 70.5 × 58.4 cm]). Collection of the Philadelphia Museum of Art.

DETAIL OF SEWING DESK shown above, with signature of Brother Eli Kidder.

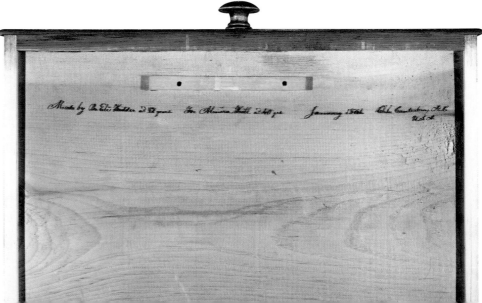

Some are built-ins; others are freestanding units. Numerous examples of the standing cupboard over drawers were built into the dwelling-house sisters' attic in the 1837 chapel wing, creating one of the most powerful examples of community style anywhere in the village. They also were built into most work areas from 1816 to 1840, and so appear in the 1816 wash house addition, the 1816 sisters' shop, the 1824 brothers' north shop, and the 1830s trustees' office.

This discussion of the development of two Canterbury Shaker furniture forms—the work counter and the standing cupboard over drawers—slights the many other forms made at Canterbury from the 1790s to the 1890s. For one hundred years the Canterbury Shakers constructed most of their own built-in and movable furniture, creating some unique American forms in the process. We now know that by 1815 a distinctive community style emerged in furniture, but we still do not know exactly who determined the design. Most likely, Shaker design in furniture was the result of collaboration between village ministries and among residents of a community. The tailoring counter and tall cupboard over drawers both may have originated at New Lebanon, and they may have been a

Below, left ❖ CASE OF DRAWERS, Canterbury, c. 1814. This case was built into the wall on the sisters' side of the dwelling house. On the opposite side of the wall is a single cupboard. Both pieces date to the 1814 renovations of the dwelling house.

Below, right ❖ BUILT-IN CUPBOARDS, ministry dining room, Canterbury, 1814. This is an early example of the standing cupboard form at Canterbury.

collaborative design, the production of a cabinetmaker advised by the elders and eldresses. The tailoring counters are sewing tool chests, comparable to the tool chests of wood-workers, and designed for maximum efficiency and operation by multiple seamstresses. Surely the cabinetmakers were designing a "machine" for women to specifications at least partly developed by the sisters or eldresses.

There is still much we do not know about Shaker furniture forms. Most of the surviving Canterbury furniture in public and private hands is from the Church Family, and was made specifically for their use. There are exceptions of course. Eli Kidder, originally from Enfield (New Hampshire), produced furniture at the Canterbury Second Family. Nevertheless, it is reasonable to assume that, generally, the best furniture was made for and used by the ministry and the Church Family and that certain forms, such as desks, were most likely permitted only among community leaders such as elders, eldresses, and trustees. Other forms, such as rocking chairs, probably were designed originally for use by the aged and infirm, but within a few decades the rocking chair was ubiquitous in the Canterbury community.

BUILT-IN CUPBOARD over case of drawers, Canterbury, 1816. This cupboard, which was made for the 1816 addition to the laundry, is unusual for Canterbury in that it has a flat panel on the single cupboard door. The raised-panel door to the left is typical of the pre-1815 period, whereas the recessed-panel door to the right is typical of the 1820–60 period.

Above, left ❖ STANDING CUPBOARD
WITH DOUBLE DOORS over case of drawers,
Canterbury, c. 1840 (76 × 44 × 19 in. [193 ×
111.8 × 48.3 cm]). This cupboard was originally
painted red, then white. It was used by Eldress
Bertha Lindsay until her death in 1990.

Above, right ❖ DOUBLE CUPBOARD over
double case of drawers, Canterbury, 1841.
The double-cupboard variation is rare at
Canterbury until the 1840s. The north shop
(1841) has built-in and freestanding double
cupboards. These yellow cupboards are from
the storerooms of the family deaconesses.

The aesthetic qualities of this quintessential Shaker furniture—which by 1815
were established in certain core forms—have been delineated in several important publications, especially *The Complete Book of Shaker Furniture,* in which Jean Burks and Tim
Rieman identify five principal design characteristics of classic Shaker furniture: balance,
hierarchy, pattern, proportion, and scale.[6]

Shaker furniture makers generally used the prevailing Western aesthetic of bi-
lateral symmetry, but one of the most unusual features of Shaker furniture design is its
regular and skillful use of asymmetry in the placement of drawers and doors in case furniture in a way that achieves an overall balance. Such furniture reveals a well-honed sense
of beauty and design sophistication that belies the stereotype of Shaker simplicity, and
helps set Shaker furniture apart from the fashionable furniture of its time. The same
sophistication is found in the Shaker application of other design principles, particularly
proportion and scale. Often, Shaker built-in furniture is the defining detail of an entire
room. Shaker interiors regularly achieve a level of integration of furniture and architecture that the outside world rarely attains apart from the work of exceptional architects
such as Frank Lloyd Wright.

WORK COUNTER with double case of drawers, Canterbury, c. 1840.

CHEST OF DRAWERS, probably designed to hold tailoring patterns and sewing equipment, c. 1840, with original red finish.

DETAIL OF MOLDING PROFILES on a built-in case of drawers in the dwelling-house sisters' attic, 1837.

Opposite ❖ CHEST OF DRAWERS, with original yellow ocher finish, 1827 (69½ × 47¼ × 23½ in. [176.5 × 120 × 59.7 cm]).

Above, left ❖ GRAY-GREEN BLANKET CHEST, Canterbury, c. 1830–40. This example has dovetailed bracket feet, two drawers, and cut-metal strap hinges. The interior of the box shows evidence of a rare pair of storage tills (33½ × 48 × 17¾ in. [85.1 × 121.9 × 45 cm]).

Above, right ❖ BLANKET CHEST with classic Canterbury bracket feet and rare blue paint, indicating that this chest was probably made for ministry use. The color matches the light blue that the Canterbury meetinghouse interior was painted in 1878. The last Shaker use of the chest was by Sister Myra Green, an Enfield Shaker who entered the community in 1849 at age 14 and died at Canterbury October 3, 1942, at age 107. The chest is pine with cherry knobs, one bone and one brass escutcheon (26¾ × 44 × 21½ in. [68 × 111.8 × 54.6 cm]). Collection of Dr. and Mrs. M. Stephen Miller.

Left ❖ RARE THREE-DRAWER CHEST, Canterbury, with lift top and traces of original red finish, c. 1830. Gift of the Monell family.

Nowhere is the success of Shaker furniture design more apparent than in its skillful use of pattern. John Kirk, one of the premier historians of American furniture, has made special note of the Shaker penchant for infinite repetition within an established grid system.[7] Drawers can be isolated in a single four-drawer chest, or multiplied into a sixteen-drawer double chest, or exploded into an entire wall of drawers. The same is true of cupboards and shelves, and of the numerous possibilities of combining drawers, cupboards, and shelves in single or double furniture units, or in entire wall systems of built-in furniture. This Shaker discovery of the practical and aesthetic appeal of pattern and repetition is one of the many reasons we acknowledge the Shakers as forerunners of modern design, whether expressed in the balanced patterns of Piet Mondrian or the practical uniformity of Ikea modular furniture.

By the 1820s, all Shaker furniture forms carried the marks of Shaker style, but in varying degrees. The most common storage unit in New England culture—the one-, two-, or three-drawer lift-top blanket chest—underwent little alteration at the hands of the Shakers. Without strong provenance, it is hard to distinguish Shaker blanket chests from their New England vernacular counterparts. But the Shakers totally transformed the traditional New England chest of drawers. They stretched it vertically, added cupboards, piled up drawers, built them into walls, and made unconventional changes in the size and gradation of the drawers.

SMALL CHEST with history of ownership at
Canterbury, c. 1840. Collection of Bob Hamilton.

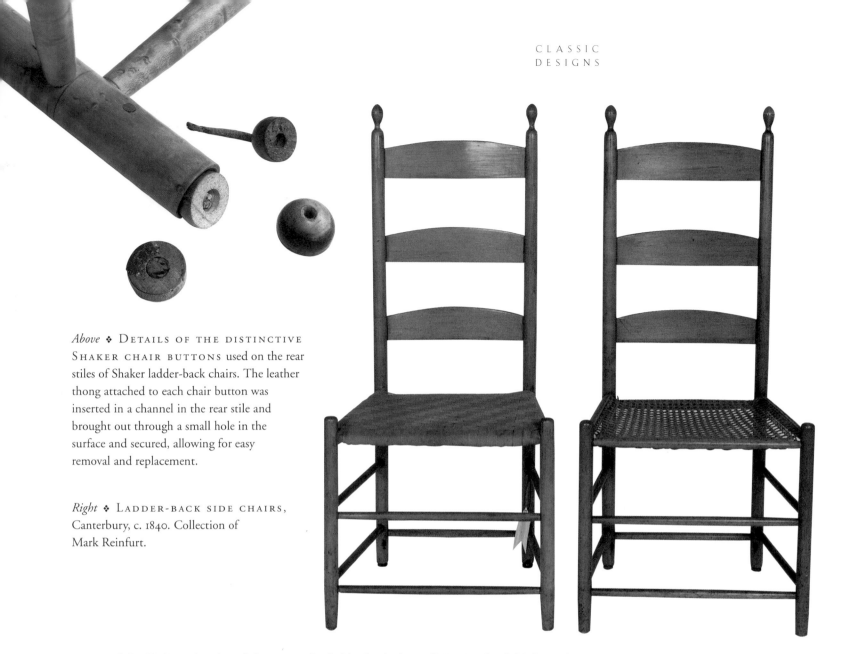

Above ❖ DETAILS OF THE DISTINCTIVE
SHAKER CHAIR BUTTONS used on the rear
stiles of Shaker ladder-back chairs. The leather
thong attached to each chair button was
inserted in a channel in the rear stile and
brought out through a small hole in the
surface and secured, allowing for easy
removal and replacement.

Right ❖ LADDER-BACK SIDE CHAIRS,
Canterbury, c. 1840. Collection of
Mark Reinfurt.

The Shakers also altered the vernacular ladder-back chair of New England. Today,
one can easily recognize the visual code of the Shakers, but within the Shaker framework
each community was permitted design flexibility, especially in the chair finials. Although
there is no documentation to suggest that one form of Shaker furniture was considered to
be more important than any other, the material history of the community strongly suggests that Shaker case furniture and chairs were the chief bearers of Shaker tradition.
These forms were used daily until the last generation of Canterbury Shakers in the 1990s,
and are still in use at the Sabbathday Lake community.

Other furniture forms, which may once have expressed an individual community's style, were significantly altered by the Shakers or abandoned, to be replaced by new
forms or designs. A symbol of Shaker Victorianization is the rocking chair. The rocker
probably originated with early-nineteenth-century improvements in health care, but in
Victorian life the rocker was a symbol of comfort and relaxation. The earliest known
Canterbury rockers date from the 1820s, when they were most likely used to provide an
extra measure of comfort for the elderly and infirm. In this use, the rocking chair is a

Above ❖ LADDER-BACK ROCKER, Canterbury, c. 1840. This chair is highly unusual in that it is constructed with only two back slats.

Right, top ❖ LOW-BACK DINING ROOM CHAIR, Canterbury, made by Micajah Tucker, c. 1830. Tucker made sixty identical chairs for use in the Church Family dining room. The chairs are made to slide under the Shaker trestle table when not in use.

Right, center ❖ LADDER-BACK SIDE CHAIR, Canterbury, with original cane seat and red finish, c. 1840.

Right, bottom ❖ LADDER-BACK ROCKER, c. 1825–30, with upright scroll armrests and original woven splint seat and traces of original red finish. This is the earliest Canterbury rocker in the village collection. Gift of Mr. and Mrs. Russell Orton.

counterpart of the adult rocking cradles of the Shaker infirmaries; at first only a few rocking chairs were made for community use.

By the 1840s the Canterbury Shakers were producing rocking chairs for daily use by eldresses and sisters. Most of these chairs lack arms, are diminutive in size, and have the woven Shaker tape seats also common on Shaker ladder-back side chairs. Early Shaker photography reveals these chairs in sisters' sitting and dwelling rooms of the 1870s and 1880s. Given the large number of surviving Shaker and Victorian factory-made rocking chairs at Canterbury and Sabbathday Lake, however, it is obvious that eventually every elder and eldress and elderly sister and brother had his or her own personal rocker, an expression of individualism that would have seemed alien to the Shakers of the early nineteenth century, and an example of the expendability of Shaker style.

Beds are perhaps the most obvious example of this category of expendable furniture. The Shakers did create a Shaker pattern for single beds, which prevailed until approximately 1860. But as the new technology of spring mattresses rendered their rope beds and straw mattresses obsolete, the Canterbury Shakers literally cast aside most of their Shaker-made beds, just as they had done with their Shaker-made clocks much earlier.

SHAKER SLAT-BOTTOM, LOW-POST BED, Canterbury, c. 1840. This bed was found under the eaves in an unfinished attic on the sisters' side of the dwelling house after Sister Ethel Hudson's death in 1992. It would have been used by several sisters.

Right ❖ DETAIL OF TRESTLE TABLE shown below.

Below ❖ TRESTLE TABLE, Canterbury, c. 1837. This is an original dining table that was converted by the Shakers into a base for a glass curiosity cabinet located in the dwelling-house library. The chair is one of a matching set of sixty low-back chairs made by Micajah Tucker in the 1830s for the dining room.

Tables fall into a middle ground in terms of their importance to Shaker style. There are several types of Shaker tables, most notably the dining trestle tables, the small candlestands, and the large communal work tables, especially laundry and ironing-room tables. There is also an important body of known ministry tables from several communities. However, the Shakers did not hesitate to make them in newer styles, and tables were among the most common furniture purchases in the late nineteenth and early twentieth centuries; the Canterbury community purchased new tables for their communal dining room in 1890 and 1947. By the late nineteenth century the Canterbury Shakers had also bought furniture forms that had never been made by the Shakers, most notably musical instruments such as pianos and organs and modern devices including Victrolas and radios.

The most common interpretation of the change in Shaker style is that the communities relaxed their rules and became more like the world around them.[8] The fundamental truth, however, is that the Shakers selectively changed, never abandoning the core furniture forms that best expressed their style, but adding new forms that contributed to their way of life. Style, in furniture as well as in architecture, was allowed to evolve to meet the needs of the community, but it retained its Shaker spirit.

Above, left ❖ CANDLESTAND, Canterbury, c. 1840–60. The chalk marking "D24" on the underside indicated its use in room 24 of building "D," the dwelling house. There is also a small pencil marking "D31," in the same handwriting, on the underside. These stands feature a metal plate screwed to the base, where the sawn feet are dovetailed to the stem. Traces of original red paint appear on the underside.

Above, right ❖ CANDLESTAND, Canterbury, 1840–60. Collection of the Philadelphia Museum of Art.

Opposite, top left ❖ SIDE TABLE with bracketed apron, Canterbury, James Daniels, c. 1820. This table was also found in the dwelling house in 1992. The bottom of the drawer is signed by Daniels (1767–1851), a carpenter and founding member of the Canterbury community.

Opposite, top right ❖ SIDE TABLE with bracketed apron, Canterbury, James Daniels, c. 1820. This table can now be attributed to Daniels based on similarities with the signed table at left.

Opposite, bottom left ❖ ONE-DRAWER TABLE, Canterbury, c. 1840. Collection of Mark Reinfurt.

Opposite, bottom right ❖ ONE-DRAWER TABLE, Canterbury, c. 1840. This is a mate to the table at left in most details except the tapering of the table legs.

Above, left ❖ WORK TABLE, from Canterbury's laundry, c. 1840–60.

Above, right ❖ SIDE TABLE WITH TWO DRAWERS, Canterbury, c. 1840.

Left ❖ WORK TABLE with overhanging ends, Canterbury's laundry, c. 1840.

WOODENWARE AND BASKETS

In rural New England at the end of the eighteenth century, wood was the most important resource for the average farmer and citizen. Most Yankees lived in wooden houses, burned wood for fuel, and sold timber for ship-building. Their tools, farm implements, furniture, wagons, casks, pails, and even tableware were made of wood. Sawmills were the most prolific small business in New England, and specialized mills produced vast quantities of woodenware.[9]

The Shakers shared their neighbors' deep reliance upon timber and its products for carrying out the routines of daily life, for creating their communities, and for their economic well-being. Not long after the founding of the Shaker villages at Canterbury in 1792 and Enfield in 1793, the New Hampshire Shakers began making wooden products for sale in their respective regions. Oval boxes, pails, tubs, sieves, brush handles, wool cards, scythes, rakes, and shovels were produced in great quantities for internal use and for sale to the outside world.

Many of the Shaker mills were devoted to the processing and production of either textiles or wood. The Canterbury Shakers had their own sawmill (1800), a wood mill for cutting firewood (1802), and a turning mill (1817) for making turned woodenware such as chair parts and handles for brushes, brooms, and tools, as well as flat staves for coopered buckets, pails, and tubs. Both Canterbury and Enfield maintained successful pail manufacturing enterprises through much of the nineteenth century.

The "Shakerness" of this woodenware is difficult to define. The Shakers were rarely the sole producers of a particular type of woodenware; however, they did develop some unusual forms for their own use—such as wooden carriers, oval boxes, and baskets—and they also developed particular shapes and details in manufacture, such as the distinctive Shaker finger lap joints of oval boxes and carriers.[10]

SHAKER-MADE PAIL found under the eaves of the Canterbury dwelling house in 1994 during a structural analysis of the building. The pail may have been placed there at one time to catch a leak, then forgotten.

Opposite ❖ SHAKER PAILS AND TUBS, most of which were made in Shaker mills at Canterbury and Enfield, New Hampshire.

Below, left ❖ EXAMPLES OF CANTERBURY WOOD TURNING, including drawer pulls, chair rail pegs, and spool, early to mid-nineteenth century.

Below, right ❖ SISTERS' SEWING BOX. Many of the sisters had their own sewing boxes, which they personalized with decorations. These boxes were generally made by Shaker brothers for the sisters, but a few were probably purchased from the outside world.

OVAL BOXES, attributed to Canterbury.
The small red box, according to Shaker tradition,
was made by Father Job Bishop, c. 1820–30.
Collection of the Philadelphia Museum of Art.

As long as wood remained the backbone of the New England economy, the Shakers flourished. They invested early in substantial tracts of land and were highly skilled in the management of wood lots to secure stands of trees for timber framing, pail manufacture, and cordwood. The Shaker craftsmen were also ingenious at combining wood with metal to manufacture new or superior products, such as wooden shovels with an iron edge and wooden washing machines with metal parts.

In the late eighteenth and early nineteenth centuries, woodworkers and blacksmiths were the "mechanics" of their communities. Many of the most skilled artisans of northern New England were in a woodworking trade, whether they were shipbuilders, wheelwrights, cabinetmakers, turners, or coopers. These artisans were usually also responsible for making and repairing machines and tools, and were often at the forefront of technological innovation, as evidenced by the patent models they made to promote and protect their ideas. However, woodworkers as a class by the nineteenth century had become traditionalists. More and more, after the mid-nineteenth century the future of the Industrial Revolution and modernization lay in machinery and buildings fabricated in metal. The innovators of that period were the clockmakers, gunsmiths, machinists, and foundrymen, as metal replaced wood as the preferred manufacturing material for machines and many household objects. Unfortunately, Shaker manufacturing never successfully navigated the complete transition from wood to metal.

Above ❖ HORSEHAIR BRUSH with turned
handle and original red finish, Canterbury, c. 1840.
Collection of Mark Reinfurt.

Right ❖ CHROME YELLOW STORAGE BOX,
most likely used in the infirmary for medicines,
c. 1850. The interior is lined with blue papers.

Opposite ❖ ASSORTMENT OF WOODEN
BOXES dating from 1800 to 1875. Many of these
were used by the sisters as sewing boxes.

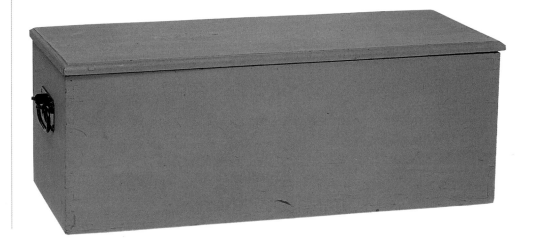

Right, top ❖ SMALL BUCKET WITH LID, Canterbury, Elijah Brown (1772–1851). Brown, one of Canterbury's master "mechanics," supervised the building of the chapel wing of the dwelling house in 1837. Collection of the Philadelphia Museum of Art.

Right, center ❖ DETAIL OF SMALL BUCKET WITH LID, showing the inscription, "This is for Dorothy Durgin, Elijah Brown." Dorothy Durgin was lead eldress of the Canterbury Church Family. Collection of the Philadelphia Museum of Art.

Above ❖ FANCY BASKET of brown ash, Canterbury, Zillah Randlett (1800–1869), mid-nineteenth century. Collection of the Philadelphia Museum of Art.

Right, bottom ❖ WORK BASKET of brown ash, Canterbury, mid-nineteenth century.

Top ❖ Pair of turned wooden candlestick stands, c. 1821–40. These rare stands were most likely made for ministry use, perhaps for use on the ministry dining table. Collection of the Philadelphia Museum of Art.

Center ❖ Applesauce bucket with bail handle and lid, c. 1875–1900. These buckets were packaged six to a crate and sold commercially.

Bottom, left ❖ Sieves made of bent wood and horsehair were a commercial Shaker product for most of the first half of the nineteenth century.

Bottom, right ❖ Oval box with spool holder, Canterbury, c. 1850. Collection of the Philadelphia Museum of Art.

CLOTHING, TEXTILES, AND FANCYWORK

Shaker clothing is one of the rarest categories of surviving Shaker-made objects. Many of the Shaker artifacts illustrated in this book have been preserved because of their associations with Shaker leaders, or because they were in buildings that were "mothballed" by the Shakers. The contents were then dispersed and acquired by collectors and museums. Clothing faced several obstacles to preservation. First, there is documentary evidence that the Shakers did not permit individuals to accumulate wardrobes of clothes, shoes, bonnets, and hats; they wore their garments until threadbare, then recycled or discarded them and made replacements. Second, since the twentieth-century Shakers at Canterbury and elsewhere lived into an era of modified Shaker fashion, they generally did not see the historical value of Shaker costume. Consequently, even the finest Shaker clothing collections today, such as the one at the Western Reserve Historical Society (Cleveland, Ohio), are modest in scope and size, and exist primarily because they were collected directly out of Shaker communities that were closing.

The rarity of eighteenth- and nineteenth-century Shaker clothing does not mean that costume was insignificant for the Shakers. Early in their history the Shakers realized that clothing was a vital element in their overall cultural system and visual code. Shaker clothing was a uniform of belief, which distinguished Shakers from their worldly counterparts and established a feeling of equality and standardization. A distinctive style of cloth-

The dress of this people [the Shakers] half a century ago [mid-nineteenth century] emphasized their separation from the world and attracted attention whenever they appeared in public. The men wore the broad brimmed hat, and clothes of a bluish shade cut in a uniform and unvarying style. The dresses of the women were a grayish tint, full in the skirt with an unadorned waist. For a head covering they had the well-known Shaker bonnet for summer use and the warm hood for winter. Their Sunday costume in the summer of 1854 is thus described by a visitor at one of their public meetings, "the adults and children were dressed nearly alike. The trousers of the brothers were of blue cloth with a wide stripe. The vest was of deeper blue, exposing a full bosomed shirt, with deep turned down collar, fastening with three buttons. The sisters had on pure white dresses, their necks and shoulders being covered with white kerchiefs. Their heads were crowned with lace caps, while over the left arm hung a pocket handkerchief. Their feet were ensconced in high-heeled, pointed-toe, cloth shoes of a brilliant ultramarine blue."

—JAMES OTIS LYFORD,
History of the Town of Canterbury, 1912

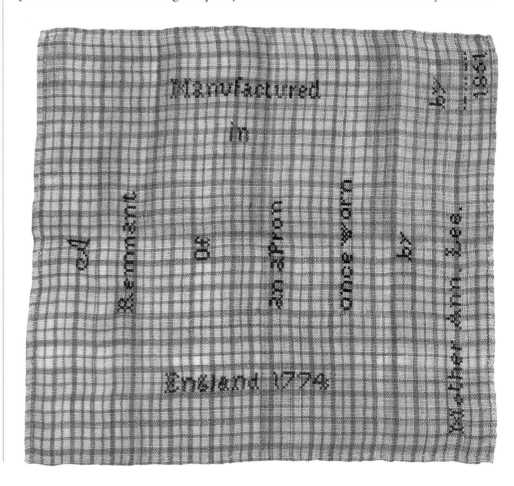

MOTHER ANN'S APRON MATERIAL, linen, 1774 (8¼ × 7¾ in. [21 × 19.7 cm]). This light blue and white plaid patterned material contains the following information cross-stitched in black: "A remnant of an apron once worn by Mother Ann Lee" and "Manufactured in England 1774."

CANTERBURY AND SABBATHDAY LAKE
ELDRESSES AND SISTERS, c. 1880, shown in
a studio portrait.

DRESS, front view, mid-nineteenth century.
Careful detailing is evident in the design and
construction of this dress, which was typical
Shaker sister attire. The striped fabric was
replaced by a modestly figured fabric called
dalaine in 1865, and the neckerchief worn
by sisters early in the nineteenth century was
replaced by the large collar known as the
bertha. See studio portrait above showing sisters
wearing both neckerchiefs and berthas.

ing was as important to the Shaker system as their community plan, their buildings, their furniture, or their distinctive rituals. Clothing was also part of the overall communication system of the Shakers, and enhanced the significance of ritual acts, such as worship dance, for which the Shakers wore special clothing and the sisters donned cloth-covered dancing slippers. Clothing was an active transmitter of Shaker ideas through style, fabric, and color. As with other aspects of their code, the Shakers generally did not try to freeze costume and demand complete compliance. Regulating costume (which they did try for a time) was nearly as difficult as enforcing sumptuary preferences. Nevertheless, the Shakers successfully suppressed extreme expressions of individualism in dress, hairstyling, and personal adornment.[11]

Achieving union of sentiment on matters of dress and establishing a Shaker uniform must have been especially difficult in the early years of the nineteenth century, when new communities were being formed and standards needed to be established in all areas of life. The rapid influx of new converts compounded the problem. Even if they had little in terms of material possessions to contribute to the cause, all converts came with some clothing from the outside world.

The potential problems in enforcing a uniform were expressed in the early nineteenth century by an exasperated David Darrow, a New Lebanon Shaker leader sent to help Union Village, Ohio. He reported on the state of Shaker clothing in a letter to Elder Rufus Bishop of New Lebanon in 1817. For five years the Union Village community had been working to bring their dress into conformity with Shakers in the east, and Darrow speculated that as soon as it was done, at great trouble and expense, a new revolution in

HANDWOVEN AND HANDSEWN VEST made for Deacon Francis Winkley (1759–1847). Rolled hems, contrasting lining, and beautiful finishing details display excellent needlework.

NECKERCHIEF, nineteenth century. A common design technique used by the Canterbury Shakers was to weave finely spun, solid-color warp with weft thread of similar grist, but another color. Here red and blue were used, with a double white-striped border. This technique produced a cloth that appears to change color based on the fabric's drape. Popularized among the Shakers as changeable cotton, this technique was also used with silk and fine wool.

outward dress would occur. Meanwhile, due to the poor state of Shaker clothmaking in the west, and the expense of changing over, the brothers wore coats of iron gray, smoke, drab, blues, and other odd colors, with the haphazard effect "that when they assemble together, in their dress they look more out of uniform than the world do. . . . They gave up buttons and double folds on their jackets and raised their collars to achieve a distinctive style, but changing the colors breaks the uniform, causing uneasiness, and throws the Believers into confusion." For his part, Darrow simply wanted a uniform dress "that will abide," serve the cause of Shaker "virtue" in clothing, and end the "convulsing" over uniform.[12]

The Shakers at New Lebanon did at various times succeed in establishing a uniform, which most Shaker communities followed with varying degrees of success. But it never did stay fixed. Henry Clay Blinn's journal notes several shifts in the uniform of the Canterbury Shakers over the course of the nineteenth century, nearly all of which involved color as well as styling, and included specific introductions such as suspenders, and even umbrellas.[13]

The Shakers identified certain colors as appropriate for clothing and other colors for use in a variety of textiles. Generally the community permitted any color that could be achieved easily with homemade dye. A rare "recipe book" from Canterbury in the 1850s reveals the colors of commonly made dyes—several shades each of black, blue, violet, red, orange, yellow, brown, and green.

The early believers inhabited a typical rural agricultural community that produced most of the textiles necessary for the home and the individual, beginning with raw materials and ending with a finished product. Textiles were a necessary part of survival, and textile needs were extensive, including clothing, household items, and labor-related articles. Joseph Blockett, an early believer, reported that in 1791, as new believers began to gather at Canterbury, the women began to weave, spin, and cook; the men, to cut wood and lumber.[14] Textile-related jobs of the early Shakers included, for the sisters, setting card teeth, carding, hetcheling, spinning, weaving, dyeing, and fashioning garments; for the brothers, making looms, wheels, wool wheels, clock reels, shuttles, and tools for linen processing, and raising flax.

The early Shakers worked primarily to provide for the community. As membership grew, products were developed for sale. As early as 1794 the list of sale items included such textile articles as hats, wool and linen wheels, and wool and cotton cards.[15] The manufacture of hand cards served a dual purpose, affording profitable employment and acting as a social meeting for the early community. A record of 1823 notes that 850 linen wheels were manufactured.[16]

To provide for community textile needs, spinning was a necessary and time-consuming job. In 1795 the spin shop was

built and the third industry building constructed. Some idea of the amount of spinning accomplished is gleaned by learning that 4,170 yards of wide cloth, 2,975 yards of binding, and 1,140 yards of tape were woven in 1796;[17] this astonishing production required the spinning of millions of yards of thread.

As the Canterbury community became firmly established, machinery and mills were added to assist textile manufacturing. The carding mill, built in 1812, was lauded so highly that Henry Clay Blinn later noted, "The hand cards are now laid aside and quite an extensive business was soon obtained in the carding of rolls . . . for Shakers and for others."[18] Spinning was added to the main Shaker industries when in 1815 a spinning jenny was purchased and in 1816 a new spin shop erected.

As they were capable of producing large quantities of thread, the Shakers developed weaving as an industry. Though there is mention of various types of yardage woven for clothing and household needs, the primary product for sale was a double-sided wool flannel, highly regarded throughout the world. Handlooms were used exclusively through 1848, and in the period between 1797 and 1848 available records show that over 42,000 yards of fabric were woven. In 1849 the addition of water-powered looms increased production; records from 1849 to 1879 show about 130,000 yards were woven, including 49,000 yards of flannel.

The Shakers were quick to realize the potential in the textile trade, and in this area for a time the Shakers marched in step with the early textile mill owners. As one examines

NECKERCHIEFS, cotton, nineteenth century. These white and blue neckerchiefs, later replaced by berthas, were a standard item of dress for Shaker sisters throughout much of the nineteenth century. Fine linen, cotton, and silk were the most common materials, and, typical of Shaker woven textiles, the neckerchiefs were usually woven in simple but delicate striped and plaid designs.

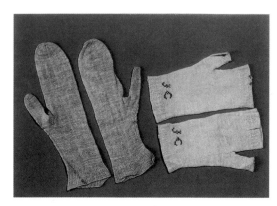

GLOVES AND MITTENS, late nineteenth and early twentieth centuries. Gloves, mittens, and wristlets knit on very fine needles and in delicate designs were an important standard sale item on Shaker sales trips. Gloves and mittens could be either practical or decorative, and were knit or crocheted of wool, silk, cotton, and raccoon.

the history of textile production at Canterbury, the parallels to the early textile industry in Rhode Island, Massachusetts, and New Hampshire are striking. Rhode Island's first textile mill, established by Samuel Slater in 1793, was expanded to mills up the Blackstone River and mill villages at Slatersville and other river towns. The first Massachusetts mills on the Merrimack River were established by Boston entrepreneurs at Waltham about 1815 and Lowell in 1822. Because the capitalist enterprises had two primary purposes, manufacturing cloth and making money, they were able to dominate the American mass market and achieve a scale that by the 1840s totally dwarfed the Shaker textile enterprises.[19] The Shakers gradually abandoned cloth production, and found specialty markets for distinctive products such as hosiery.

Throughout the nineteenth century the textile industries of the Shakers were still quite profitable. In the first half of the century the industry was a cooperative one, with the sisters spinning, weaving, and hand carding, and the brothers carding, fulling, and dressing the cloth in the mills. Other textile industries developed in the late nineteenth century, most notably the knitting of sweaters and cloak making.

By 1865 the increased production of cheaper material by other mills hurt the demand for Shaker fabric. While yard goods were their most important textile product, they also developed and sold other items. Rugs were knitted, braided, hooked, and woven. Shaker rag rugs (actually not made of rags) made use of leftovers from the weaving and spinning mills. Chair tapes provided colorful, comfortable woven seating and were a unique Shaker product, as were bonnets woven of oat or rye straw or palm leaf imported from Cuba. Palm was also used to produce table mats and fans. From 1856 to 1866 another small but active industry flourished, the production of "shirt bosoms," a men's

CHAIR TAPES, wool. A uniquely Shaker product, original Shaker chair tapes were a colorful, comfortable complement to Shaker chairs. Usually made of wool, they were characterized by symmetrical striped designs, which sometimes included a twisted warp design reminiscent of the twisted weft of Shaker rugs.

dickey worn with a suit. Records for this industry show that almost 120,000 shirt bosoms were produced during this period.

Following the Civil War many changes occurred in textile production. Sales became more important as total self-sufficiency became less possible for the increasingly female community. A frustration with machinery led to products less technologically oriented. Specialty products were developed and successfully marketed, often by the Shaker sisters with minimal assistance from the brothers. Hart and Shepard, the trade name for the sisters' industry products (named after Canterbury sisters Emmeline Hart and Lucy Shepard), is an example of the increasing business responsibilities of the Shaker sisters. Several products dominated production and sales in the late nineteenth century, namely, the Shaker sweater, the Dorothy cloak, and poplarware.

Knitting was another important industry for the sisters; they produced stockings in the mid-nineteenth century, and sweaters in the second half of the century. The Shakers were pioneers in production from modern knitting machines. The sisters reported the story of one of their most ambitious knitting orders: in 1886 a man who had been to England asked if they could provide a large order of sweaters; although they had only one Aiken flatbed knitting machine, the sisters agreed. "We commenced to knit on the machine and before December 25 had shipped an order of 60 dozen sweaters." Two types of sweaters were produced: a turtleneck pullover used as a letter sweater for Dartmouth, Yale, Harvard, and Princeton; and a jacket or coat sweater manufactured for popular use. Three types of coat sweaters—with a V-neck, military collar, and auto collar (a type of rolled collar), ranging in weight from lightest to heaviest—were produced using imported Australian wool, in white, black, blue, and garnet. To facilitate production, five Lamb knitting machines were purchased between 1887 and 1903, ranging in cost from $195 to $904.[20] These machines were installed in the laundry building, where they were powered by a steam engine. During World War I some of the white sweaters were dyed khaki and given to the war effort by the Shaker Auxiliary of the Concord chapter of the Red Cross.[21] In 1910 alone, 1,489 sweaters were produced.[22] Later knitted products included socks, stockings, undergarments, gloves, mittens, wristlets, fingerless gloves or mitts, chair seat covers, and rugs. Materials included cotton, linen, silk, and wool. In 1917 the Jordan Marsh department store commissioned knitted scarves, shawls, and kimonos.[23] The knitting industry closed in 1923.

Another important sales item, the Dorothy cloak, is attributable to Eldress Dorothy Durgin (1825–1898). Durgin based her unique design for the cloak on a raincoat she owned and found to be exceptional in design and function. An excellent tailor, she

SHAKER JACKET OR COAT SWEATER, heavyweight wool, 1886 to early twentieth century. Knit in various weights of wool, in pullover "letter sweater" or jacket styles, the Shaker sweater was a popular sale item. Knit on Lamb knitting machines with Australian wool, Shaker sweaters were commonly gray for community members, but could be ordered by the outside world in white, blue, black, and garnet.

Above, left ❖ CLOAK, wool, late nineteenth to early twentieth century. Canterbury Shaker sisters made cloaks, a popular item of women's clothing, for personal use and for sale to the world's people. Although the sisters preferred gray for themselves, cloaks for sale were made in many colors. The Canterbury Shakers had an extensive cloak industry during the late nineteenth and early twentieth centuries.

Above, right ❖ POPLAR BOXES, wood, satin, and kid leather, late nineteenth to mid-twentieth century. Finely constructed of beautiful materials, lined and beribboned in fashionable colors, these boxes were designed for many uses, including handkerchief boxes, diamond card trays, long and short bead boxes, and button boxes. This final set of poplar boxes was made by the Shaker sisters under the direction of Sister Bertha Lindsay for Charles "Bud" Thompson at the close of the industry in 1958.

dismantled the coat to provide a pattern for a woolen cloak she made for herself. At various sales trips, customers questioned the availability of the cloak for purchase and, in true Shaker style, orders were taken and the cloak business was begun in the 1890s. The earliest cloaks were made of Shaker fabric, but as demand grew and as cloth was no longer woven in quantity at Canterbury, high-quality French broadcloth was substituted. Each person was individually measured, and sizes ranged from doll to adult. The cloaks were tailored with a choice of lining, hood, cape, ribbons, and color. The available colors included at least white, black, tan, yellow, three shades each of gray, purple, and red, and eight of blue. Prices ranged from $1.30 to $58. Sales were brisk and figures cannot be obtained for all years, but from 1927 to 1942 sales of the Dorothy cloak averaged about 25 percent of the total for Shaker sales trips.[24] In 1903 the trademark "The Dorothy" was issued, which protected the design and manufacture of these cloaks around the world.

The last major Shaker textile industry, poplarware, typified the "fancywork" that characterizes Shaker sales throughout the late nineteenth and twentieth centuries. Textile and agricultural products declined, as first brothers, then sisters grew less in number. With less dependence on major machinery, the manufacture of fancy goods provided needed financial support. Sisters could produce these small items and yet care for domestic duties. Poplarware, still dependent on machines, demanded presses, stamping machines, vertical planes, and gauges. Poplar strips were woven through a cotton warp to make high-quality poplar cloth; products were luxuriously decorated with satin and velvet linings, kid leather trim, and ribbons. Over twenty different items are known and more than twenty-five colors are noted in sales records. Although accounts are not available for all years, over 11,000 pieces of poplarware were crafted at Canterbury from 1930 to 1958, when the industry was closed by Eldress Bertha Lindsay due to reduced interest in the product, lack of trained people, and loss of equipment.[25]

Fancywork (other than poplarware), begun in the late nineteenth century, continued into the twentieth century and was the major source of income for that period. Fancywork products varied; some were standard items, some appeared only occasionally. Crocheted items, which had gained popularity throughout America during the Victorian period, included shawls, mantillas, doilies, hats, toys, potholders, belts, and curtain pulls. Other standard products included aprons, tablemats, darning sets, sewing sets, wooden sewing baskets, and writing equipment.

Fancywork was sold through sales trips. Sisters traveled to beach and mountain resorts throughout New Hampshire and to cities in Massachusetts, Connecticut, Rhode Island, New York, New Jersey, Pennsylvania, the District of Columbia, and Florida. At first they were driven to these destinations by brothers, but the trips continued even when the sisters were forced to travel by boat or train or hire a driver. As the number of sisters dwindled further, sales trips were abandoned and the bazaar at the village provided the last venue for Shaker textile products.

Below, left ❖ CROSS-STITCHED SAMPLER. Shaker samplers were simple, unornamented projects used to teach cross-stitch alphabets. Because embroidery was used mostly for identification of clothing and textiles, the lavish decorations of other embroidery samplers and schools are not found at Canterbury. Cross-stitched with the initials "JE" in red and black on a white background, this sampler features single numbers and alphabets in both block and cursive lettering.

Below, right ❖ CROSS-STITCHED SAMPLER, November 1834. This red and black alphabet sampler contains the motto, "Open rebuke is better than secret love."

MAPS, PAINTINGS, AND DRAWINGS

Shaker works of art on paper are classics of American folk art in the minds of many museums and collectors. Since the Shakers were part of the iconoclastic Protestant movement of the seventeenth and eighteenth centuries that eschewed individualistic artistic expression, the intricate Shaker "spirit" drawings are remarkable works of art.[26]

The Era of Spirit Manifestations was powerful and prolonged at Canterbury, and manifested itself in many forms of "gifts," including songs, messages, and dances. Only a few spirit drawings survive with a known Canterbury origin, the most famous of which is the Hester Ann Adams manuscript. If more spirit drawings were done at Canterbury, they have been subsequently lost or destroyed.

Right ❖ BOTANICAL DRAWINGS, Sister Cora Helena Sarle of Canterbury, 1886–87. This is one page from the two botanical notebooks drawn and watercolored by Sister Helena in collaboration with Henry Clay Blinn, who provided the written plant titles and descriptions.

Opposite ❖ SISTER HESTER ANN ADAMS, who made this spirit drawing, was eldress in the Canterbury Church Family, and was transferred in 1859 to the Sabbathday Lake community in Maine. This spirit drawing is now in the collections of the Sabbathday Lake Library in New Gloucester, Maine.

Right, top ❖ *CANTERBURY MEETINGHOUSE*, Sister Cora Helena Sarle of Canterbury, watercolor on Masonite, October 15, 1940 (12 × 14 in. [30.4 × 35.6 cm]).

Right, bottom ❖ OVAL BOX, Canterbury, 1857. The lid, painted by Sister Cora Helena Sarle, was completed about 1921, after the opening of Enfield House—the building pictured on the lid. Collection of the Philadelphia Museum of Art.

Below ❖ OIL ON WOOD OF ROSES, Sister Cora Helena Sarle of Canterbury, c. 1920 (36 × 16 in. [91.4 × 40.1 cm]. This piece was painted for the sisters' enjoyment in the dwelling house.

What do survive are excellent examples of Shaker maps, as comprehensively analyzed in Robert Emlen's *Shaker Village Views*. Four of the finest village maps from any Shaker communities are those by Henry Clay Blinn of Watervliet (1842–44), New Lebanon (1842–48), and Canterbury (1848), and the Peter Foster map of Canterbury (1849). The two maps of Canterbury portray the community near its peak, and except for a few woodcut illustrations, offer the only visual documentation of the village before the widespread use of photography.

In the Victorian era the concept of art as being created for visual pleasure and individual expression began to appear in Shaker life. Victorian wall mottoes with domestic or religious sentiments were popular for the decoration of Shaker offices.

At Canterbury in 1886 and 1887 Cora Helena Sarle began a collaborative project with Blinn to record the known plants and wildflowers of the Canterbury community. Sarle's plant journals, with delicate watercolor renderings, were annotated by Blinn, who listed the common and Latin botanical names as well as a brief description of growing conditions. Most likely the journals were intended for instruction of young people within the community, as well as an outdoor avocation for Sarle, who collected the plant specimens. Whatever the intent and use of the plant journals, Sarle continued to paint throughout her life at Canterbury. Her most important works are large floral and landscape scenes done for eldresses or for specific locations within the community, such as the sisters' common rooms in the dwelling house. She also decorated many utilitarian objects used by the sisters, such as umbrella stands and globes for newly installed ceiling lights in the dwelling house and Enfield House. As sources of income dwindled after World War II, Sister Helena painted many small pictures for sale to visitors to Canterbury. These were often done on Masonite panels, but she also used other mediums readily at hand. Some of her most charming works are on metal buttons, metal pin boxes, typewriter ribbon boxes, and even Band-Aid boxes.

Sister Helena was not the only Shaker sister at Canterbury to take up the brush, but she is the best known because of her long career—from 1886 to her death in 1956— and the availability of her works. Her plant journals, recently acquired by Canterbury Shaker Village, were published in a facsimile edition as *A Shaker Sister's Drawings* (1997).[27]

The other notable artist at Canterbury in the twentieth century was Alice P. Howland. Sister Alice was a beekeeping protégé of Blinn's. In her later years Sister Alice developed strong interests in painting and producing craft items made with buttons. Sister Alice gave her paintings, which generally portray flowers, landscapes, or animals, to sisters and to non-Shaker friends.

STONEWORK

Shaker stonework deserves far more recognition than it has received to date. In the eastern communities the Shakers built mostly in wood, but there were notable exceptions in brick and stone. The Great Stone Dwelling at Enfield is the apex of Shaker stone construction, although the Shakers hired outside help in the form of architect Ammi Young and a crew of masons from Boston.

UMBRELLA STAND, Sister Cora Helena Sarle, c. 1920. Sister Helena decorated ceiling light globes and various practical boxes and painted pictures on wood panels, masonite, or canvas.

The eastern Shaker achievement in stonework lies less in stone buildings than in stone's comprehensive application throughout the communities. At Canterbury the Shaker accomplishments in stone are seen in foundation or sill blocks, walkways, steps, gateposts, walls, drains, bridges, dams, culverts, and tombstones. Whether rough cut or dressed, the ubiquitous stonework conveys a message of permanence. Like the peg rail of Shaker interiors, the ribbons of stone that demarcate the Shaker community identify a Shaker space. The stonework is a defining detail of the Canterbury community, from the stone watering trough at the bottom of the hill to the stone gatekeepers marking village entryways.

Stone walls are a common phenomenon in rocky New England, but it is clear that Shaker stonework was not just the practical solution to field clearing. The Shakers began building the meetinghouse field wall along Shaker Road as early as 1797. This stone fence is not composed just of rubble or fieldstone; its face, along Shaker Road, has been expertly fitted together like a jigsaw puzzle and presents a flat finished surface to the travelers up Shaker Road.

Other stone fences at Canterbury are double-walled fieldstone structures that taper from bottom to top. The largest of these measures up to four feet (1.2 m) thick at the base and rises up to eight feet (3.1 m) in height. These fences are filled in with rubble and

Above ❖ GRANITE SIGNPOST AND WATERING TROUGH at the intersection of Shaker Road and Ashby Road. This trough lies at the bottom of the hill leading to Canterbury Shaker Village. The watering trough was fed by gravity from a nearby spring and was accessible to all travelers on the stage route from Concord to Laconia. The "fountain" was featured in a short story by Nathaniel Hawthorne called "The Canterbury Pilgrims."

Right ❖ GRANITE STEPS leading to the interior privy of the 1825 carriage house, commonly called the "yellow building" by the Shakers.

Opposite, top ❖ GRANITE GATEPOSTS, set out in 1834 as part of the south fencerow along Meetinghouse Lane.

Opposite, bottom ❖ DOUBLE STONE WALLS line Shaker Road and the Shaker cemetery.

Opposite ❖ GRANITE WALK AND FENCE POSTS, c. 1830, supporting the meetinghouse picket fence. Polished granite posts such as these were reserved for the special enclosure around the meetinghouse.

Far left ❖ DETAIL OF GRANITE WALK laid out in the south dooryard of Dwelling House Row in 1835 by Brother Micajah Tucker (1764–1848), a founding member of the Canterbury community. In summer he was a stone carver, in winter he was a woodworker—until 1845, when he cut off two fingers on a circular saw, which some Shakers claimed he had invented.

Left ❖ GRAVESTONE OF MARY HATCH. Headstones of identical size were the standard for the Shaker graves throughout the nineteenth century. In the early twentieth century all existing headstones were removed and replaced with one large marker, inscribed "Shakers." The old individual stones were recycled into ironing tables and used for wash lines and as dripstones under the edges of porch and building roofs.

sometimes capped with large, flat headers. Other walls are vertical on the road side and slope on the inside. While the outside wall was carefully built up with large stones, the inside wall was laid in a more random fashion and provides a stone buttress for the vertical facing wall. Away from Shaker Road, the primary access and trade route for all Shaker families, the stonework becomes less Shaker and more generically Yankee. The walls that divide fields and line roads are generally the same single-wall type found throughout northern New England.

The other extraordinary use of stonework to define spaces in the Canterbury community is the network of granite walks that connects most buildings in the Church Family. These geometric ribbons of giant pavers announce the pedestrian circulation patterns of the village. The dwelling-house path, laid out by Brother Micajah Tucker in 1835 with stones chiseled with Roman numerals, is the longest and most spectacular of these walkways.

❖

AFTERWORD

Of all the nineteenth-century visitors to Canterbury from Europe, one of the most distinguished was the articulate and widely traveled Frederika Bremer of Sweden, who published her impressions of America in 1853. Bremer was enchanted with the Shaker form of community life:

> *The Shaker communities are the most rational, and probably the happiest of all conventual institutions. I should be glad if similar ones are found in all countries. People may say what they will, and do the best they can in the great community, but there will always exist the need of places where the shipwrecked in life, the wearied in life, the solitary and feeble, may escape as to refuge, and where their goodwill and their powers of labor may, under a wise and affectionate management, be turned to account; where the children of misfortune or misery may be brought up in purity and love; where men and women may meet and associate as brethren and sisters in a goodwill and friendship, laboring all for the benefit and advantage of each other. And this is the case here. The Shaker community is—admitting some small, narrowed peculiarities—one of the best small communities in the world, and one of the most useful in the great community.*[1]

Pages 206–7 ❖ View of village from Turning Mill Pond.

Right ❖ Eldress Bertha Lindsay and Penny, c. 1980.

Opposite ❖ Detail of hand rail and stair balusters at the end of the brothers' staircase on the third floor of the trustees' office, 1833.

VIEW OF VILLAGE FROM TURNING MILL
POND, looking west.

Bremer's assessment differs from some of the other nineteenth-century accounts we have seen so far. Bremer saw the community as a refuge of order and a place of cheerful, compassionate camaraderie. She recognized—as this study of Shaker life shows—that Shaker villages were environments that nurtured the improvement and harmony of body and soul.

We can see now that Shaker village planning formed the backbone of that integration of the material and spiritual aspects of life. Everything the Shakers created, from the layout of their roads and buildings to the manufacturing of everyday objects and tools, fulfilled their vision of an ordered society and synthesized elements of the physical and spiritual, work and worship. In the development of their community plans and the construction of their buildings, the Shakers translated complex ideas of their faith into physical forms. They believed that their model for community planning, the so-called pattern from the Mount, was a gift from God that would continue to unfold through progressive revelation. The entire village plan became an operating machine for realizing heaven on earth.

Shakerism offered alternatives to the prevailing forms of social organization and religious practice in eighteenth-century America, and Shaker innovations in community planning, architecture, and art each served this revolutionary worldview. But even Bremer's sympathetic remarks show that in spite of its progressive and humane attitudes, Shakerism

was not for everyone. Shaker socialism was discredited and undermined by the emergence of revolutionary Marxism and labor militancy. The millennialist appeal of the Shaker faith was blunted by the liberalization of Protestantism. Above all, Shaker celibacy was rejected by the vast majority of Americans as unnatural, impractical, and a threat to the expansive American dream. Ultimately, the Shaker way did not become the American way, and the Shaker village did not become the social norm. But for most of its history, the Shaker movement was highly successful in creating and sustaining intentional communities, promoting viable business enterprises, and developing sympathetic environments for worship and human interaction.

Perhaps the essence of Shaker achievement in art and architecture lies in the process of creating a spirit-filled village plan, in which the Shakers differentiated raw space with a set of distinctive visual codes in service of their belief system. The history of the village at Canterbury shows that the Shaker community was one in which egoless individuals and timeless ways lived, breathed, and grew. Shakers no longer work and worship among Canterbury's lanes and buildings, but the structures, setting, memories, and legacy of the preserved Canterbury Shaker Village continue to inspire new life.

VIEW OF BOY'S ISLAND AND TURNING MILL POND.

❖

NOTES

Abbreviations of frequently cited sources

Blinn, "Church Record": Henry Clay Blinn, "Church Record by Henry Clay Blinn," ms. #764, c. 1895.

Blinn, "Historical Record": Henry Clay Blinn, "A Historical Record of the Society of Believers in Canterbury, New Hampshire, 1792–1848," ms. #763 [1891], Canterbury Shaker Village Archives.

Blinn, "Historical Notes . . . Enfield": Henry Clay Blinn, "Historical Notes Having Reference to the Believers in Enfield, New Hampshire," vol. 1, ms. #761 [1782–1847]; vol. 2, ms. #762 [1847–1902].

CSVA: Canterbury Shaker Village Archives

INTRODUCTION

1. Dolores Hayden, *Seven American Utopias: The Architecture of Communitarian Socialism, 1790–1975* (Cambridge, Mass.: MIT Press, 1976), 6.

2. Counting Shakers has always been problematic. In 1823 the Shakers claimed over 4,000 adherents. The number 6,000 was used by scholars as the maximum number of Shakers in all villages at one time, but that figure is open to question due to the fluidity of Shaker membership. The federal census records the peak membership at 3,842 in 1850. See William Sims Bainbridge, "Shaker Demographics, 1840–1900," *Journal for the Scientific Study of Religion* (1982) 21, and Priscilla J. Brewer, *Shaker Communities, Shaker Lives* (Hanover, N.H.: University Press of New England, 1986), 203. See also Richard C. Borges, "The Canterbury Shakers: A Demographic Study," *Historic New Hampshire* 48, nos. 2–3 (summer–fall 1993), 155–81, which is adapted from "Canterbury Shaker Village: A Demographic Analysis" (Ph.D. dissertation, University of New Hampshire, 1989).

   Studies of specific communities are critical to correcting generalizations about the Shakers. Several of the most important works are Deborah E. Burns, *Shaker Cities of Peace, Love, and Union: A History of the Hancock Bishopric* (Hanover, N.H.: University Press of New England, 1993); Edward R. Horgan, *The Shaker Holy Land: A Community Portrait* (Harvard, Mass.: Harvard Common Press, 1982); Suzanne R. Thurman, "The Order of Nature, the Order of Grace: Community Formation, Female Status, and Relations with the World in the Shaker Villages of Harvard and Shirley, Massachusetts, 1781–1875" (Ph.D. dissertation, Indiana University, 1994); and John B. Wolford, "The South Union, Kentucky Shakers and Tradition: A Study of Business, Work and Commerce" (Ph.D. dissertation, Indiana University, 1992). Short, helpful introductions to other communities include those by John Ott (Hancock), Thomas Clark (Pleasant Hill), Wendell Hess (Enfield, New Hampshire), Dorothy M. Filley (Watervliet), and Fran Kramer (Groveland).

3. The most comprehensive study and standard reference work on the Shakers as a religious movement is Stephen J. Stein's monumental *The Shaker Experience in America* (New Haven and London: Yale University Press, 1992). Clarke Garrett, *Spirit Possession and Popular Religion from the Camisards to the Shakers* (Baltimore: Johns Hopkins University Press, 1989) is essential reading for understanding the religious context of the birth of Shakerism. There are many excellent studies of the "Great Awakenings" in England and America, from which the Shaker movement emerged, and which altered the course of American religious history. The scholarly works of William McLaughlin and Richard Bushman are particularly noteworthy. For studies that place the Shakers in the context of American religious history, see Stephen A. Marini, *Radical Sects of Revolutionary New England* (Cambridge, Mass.: Harvard University Press, 1992) and "A New View of Mother Ann Lee and the Rise of American Shakerism," parts 1 and 2, *Shaker Quarterly* 18 (summer 1990), 47–52, 56–62; (fall 1990), 95–114.

4. James Thacher, M.D., *A Military Journal During the American Revolutionary War from 1775 to 1783* (Boston: Cottons and Barnard, 1823, 1827), 169–70.

5. Charles Dickens, *American Notes for General Circulation,* 2 vols. (London: Chapman and Hall, 1842), 2:217–220.

6. June Sprigg, *Shaker Design* (New York and London: Whitney Museum of American Art, in association with W. W. Norton and Company, 1986), 11, 21–22.

7. Rosabeth Moss Kanter, *Commitment and Community: Communes and Utopias in Sociological Perspective* (Cambridge, Mass.: Harvard University Press, 1972) is the classic study of commitment mechanisms and behavioral psychology in communitarian societies. For a more personal perspective, and a contemporary look at daily life and commitment in a religious community, see Kathleen Norris, *The Cloister Walk* (New York: Riverhead Books, 1996).

VILLAGE LIFE

THE BUILDING PROCESS OF A PLANNED COMMUNITY

1. Norman Holmes Pearson, "Hawthorne and the Mannings," *Essex Institute Historical Collections* (July 1958), 185.

2. The new office cost $7,440, exclusive of Shaker labor and Shaker-supplied bricks and granite. Blinn, "Historical Record," 237.

3. James Otis Lyford, *History of the Town of Canterbury, New Hampshire, 1727–1912* (Canterbury, N.H.: Canterbury Historical Society, 1973), 443.

4. Edward Deming Andrews, *The People Called Shakers: A Search for the Perfect Society* (New York: Dover Publications, 1963), 285.

5. A. Donald Emerich, "American Monastic; or, The Meaning of Shaker Architecture," *Journal of the Victorian Society in America* 11, nos. 3–4 (1992), 3–11.

6. Blinn, "Historical Record," 47.

7. Henry Clay Blinn, "Job Bishop," *Shaker Manifesto* 22, no. 5 (May 1882), 102. "[H]e would allow of no variation in the style of dress, in the form of a building, in the color of the paint, or in the attachments or capacity of anything that was manufactured, beyond the pattern shown in the Mount."

8. A gambrel roof has two pitches to either side of a central ridge. A low-sloping upper section adjoins a steeper sloped section below. The Canterbury Shakers called this a "curb" roof. The Reverend Timothy Walker House in Concord (1733–35) and the Major Caleb Stark Mansion in Dunbarton (1785) are the only surviving examples of eighteenth-century two-story gambrel-roof houses within the Upper Merrimack Valley region of New Hampshire. Both were considered to be mansions in the eighteenth century.

9. "Francis Winkley Daybook," Oct. 9, 1795, ms. #25, 13, CSVA.

10. Ibid., May 18, 1803, 28.

11. Penelope S. Watson, "Architectural Survey and Analysis: Canterbury Shaker Village" (Canterbury, N.H., n.d.), unpublished manuscript, CSVA.

12. Blinn, "Historical Record," 89.

13. Blinn, "Historical Record," 258.

14. The most detailed early description of Canterbury Shaker Village is provided by Isaac Hill in *Farmer's Monthly Visitor* (Concord, N.H.) 2, no. 3 (August 31, 1840), 113–118.

15. Jerry V. Grant and Douglas Allen, *Shaker Furniture Makers* (Hanover, N.H.: University Press of New England, 1989), 142–43.

16. From 1940 through 1975 many Canterbury Shaker buildings were torn down, destroyed by fire, or sold and moved. The Canterbury horse stand was sold in 1951 to Electra Havermeyer Webb for the Shelburne Museum in Vermont, where it is now known as the "Shaker shed."

ARCHITECTURAL DESIGN AND AESTHETICS

1. Shaker architecture and design are nationally and internationally recognized as uniquely American. The impact of Shaker ideas on modern trends in the design of architecture and furniture is well established, for the Shakers are seen as precursors of the "form follows function" ideology. The Historic American Buildings Survey (HABS) recognized the importance of Shaker architecture since its inception as a national survey. The HABS Shaker collection is the survey's single largest collection of architectural photographs and measured drawings, and is described in "Shaker Material in the Historic American Buildings Survey," *Shaker Quarterly* 9, no. 4 (winter 1969), 107–32.

2. Seth Y. Wells and Calvin Green, eds., *Testimonies Concerning the Character and Ministry of Mother Ann Lee* (Albany: Weed, Parsons & Co., 1827, 1888), 239. The reference to the Ashfield Shaker meetinghouse as a log, gambrel-roofed building is based on a conversation with David D. Newell, a resident of Ashfield, in 1997.

3. The Shakers' skillful architectural manipulation of light exceeds that of both the German American communitarian builders and vernacular builders in New England. The Shakers improved their techniques as they gained building experience from the 1790s into the 1820s. The importance of light in Shaker architecture can hardly be overemphasized, yet there is no satisfactory treatment of the subject. Edward T. Hall, *The Hidden Dimension* (Garden City, N.Y.: Anchor Books, Doubleday and Company, 1966), 747 ff, and Christopher Alexander, *A Pattern Language: Towns, Buildings, Construction* (New York: Oxford University Press, 1977), 526–27, provide helpful introductions to the role of light in buildings.

4. An example of this two-way communication in a Shaker community is revealed in the following eighteenth-century account: "The Rev. William Bentley Visits the Shakers," *Shaker Quarterly* 4, no. 1 (spring 1964), 8.

5. Alexander, *Pattern Language*, 898–99.

6. The two standard works on nineteenth-century American color preferences are Roger W. Moss and Gail Caskey Winkler, *Victorian Decoration: American Interiors, 1830–1900* (1986) and *Victorian Exterior Decoration: How to Paint Your Nineteenth-Century American House Historically* (1987), both published by Henry Holt and Company of New York. Moss and Winkler's books develop the idea that color is both a technological and a cultural phenomenon.

7. The use of color by the Shakers is one of the premier topics among Shaker furniture historians and conservators. The essential sources on the topic are Susan Buck, "Interpreting Paint and Finish Evidence on the Mount Lebanon Shaker Collection," in Timothy D. Rieman, *Shaker: The Art of Craftsmanship* (Alexandria, Va.: Art Services International, 1995), 46–57; Susan Buck, "Bedsteads Should Be Painted Green: Shaker Paints and Varnishes," *Old Time New England* 73 (fall 1995), 16–35; and John T. Kirk, *The Shaker World: Art, Life, Belief* (New York: Harry N. Abrams, 1997), particularly chapter 7, "Color and Varnish: History and Worldly Practices, and Shaker Use," 124–55.

8. Blinn, "Historical Record," 141.

9. Andrews, *People Called Shakers*, 286.

10. Jessie Evans Diary, ms. #1985.6, 43, CSVA.

11. Two closets on the first floor of the ministry shop (elders' quarters) contain gold and white wallpaper that matches the wallpaper found inside Elder Henry Clay Blinn's desk in the Shaker Museum and Library. At one time this wallpaper probably adorned at least the entire west room, and perhaps the whole first floor, of the ministry shop.

12. For this practice, see Jessie Evans, "Data of Probable Importance," ms. #1992.10, 120, CSVA; Irving Greenwood, Building Journal, 1939, ms. #1992.2, CSVA.

WORSHIP AND INDUSTRY

1. William H. McNeill, *Keeping Together in Time: Dance and Drill in Human History* (Cambridge, Mass.: Harvard University Press, 1995), 45. McNeill is not a specialist in Shaker dance ritual; a more comprehensive treatment is Suzanne Youngerman, "Shaking Is No Foolish Play: An Anthropological Perspective on the American Shakers—Person, Time, Space, Dance Ritual" (Ph.D. dissertation, Columbia University, 1983).

2. Edward Deming Andrews and Faith Andrews, *The Gift to Be Simple* (New York: J. J. Augustin, 1940) is still a useful starting point for the study of Shaker music and dance. Daniel W. Patterson's *Gift Drawing and Gift Song* (Sabbathday Lake, Maine: United Society of Shakers, 1983) is essential for understanding the Era of Spirit Manifestations. Harold E. Cook, *Shaker Music: A Manifestation of American Folk Culture* (Lewisburg, Penn.: Bucknell University Press, 1973) provides a valuable introduction to Shaker musicology. The most comprehensive, authoritative study is Daniel W. Patterson, *The Shaker Spiritual* (Princeton, N.J.: Princeton University Press, 1979).

3. Julia Briggs, "Dance Manual," c. 1890, ms. #1997.1, CSVA.

4. Patterson, *Shaker Spiritual*, 454.

5. Blinn, "Historical Notes . . . Enfield," 91.

6. *A Shaker Hymnal: A Facsimile Edition of the 1908 Hymnal of the Canterbury Shakers* (Woodstock, N.H.: Overlook Press, 1990). The introduction by Cheryl A. Anderson discusses the limited use of hymns and hymnals by the Shakers, whose active and at times spontaneous worship favored short hymns, which could easily be sung in unison from memory, or repetitive, one-verse "laboring songs" for dancing.

7. Edward Deming Andrews, *Community Industries of the Shakers* (1933) was enlarged, revised, and republished as *Work and Worship among the Shakers: Their Craftsmanship and Economic Order* (Greenwich, Conn.: New York Graphic Society, 1974). A complementary catalog is *Community Industries of the Shakers: A New Look* (Albany: Shaker Heritage Society, 1983), based on a 1983 exhibit at the New York State Museum in Albany.

8. Isaac Hill, *Farmer's Monthly Visitor* (Concord, N.H.) 2, no. 3 (August 31, 1840), 113–18.

9. One of the most successful Canterbury Shaker enterprises was the manufacture of commercial washing machines, based on an invention patented by Parker, advertised nationally, and sold to urban and resort hotels throughout the northeast. See "The Shaker Washing Machine," *Scientific American,* n.s. 2, no. 2 (March 10, 1860), 161.

10. David Starbuck, "The Archaeology of Canterbury Shaker Village," *New Hampshire Archaeologist* 21 (1980), 67–79.

11. Blinn, "Historical Record," 47–48.

12. The role of the Shakers in American industrialization, and their relationship to technological innovation and change, is a fruitful area for future study. Shaker achievements in milling and manufacturing have not been interpreted in light of regional and national economic trends, even though those trends have been outlined in Steven Hahn and Jonathan Prude, eds., *The Countryside in the Age of Capitalist Transformation* (Chapel Hill, N.C.: University of North Carolina Press, 1985), and in Brian J. L. Berry, *America's Utopian Experiments: Communal Havens from Long-Wave Crises* (Hanover, N.H.: University Press of New England, 1992). The most substantial analysis of technological change in one Shaker community is in Andrew J. Vadnais, "Machines among the Shakers: The Adoption of Technology by the Mount Lebanon Community, 1790–1865" (M.A. thesis, University of Delaware, 1990).

The Shakers also pursued a parallel modernizing track to industrialization, namely, the commercialization of agriculture, livestock breeding, and woodlot management. The same openness to innovation and improvement prevailed in farming, which led to Shaker leadership in stock breeding, plant hybridization, and adoption of new machinery and techniques (such as the use of silage for cattle feed). This is another area wide-open for research. An important Canterbury study is Darryl Thompson, "Shaker-Originated Plant Varieties" (M.A. thesis, University of New Hampshire, 1996). For the Shaker role in forestry management, see Robert McCullough, *The Landscape of Community: A History of Communal Forests in New England* (Hanover, N.H.: University Press of New England, 1995), 37–46.

13. The "Records of Office Conferences" start in 1883, although the practice of gathering both ministry elders and trustees to discuss business was probably a long-standing tradition. As the Records indicate, eldresses were frequently called upon to represent the sisterhood in business discussions. In 1883 the chief issues were how to obtain water rights from neighbors to the north, and how much firewood and lumber would be needed for the coming year. In 1884 the issues still included water rights, but also livestock, hired men, building maintenance, and milk production (ms. #24, CSVA).

14. Mary Rose Boswell, "Women's Work: The Canterbury Shakers' Fancy Work Industry," *Historical New Hampshire* 48, nos. 2–3 (summer/fall 1993), 133–54. For the broader Shaker context see Beverly Gordon, "Shaker Fancy Goods: Women's Work and Presentation of Self in the Community Context in the Victorian Era," in *Women in Spiritual and Communitarian Societies in the United States* (Syracuse, N.Y.: Syracuse University Press, 1992), 89–103.

MIND AND BODY

1. The history of Shaker education is most comprehensively treated by Frank G. Taylor, "An Analysis of Shaker Education: The Life and Death of an Alternative Educational System, 1774–1950" (Ph.D. dissertation, University of Connecticut, 1976). The Canterbury story from 1792 through the mid-nineteenth century has been told by Henry Blinn in his "Historical Record." Much of Blinn's knowledge was from the direct experience of going to the Canterbury Shaker school as a boy, and then becoming the teacher. The most recent study of Canterbury Shaker education is Judith A. Livingston's "The Industrial Shakers: Closing the Gap," a senior honors thesis at the University of New Hampshire, 1997. See chapter 2, "Industrial Education: The Adoption of the World's Ideas."

2. Carl F. Kaestle, *Joseph Lancaster and the Monitorial School Movement* (New York: Columbia University Teacher's College Press, 1973), and Kaestle, *Pillars of the Republic* (New York: Hill and Wang, 1983).

3. Elizabeth Anna DeWolfe, "Erroneous Principles, Base Deceptions and Pious Frauds: Anti-Shaker Writing, Mary Marshall Dyer, and the Public Theater of Apostasy" (Ph.D. dissertation, Boston University, 1996).

4. "School Regulations," 1823, ms. #1993.6, CSVA.

5. Jean McClintock and Robert McClintock, eds., *Henry Barnard's School Architecture* (New York: Columbia University Teacher's College Press, 1970) includes a reprint of *Barnard's School Architecture; or, Contributions to the Improvement of School-Houses in the United States* (1848).

6. Diocletian Lewis, M.D., *The New Gymnastics for Men, Women, and Children* (Boston: Ticknor and Fields, 1862).

7. Blinn, "Historical Record," 190–91.

8. Oliver Wendell Holmes published a series of articles on the stereoscope in *Atlantic Monthly* from 1859 to 1863. Those Shakers interested in photography might also have seen an article in *Scientific American* n.s. 2, no. 2 (June 2, 1860), 36, which explained the process of producing stereoscopic photographs.

9. Both the Enfield and Canterbury communities allowed commercial photographers to prepare sets of viewcards of their villages. The earliest Enfield views are by E. T. Brigham, of Lebanon, New Hampshire. One of these, now in the CSVA, shows a panoramic view of the fertile Shaker fields along Mascoma Lake at Enfield, with a lone Shaker brother standing in the middle of the vast landscape. On the reverse is a handwritten inscription, "Field between the Church and 2nd family. Elder Nelson Chase at rest." The handwriting is probably that of Henry Clay Blinn. The earliest views of Canterbury were taken by the Kimball Studio in Concord, New Hampshire.

10. This summary and the entire chapter owe a debt to the volunteer research of Sabra Welch, who over three years read all Canterbury archival material pertaining to the village's medical history. Her unpublished work is complemented by the unpublished research on Dr. Thomas Corbett by Heidi Herzberger and the important book by Galen Beale and Mary Rose Boswell, *The Earth Shall Blossom: Shaker Herbs and Gardening* (Woodstock, Vt.: Countryman Press, 1991). Amy Bess Miller's dated *Shaker Herbs* (1976) is slated for revision and reprinting. M. Stephen Miller's *A Century of Shaker Ephemera* (New Britain, Conn.: M. Stephen Miller, 1988) and his articles on Shaker medical and dental products are the best sources of information on these products.

11. In that same year Corbett's seed inventory had a value of $1,378, and he had $3,697 in capital to run the business. Blinn, "Church Record," 79.

12. Letters, November 27, 1835, and January 4, 1836, Garret Lawrence to Thomas Corbett, University of New Hampshire Special Collections.

13. For the devastating effect of tuberculosis on Shaker communities, see John Edward Murray, "Communal Living Standards and Membership Incentives: The Shakers, 1780–1880" (Ph.D. dissertation, Ohio State University, 1992), 50, 61.

14. Blinn, "Church Record," 121.

15. Barbara Rotundo, "Crossing the Dark River: Shaker Funerals and Cemeteries," *Communal Societies* 7 (1987), 36.

16. "An Obituary Journal of Members," III, ms. #760, 34, CSVA; Etta M. Madden, "Bodies of Life: Shaker Literacies and Literature" (Ph.D. dissertation, University of New Hampshire, 1995), 243–44. Madden's chapter 6, "Preserving the Body in Poetry: The Canterbury Obituary Journal," 243–311, is the best treatment to date of the Shaker practice of ritual commemoration, which is vital to the bonding of a communal society. Ritual commemoration is common in Shaker material culture as well as in Shaker poetry and literature.

17. Journal, New Lebanon or Watervliet, May 1835, Edward Deming Andrews Collection, #636, Winterthur Library.

DAILY LIFE AND WORK

1. Shaker dwelling houses are only beginning to receive the scholarly attention they deserve. The only full-scale study is Julie Nicoletta, "Structures for Communal Life: Shaker Dwelling Houses at Mount Lebanon, New York" (Ph.D. dissertation, Yale University, 1993).

2. Nicoletta, *The Architecture of the Shakers,* 49–76, based partly on the journal of Isaac N. Youngs, "A Concise View of the Church of God and of Christ on Earth . . . ," 1856, ms. #861, Andrews Collection, Winterthur Library. At Canterbury, the meetinghouse and dwelling house were each built in a full building season, from April through early November. Both original buildings reveal meticulous, skillful framing and finish carpentry. The meetinghouse and the 1793 dwelling house frames show evidence of scribe rule joinery, whereby each timber frame joint is custom fit. In the dwelling-house addition of 1814, the frame reveals evidence of a major shift in joinery techniques, as the Shaker builders adopted square rule joinery, by which joints were precut and numbered. For explanation of the difference between these techniques I am indebted to Conor Power of Boston, a consulting structural engineer on the dwelling-house restoration at Canterbury.

3. Robert P. Emlen, "The Great Stone Dwelling at Enfield, New Hampshire," *Old Time New England* 69, nos. 3–4 (winter/spring 1979), 69–85. For more information on Dartmouth College architecture and Ammi Young see Bryant Tolles, "The Evolution of a Campus: Dartmouth College Architecture before 1860," *Historical New Hampshire* 42, no. 4 (winter 1987), 329–82.

4. The primacy of the square in early Shaker architecture may trace back to Mother Ann Lee, who regarded the "Square House" in Harvard as a place of special importance. It was here that she witnessed the embodiment of a vision she had experienced in England in 1772. See Wells and Green, *Testimonies,* 67. At Canterbury the square appears within buildings, in enclosures such as that for the meetinghouse, and even in the 1797 vegetable garden layout. The square also figures prominently in Shaker dance and in dining, where the tables are set "four square."

The 1792 meetinghouse at Canterbury had an approximately 30-foot-square worship area until 1815, when it was enlarged by the removal of fireplaces and staircases. The 1793 Canterbury dwelling house had two 20-by-20-foot meeting rooms on the first floor, with one or more folding partitions between men's and women's sides that could be opened to make a 20-by-40-foot space. The two 15-foot-square dining rooms on the ground level had no partition, and appear as an open 15-by-30-foot space, but there was an invisible barrier between the men's and women's sides. Other later Shaker dwelling houses retain the square meeting room and dining room. Dimensions in dwellings vary, from 20-foot square, to 24-foot square, to 30-foot square and more, but the square remains the principal spatial symbol in core Shaker buildings of varying dimensions at least through the 1820s. The Shaker meetinghouses of the 1820s appear to abandon the square, but the men's and women's sides are each approximately square. Some later dwelling houses have square retiring rooms (e.g., Enfield's Great Stone Dwelling), and squares still characterize some dining and meeting rooms into the 1870s and 1880s.

5. Blinn, "Historical Notes . . . Enfield," 12, 31.

6. The 1848 ministry shop is essentially a vernacular domestic dwelling with a central hall and single staircase. However, as the Shakers creatively adapted the vernacular plan, they developed equal entries for elders and eldresses, and oriented the staircase to the south for the convenience of the eldresses, who worked on the second floor. A later addition on the south and a hood over the elders' entrance on the north, created a front/back impression for the ministry that had not been the intent in 1848.

7. Blinn, "Historical Record . . . Enfield," 51.

8. Letter, Sister Amanda to Sister Edith Green, Easter, April 1908, ms. #1997.7, CSVA.

9. Edward Deming Andrews and Faith Andrews, *Work and Worship among the Shakers: Their Craftsmanship and Economic Order* (Greenwich, Conn.: New York Graphic Society, 1974, 1982), 37, 174 ff.

10. Blinn, "Historical Record," 48.

11. The literature on women's work and the "cult of domesticity" is vast and cannot be cited here, but several works are essential in comparing the domestic life of the Shaker women to that of their nineteenth-century counterparts. Catherine E. Beecher, *A Treatise on Domestic Economy, for the Use of Young Ladies at Home, and at School* (Boston: Marsh, Capen, Lyon, and Webb, 1841) provides a contemporary context. Sigfried Giedion's *Mechanization Takes Command* (New York and London: W. W. Norton and Company, 1948, 1969) provides a historical treatment of the technological innovations that influenced nineteenth-century domestic economy. Elizabeth D. Garrett's *At Home: The American Family, 1750–1850* (New York: Harry N. Abrams, 1990) and Jane C. Nylander's *Our Own Snug Fireside: Images of the New England Home, 1760–1860* (New York: Alfred A. Knopf, 1993) both treat the material culture of the homes of prosperous Americans of the eastern seaboard. An introduction to the issues of gender can be gained from Carroll Smith-Rosenberg, *Disorderly Conduct: Visions of Gender in Victorian America* (New York: Alfred A. Knopf, 1985).

12. The history of women as workers in the early textile mills of New England is the subject of Thomas Dublin's *Women at Work: The Transformation of Work and Community in Lowell, Massachusetts, 1826–1860* (New York: Columbia University Press, 1979) and Thomas Dublin, ed., *Farm to Factory: Women's Letters, 1830–1860* (New York: Columbia University Press, 1981, 1993). The lives of Shaker women have been the focus of excellent, pathbreaking scholarship in the writings of Jean M. Humez, Priscilla Brewer, Diane Sasson, Lawrence Foster, Louis J. Kern, D'Ann Campbell, Sally

Kitch, and Marjorie Proctor-Smith. See also Marsha Mihok, "Women in the Authority Structure of Shakerism" (Ph.D. dissertation, Drew University, 1989), and Karen K. Nickless and Pamela J. Nickless, "Sexual Equality and Economic Authority: The Shaker Experience, 1784–1900," in Wendy E. Chmielewski, et al., *Women in Spiritual and Communitarian Societies in the United States* (Syracuse, N.Y.: Syracuse University Press, 1993), 119–32.

13. David Starbuck and Scott T. Swank, *A Shaker Family Album* (Hanover, N.H.: University Press of New England, 1998).

14. Miriam Wall and Aida Elam, *History of the Shakers: Education and Recreation* (Canterbury, N.H.: Canterbury Shaker Village, n.d.).

COMMUNITY ORDER

REGULATING EVERYDAY LIFE

1. Stein, *Shaker Experience,* 218. For a comprehensive analysis of fictional treatments of the Shakers, see Michael Pugh, "A Thorn in the Text: Shakerism and the Marriage Narrative" (Ph.D. dissertation, University of New Hampshire, 1994).

2. Thomas Barrie, *Spiritual Path, Sacred Place: Myth, Ritual, and Meaning in Architecture* (Boston and London: Shambhala Publications, 1996), 6, 27, 31, 38, 39.

3. Marking by letters and numbers was characteristic on Shaker textiles, baskets, and other household objects. They made communal life easier and less fractious: Roman numerals on granite stones simplified the process of laying walks; numbers on drawer parts simplified the assembly of a drawer. This practice of marking was not unique to the Shakers, for nearly all eighteenth-century woodworkers used marking systems—but the Shakers extended the practice to most aspects of life.

4. June Sprigg, *By Shaker Hands* (Hanover, N.H., and London: University Press of New England, 1975, 1900), 50–51.

5. Peg rail was the first line of the Shaker storage system. Its overt presence was a constant reminder to hang one's hat or coat, or put away one's chair. From this surface storage device, the system flowed throughout the village, into progressively smaller and more remote spaces. The Shakers seemed to delight in conceiving a storage solution for spaces that yielded little practical return for the amount of effort needed to enclose them. To ensure proper use, the Shakers placed chalk instructions on attic rafters, closet doors, posts, etc. For example, a nail on an attic post in the north shop has the word "scissors" written above it.

6. Jessie Evans Diary, ms. #1986.14, CSVA.

7. Blinn, "Church Record," 185.

8. This brief summary of the Canterbury Shaker attitude toward cleanliness does not do justice to a topic in Shaker history that deserves full scholarly treatment. The legacy of Shaker water systems, wash houses, laundries, cisterns, and plumbing is extensive, and rivals that of the Moravians in significance, for both communitarian groups were in fact developing small municipal water systems. For an excellent social history of cleanliness, see Suellen Hoy, *Chasing Dirt: The American Pursuit of Cleanliness* (New York

and Oxford: Oxford University Press, 1983). On technological innovations in domestic plumbing, see Giedion, *Mechanization Takes Command.* For laundry practices in New England, see Nylander, *Our Own Snug Fireside,* particularly chapter 6, "Clean and Decent: A Family's Clothing," 143–62.

9. See Nylander's *Our Own Snug Fireside,* which places the Canterbury Shaker experience in a broader New England context, especially chapter 4, "Frosty Mornings and Stinging Fingers: The Effects of Winter," 74–102.

10. Blinn, "Historical Record," 165.

11. Although there are no specific accounts detailing the Canterbury production of firewood, comparable accounts do exist for New Lebanon. In general a Shaker brother, several hired men, and several ox and horse teamsters would work three "man days" to produce a cord of wood in 1840 (split and stacked in woodhouses), and two man days per cord in 1900. A dwelling house would need approximately fifty cords of wood per winter, with another twenty per winter for baking and cooking. The ministry might require eight to ten cords per winter, the office fifteen to twenty-five cords, and shops from five to fifteen cords.

12. Blinn, "Historical Record," 198.

13. Ibid., 119.

14. Blinn, "Church Record," 184.

15. Irving Greenwood, "Electrical Journal," c. 1913, Sister Ethel Hudson Collection, box 4, folder 5, CSVA.

16. Madden, "Bodies of Life," 243–311.

SHAKER STYLE

CLASSIC DESIGNS

1. Shaker style, defined in art-historical terms as a distinctive set of aesthetic principles applied to the making of art, is an elusive phenomenon. The literature on the subject has been dominated by the work of Edward Deming Andrews and June Sprigg, as noted in the introduction to this book. John Kirk's *The Shaker World* encompasses their previous work and will be the standard art-historical treatment of the Shakers. Although Kirk is primarily a furniture historian, in *The Shaker World* he develops an integrated theory about Shaker design, style, and beauty.

2. *Shaker Manifesto* 12, no. 8 (August 1892), 173.

3. Edward Deming Andrews and Faith Andrews, *Shaker Furniture: The Craftsmanship of an American Communal Sect* (New Haven: Yale University Press, 1937), chapter 2.

4. Jean M. Burks, *Documented Furniture: An Introduction to the Collections* (Canterbury, N.H.: Canterbury Shaker Village, 1989); Jerry V. Grant and Douglas R. Allen, *Shaker Furniture Makers*; Charles R. Muller and Timothy D. Rieman, *The Shaker Chair* (Amherst, Mass.: University of Massachusetts Press, 1992); Timothy D. Rieman and Jean M. Burks, *The Complete Book of Shaker Furniture* (New York: Harry N. Abrams, 1993). One of the best-known Shaker furniture makers is featured in Erin M. Budis, *Making His Mark: The Work of Shaker Craftsman Orren Haskins* (Old Chatham, N.Y.: Shaker Museum and Library, 1997).

5. Rieman and Burks, *Complete Book of Shaker Furniture*, 134, 236–38.

6. Ibid., 55–58.

7. Kirk, *Shaker World*, 87–100.

8. Kirk, *Shaker World*, chapter 9, "After 1860: Very much like the inhabitants of the section of the country where they reside," 190–239. See also the earlier work of Mary Lynn Ray, "A Reappraisal of Shaker Furniture and Society," *Winterthur Portfolio* 8 (1973).

9. Brooke Hindle, ed., *America's Wooden Age: Aspects of Its Early Technology* (Tarrytown, N.Y.: Sleepy Hollow Press, 1975, 1985). This standard work illustrates American dependency on wood from 1607 through the 1840s.

10. The classic work on Shaker baskets is Martha Weatherbee and Nate Taylor, *Shaker Baskets* (Sanbornton, N.H.: Martha Weatherbee Basket Shop, 1993). The most useful books on Shaker woodenwares are in the Shaker Field Guide Series by June Sprigg and Jim Johnson, *Shaker Woodenware*, vol. 1 (1991), on Shaker carriers, oval boxes, pails, and tubs, and vol. 2 (1992), on Shaker tools and household and craft equipment. The field guides are published by Berkshire House Publishers, Stockbridge, Mass.

11. The standard work on Shaker textiles is Beverly Gordon, *Shaker Textile Arts* (Hanover, N.H., and London: University Press of New England, 1980). See also Beverly Gordon, "Victorian Fancy Goods: Another Reappraisal of Shaker Material Culture," *Winterthur Portfolio* 25 (summer/autumn 1990), and Richard M. Candee, "The 'Shaker Sock': A New Hampshire Contribution to Nineteenth-Century Machine Knitting," *Historical New Hampshire*, 52, nos. 3–4 (fall/winter 1997), 61–77.

12. Letter from Father David Darrow, Union Village, Warren County, Ohio, to "Beloved and Much Respected Brother Rufus," October 20, 1817. Western Reserve Historical Society, Cleveland, microfilm reel IV: B-34, 54–56.

13. Henry Blinn's "Historical Record" and "Church Record" are the primary sources for the history of Canterbury's textile production. He frequently closed a year's entries with a statistical summary of textile production.

14. A rare manuscript "Receipt Book" of dye recipes for cloth was compiled in 1857 by Mary Ann Hill, a deaconess of Canterbury from 1830 until 1859, when she moved to Sabbathday Lake. See Brother Arnold Hadd and John Cutrone, eds., *Mary Ann Hill's Receipt Book* (Sabbathday Lake, Maine: Red Wagon Press at the Shaker Press, 1997).

15. Blinn, "Historical Record," 1794 "Yearly Report."

16. Ibid., 1823 "Yearly Report."

17. Ibid., 1796 "Yearly Report."

18. Ibid., 1812 "Yearly Report."

19. The standard works on early industrial mill architecture are John Coolidge, *Mill and Mansion: A Study of Architecture and Society in Lowell, Massachusetts, 1820–1865* (New York: Columbia University Press, 1942) and John S. Gardner, ed., *The Company Town: Architecture and Society in the Early Industrial Age* (New York and Oxford: Oxford University Press, 1992). These general works need to be supplemented by specialized surveys and studies, such as those by Gary Kulik for Rhode Island.

20. See the unpublished modern papers "History of the Shaker Sweater" and "About the Shaker Sweater," CSVA.

21. "Knitting Machine and Winder," ms. #28, CSVA; Josephine E. Wilson Diary, January 23, 1918, ms. #1985.52, CSVA.

22. Jessie Evans Diary, 1910, ms. #1985.24, CSVA.

23. Ibid., 1917.

24. "Account Book Sales Trips," 1923–42, ms. #1034, CSVA.

25. "Orders for Poplar Work," October 1, 1930, ms. #659, CSVA.

26. The standard treatment of Shaker spirit drawings as art is *Visions of the Heavenly Sphere: A Study in Shaker Religious Art* (Charlottesville, Va.: University Press of Virginia, 1969). The newest scholarly study from a historical perspective is Sally M. Promey, *Spiritual Spectacles: Vision and Image in Mid-Nineteenth Century Shakerism* (Bloomington: Indiana University Press, 1993).

27. Cora Helena Sarle, *A Shaker Sister's Drawings* (New York: Monacelli Press, 1997).

AFTERWORD

1. Bremer, Frederika, *The Homes of the New World: Impressions of America*, vol. 2 (New York: Harper and Brothers, 1853), 579–80.

CHRONOLOGY OF CANTERBURY SHAKER EVENTS

Darryl Thompson

1736

❖ February 29—Ann Lee is born to John Lees, a blacksmith, and his wife in Manchester, England. (The family will later drop the "s" from their surname.)

1747

❖ James and Jane Wardley, longtime Quakers by belief, secede from the Society of Friends and begin worshiping in their home. Friends and neighbors, mostly lower- and working-class, begin to attend religious meetings at the Wardley home. A new religious society forms; they call themselves the United Society of Believers in Christ's Second Appearing, but come to be known as the "Shaking Quakers" or "Shakers" because of their tendency to shake, tremble, and express their religious emotions in spontaneous dance. The group later officially adopts the name. They practice oral confession of sins, separation from "worldliness," and use of the charismatic gifts of the spirit.

1758

❖ Ann Lee and her relatives join the Wardley's religious society.

1762

❖ January 5—Lee marries Abraham Standerin, a blacksmith. The couple eventually conceives four children, but each will die at birth or in infancy.

1770s

❖ Lee, in great emotional and physical distress, has a series of transforming spiritual experiences. She becomes known as "Mother Ann" to her followers. Within the new Quaker community she begins to preach the way of celibacy—a stricter form of "taking up the cross" against one's own sinful nature. More and more members of the society look to her for leadership, but faced with mounting opposition, eventually Lee and her followers are subjected to persecution and imprisonment.

1774

❖ Mother Ann Lee, accompanied by a small band of followers from Wardley's society, emigrates to America in search of religious freedom and new converts.

1775

❖ War breaks out at Lexington and Concord, Massachusetts.

1780

❖ The American colonies undergo social, political, and economic stress due to the long war with Great Britain. These conditions foster a religious revival throughout New Hampshire and Maine by a charismatic group called Free Will Baptists, or Randallites, who oppose Calvinism and emphasize the role of human free will in salvation.

1781–1782

❖ Free Will Baptists from Canterbury, New Hampshire, hear about the Shakers from Benjamin Thompson, who had encountered members while in the general area of New Lebanon, New York. Edward Locke and John Shepard, pastors of the Loudon and Canterbury Free Will Baptist churches, travel to Harvard, Massachusetts, to meet with the Shakers there and with visiting Shaker preachers from New Lebanon.
❖ September 1782—First Shaker presentation is held in Loudon, New Hampshire. Before the year ends, Shaker meetings are held regularly in Canterbury at the farm of Benjamin Whitcher.

1783

❖ America wins its battle for independence.
❖ A few of the newly formed Canterbury Shaker congregation move in with the Whitcher family and live communally.

1784

❖ Mother Ann, worn out from years of hardship, exertion, missionary travels, and violent persecution, dies in New York State at age forty-eight. Father James Whittaker, her younger cousin and foster son, becomes head of the Shaker Society.

1787–1793

❖ Eleven Shaker communities are "called to order": these include

Watervliet (at first called Niskeyuna) and New Lebanon, N.Y.; Hancock, Shirley, Harvard, and Tyringham, Massachusetts; Canterbury and Enfield, New Hampshire; and Alfred and Sabbathday Lake, Maine. Father James Whittaker initiates this process; after his death in 1787 his successor, Father Joseph Meacham, completes it.

1792

❖ The Whitcher family turns over their farm to the Shaker Society. Father Joseph Meacham entrusts Job Bishop with formally organizing the society at Canterbury and taking charge of the believers at Enfield.

❖ February—Father Job Bishop and Edmund Lougee arrive at Canterbury.

❖ May 9—The frame of the meetinghouse is raised in one day, and with such solemn reverence that "scarcely a word is spoken during the framing and raising of the building, except in whisper."

❖ May 11—Mother Hannah Goodrich of New Lebanon and Anna Burdick arrive to take spiritual charge of the sisters at Canterbury and Enfield. In the new governmental system that is instituted, elders and eldresses serve as spiritual and administrative leaders, and, under their oversight, deacons and deaconesses direct work activities and trustees look over financial affairs.

❖ November 10—A tannery is erected to provide income for the community.

1793

❖ April 30—Construction begins on the dwelling house, a dormitory for the growing community.

❖ May 29—Father Joseph Meacham and Mother Lucy Wright make a five-day visit to Canterbury and observe the construction of the new building.

❖ November 11—The dwelling house is ready for its first occupants.

❖ November 13—The brethren begin to build a blacksmith shop and start a second business, the manufacturing of hoes, axes, and scythes.

1794

❖ April 1—It is decided to paint the meetinghouse for the first time.

❖ September 30—A second dwelling house is framed to accommodate the expanding population. During the year a stable is built for the ministry and construction of the first trustees' office is begun.

1795

❖ March 25—Construction of a spin shop is begun for the sisters' textile production.

❖ July 29—A workshop is begun for the brothers to house a hatter's shop on the lower loft; a cooper's shop on the second loft; a wool card makers' shop (east end); and a tailor's shop (west end) on the third loft.

By this year garden seeds are sold by the Shakers at Canterbury and Enfield, New Hampshire; New Lebanon, New York; and Hancock, Massachusetts.

1796

❖ Spring—One-half of a large orchard, covering some six acres, is set out. There were already some fruit trees growing on the Whitcher farm.

❖ May 12 and 16—A written covenant is drawn up and signed by all of lawful age, in the presence of the Church Family.

❖ July 8—Father Joseph Meacham, who had been to visit the Maine Shakers, visits for two days, accompanied by two colleagues.

❖ August 20—Father Joseph Meacham dies at New Lebanon; Mother Lucy Wright assumes full executive authority as head of the Shaker church.

❖ Fall—The directors of Canterbury's Second Family (established already for several years) are given the title of elders.

1798

❖ The Shaker ministry reopens Shaker worship to the outside world after a period of building and economically consolidating eleven communities. A new form of dance worship is introduced that features a more disciplined walk or march and a quick shuffle step.

Land is set aside for a cemetery, and a stone wall is built around it. The brothers begin building stone walls around the fields and orchards.

1800

❖ Water power is established at the Shaker village at Canterbury: "A reservoir was made this season, some three miles north of the Village. . . . From this a canal was made to bring the water into the pond east of the North Family. After this had been completed, a small mill for the grinding of grain and the sawing of lumber was built at a point about one hundred and fifty rods S.W. from the Meeting House." Work begins on the "long ditch," the canal that supplies water to the Shaker mills. A fulling mill for the dressing of cloth is also established.

This year there are forty-one brothers and forty-two sisters in the Church Family and thirty-one residents in the Second Family.

1801

❖ The North Family is organized for new converts who "needed farther instruction" in the principles of the group's faith and worship "before they could be reasonably admitted into a Church relation." Several buildings are erected at the Church and North Families.

Commercial dairy and cider production begins in earnest at the village. The dairy—run by the sisters—produces butter and cheese for market.

1805

❖ Shaker evangelists begin a twenty-five-year campaign into frontier areas, forming eight new communities: one in western New York, two in Kentucky, four in Ohio, and one in Indiana.

1806

❖ Formal schooling of Shaker girls begins at Canterbury with instruction in penmanship (writing on bark) for one hour, six evenings each week.

The West Family, a branch of the North Family, is founded.

1808

❖ A religious revival occurs at Canterbury, characterized by "a sharp testimony against all sin and with powerful operations in the manifestations of diverse gifts."

❖ For the first time, roofs are painted—red. "It was thought to be a preservative of the shingles."

1812

❖ The New Lebanon Shakers establish the first Shaker medicinal herb garden.

❖ Canterbury builds a new carding mill.

1813

❖ Brother Thomas Corbett of Canterbury is credentialed as a physician.

1815–1818

❖ Eunice Chapman, whose husband, James, has joined the New York Shakers and taken the couple's children with him, wages a successful three-year battle to gain custody of her youngsters. She wins when the New York legislature signs a bill dissolving the Chapman marriage. Her victory stimulates anti-Shaker accounts, and leads to efforts to pass anti-Shaker legislation (most of which is eventually defeated). It also prompts others to claim children that relatives had entrusted to the Shakers, personal property that families had left to the Shakers, and compensation for labor done while living in Shaker communities.

1816

❖ Thomas Corbett begins the production of medicinal herbs at Canterbury by laying out the physicians' botanical garden.

1819

❖ The New Hampshire legislature passes the Toleration Bill, which recognizes the Shakers' pacifism and exempts them from military service and equivalency payments.

❖ The Canterbury West Family closes.

1821

❖ The Millennial Laws of 1821, the Shakers' first systematic codification of rules, culminates the institutionalization that began under Father Joseph Meacham in 1787.

1823

The Canterbury Shakers build their first schoolhouse. A legal school district is established at the Church Family. Textbooks in the curriculum include the *New Testament*, the *Millennial Church*, *Easy Lessons*, *Webster's Spelling Book*, *Jackson's Arithmetic*, *Leavitt's Small Arithmetic*, the *New York Reader*, *Ingersol's Grammar*, *Gould's Penmanship*, and *Arithmetical Tables*. Lead pencils are introduced to the classroom.

1828

❖ Ralph Waldo Emerson makes his first visit to the Canterbury Shakers.

The New Hampshire Temperance Society is chartered; a temperance wave also hits the New Hampshire Shakers. The Canterbury Shakers perform a symbolic "funeral" ceremony in which they give a ritual burial to "alcoholic drams." They continue to drink cider, but in restricted quantities.

1829

❖ Ralph Waldo Emerson, accompanied by his new wife, Ellen Tucker of Concord, New Hampshire, makes his second visit to Canterbury. The philosopher is critical of the Shakers; at mealtime he and his wife receive a long sermon from Sister Winkley on "the beauty of virginity."

1830–1833

❖ A brick trustees' office of two stories (five levels) is built to contain the offices and retiring rooms of the trustees responsible for business dealings with the outside world.

1831

❖ Nathaniel Hawthorne visits the Canterbury Shakers.

1835

❖ Canterbury publishes its first herb catalog, with 180 offerings. While the Enfield, New Hampshire, Shakers focus on seed production, Canterbury stresses herb culture.

1837

❖ An intense Shaker religious revival movement, triggered by the trances of young girls at the Watervliet colony, sweeps through all the Shaker communities and thrives for a decade. Spiritual manifestations and psychic phenomena abound. Worship meetings are closed to outsiders because of the intensity of the "spiritual exercises." The Canterbury Shakers hold their first outdoor meeting at Pleasant Grove, a worship area in the nearby woods.

1840

❖ Aided by new technical developments in printing type, Canterbury becomes one of the Shaker movement's printing centers. Under Henry Clay Blinn, the print shop handles Shaker business printing needs, children's educational materials, internal communications, and evangelistic materials for distribution to the outside world.

1845

❖ The Millennial Laws of 1845 are written. A more extended and elaborate version of the 1821 laws, they reflect the society's increased preoccupation with purifying itself of worldly influences by separatism, communal asceticism, and restoring the pristine spirituality of the Shakers' founders.

1846

❖ The Shakers at Canterbury, already making deerskin and fur gloves by this time, begin their broom industry.

1847

❖ Mary Dyer, a former Enfield Shaker, publishes *The Rise and Progress of the Serpent from the Garden of Eden,* a book harshly critical of Shaker doctrine and life.

Canterbury begins raising culinary herbs, as well as medicinal plants, for sale.

1848

❖ Alarmed by the charges of Mary Dyer and other Shaker apostates, the New Hampshire legislature considers restrictive anti-Shaker legislation. The Shakers retain Franklin Pierce and two other New Hampshire attorneys as their legal counsel; they are successfully defended and the legislation is not passed.

A sewing machine, "the first that . . . [has] ever been seen in this section of the country," is purchased by the Canterbury Shakers. It works "only on full cloth and on strait seams" but its introduction is "hailed with joy by the Sisters."

1860

❖ The Millennial Laws are revised once again by the Central Ministry at Mount Lebanon, New York. Some of the more exotic regulations of the 1845 code are eliminated; the new code allows more flexibility with the outside world.

Canterbury obtains another sewing machine, "for heavy work," in order to sew palm leaf table mats for sale.

This year the village produces 36,096 brooms; 1,795 pounds of butter; 3,068 pounds of cheese; and 122 barrels of maple sugar cakes.

1861–1865

❖ Thirty thousand New Hampshire men fight in the Civil War; a few Canterbury Shakers are drafted and ordered to appear for physical examinations, but they are eventually exempted due to their pacifist beliefs.

Mount Lebanon Shaker leaders meet with Abraham Lincoln to discuss their objections to military service. Canterbury trustee David Parker travels to Washington to explain the Shakers' objections to military service to the secretary of war, Edwin Stanton; the Shakers are granted exemption. The Mount Lebanon Shakers develop deep regard for Lincoln and send him a chair; they later try to persuade him to come to their village to rest.

Sister Cecelia DeVere of Mount Lebanon dreams of a "great crime" committed in a theater. Eleven days later, Lincoln is assassinated at Ford's Theater in Washington, D.C.

1869

❖ Franklin Pierce, who has been nearly an outcast even in his native

New Hampshire ever since his endorsement of the Kansas-Nebraska Bill, which permitted slavery in those states, stays with the Canterbury Shakers for a few days. Although the Shakers are opposed to slavery, they remain devoted to Pierce because of his defense of them in the Mary Dyer case.

1870s

❖ Reform movements regain momentum. Temperance, diet reform, women's rights, and fair labor conditions are frequently discussed in the press and among the Shakers.

1871

❖ The Second Family is made a branch of the Church Family.

1873

❖ A financial panic grips the nation; destitute men asking for food and lodging call at many of the Shaker villages.

1874

❖ The Shakers celebrate their centennial. An editorial in the *New York World* remarks that perhaps no group has done more for the country than the Shakers, considering their small numbers.

1876

❖ America's "Gilded Age" is in full swing. The nation's first world's fair, the Centennial Exposition, is held in Philadelphia. Shaker products exhibited include Mount Lebanon's famed chairs; the Canterbury community wins gold medals for their "Corbett's Compound Concentrated Syrup of Sarsaparilla" and for their improved steam-driven washing machine, which they manufacture and sell to hotels, boardinghouses, and residential institutions.

1880s

❖ Agricultural production becomes more focused on the dairy business. The herbal medicine business continues, although production declines. The Dorothy cloak becomes a lucrative business; one is sold to Alice Roosevelt Longworth, daughter of Theodore Roosevelt. Commercial production of baskets at Canterbury ends.

1886

❖ Mary Baker Eddy, who grew up in the region surrounding the Canterbury Shakers, founds the Christian Science Association. Later Canterbury Shaker tradition would assert that she occasionally vis-

ited the village and maintained friendships with Sister Blanche Gardner and Eldress Dorothy Durgin.

1894

❖ Canterbury's North Family closes, and the surviving members merge with the Second Family. The merged family is usually called the "Branch Family" but is still often referred to as the North Family.

1897

❖ Sarah Orne Jewett, author of *The Country of the Pointed Firs* and other works, and a longtime friend of the Maine Shakers, visits Canterbury and is reminded of the great monastic houses of Europe and the landscape of Italy.

1901

❖ The Canterbury Shakers obtain telephone service from New England Telephone Company.

1905

❖ A new creamery is built. The Canterbury Shakers become renowned for their "Golden Guernsey Butter."

The New Lebanon Shaker Village hosts an international nongovernmental conference on world peace, inspired and organized by Anna White and Leila Taylor of that community. The resolutions are forwarded to the Hague, to Congress, and to President Theodore Roosevelt, who responds by saying that the measures are regrettably impracticable under existing world conditions.

1907

❖ The Canterbury Shakers buy their first car, an REO.

1910

❖ The Canterbury community obtains DC electricity from its own generator and batteries set up in the powerhouse, a small tin-sided building erected for the Church Family.

1914

❖ World War 1 breaks out. The Canterbury Shakers raise food for the servicemen.

1916

❖ The Branch Family closes, and its surviving members merge with the Church Family.

1918
❖ World War I ends.

1920
❖ Canterbury's cattle are sold and the village begins to buy dairy products. The farm now focuses on raising purebred horses for sale as carriage horses, a business managed by Elder Arthur Bruce and Brother Irving Greenwood. The Canterbury Shakers continue to engage in beekeeping and raising their own fruits and vegetables.

1925
❖ Canterbury is hooked up to AC electrical power.

1927
❖ Charles Lindbergh crosses the Atlantic in an airplane. The Canterbury Shakers travel to the airport in Concord, New Hampshire, to see Lindbergh and his plane, the *Spirit of St. Louis.*

1929
❖ The stock market crashes and the Great Depression begins. The Canterbury Shakers begin weaving their own poplar cloth around this time (they formerly had purchased rolls of the material from the Mount Lebanon and Sabbathday Lake communities).

1937
❖ The Canterbury Shakers resort to the outside world for their electric power.

1939
❖ Irving Greenwood, the last Canterbury Shaker brother, dies.

1941–1945
❖ The United States fights World War II; the Canterbury Shakers raise "victory gardens."

1950
❖ Sixteen sisters, middle-aged to elderly, make up the Canterbury community.

1958
❖ The poplarware business, the last Shaker industry at Canterbury, officially closes. The sisters continue to make small handcrafts for the gift shop and the "bazaar," which they run on the property.

1959
❖ Charles "Bud" Thompson, a close friend of the Canterbury sisters, comes to work for them full-time. He brings his family and founds the small museum that will—with the support of the Shakers, their attorneys, and area residents—develop into the public historical restoration known as Canterbury Shaker Village, Inc.

1965
❖ Canterbury officially closes the doors to new members, although the Shaker religion will continue to be practiced there.

1969
❖ The administration of Canterbury is handed over to a nonprofit corporation. The sisters retain the right to life residency and continue to practice their faith at the site. Several sisters sit on the board of the new organization.

1973
❖ Canterbury Shaker Village's "great barn," once the largest wood-framed cow barn in the state of New Hampshire, is destroyed by fire.

1974
❖ The Shakers celebrate two hundred years in America.

1976
❖ The United States celebrates its bicentennial.

1990
❖ Eldress Bertha Lindsay, the last spiritual leader of the Canterbury Shakers, dies.

1992
❖ Canterbury Shaker Village celebrates the two hundredth anniversary of its "calling to order."
❖ Sister Ethel Hudson, the last Canterbury Shaker, dies.

1998
❖ Shakerism survives as an organized religion at the Sabbathday Lake community.

SELECTED BIBLIOGRAPHY

Scott T. Swank and Darryl Thompson

This bibliography identifies the major books on Shaker life and art, but there are other studies, including articles and dissertations on more specialized issues, that are worth discussing here because of their relevance to Shaker architecture and community planning.

In spite of the significance of Shaker architecture, scholarly treatments of the topic are rare. Existing publications such as June Sprigg and Paul Rocheleau's *Shaker Built: The Form and Function of Shaker Architecture* (New York: Monacelli Press, 1994) are oriented to general audiences and endeavor to make sweeping generalizations about Shaker architecture. The scholarly study of Shaker architecture thus remains a wide-open field, with no thorough case study of a single community. One of the most helpful works to date is Robert Emlen's *Shaker Village Views: Illustrated Maps and Landscape Drawings by Shaker Artists of the Nineteenth Century* (Hanover, N.H.: University Press of New England, 1987), which concentrates on a distinctive genre of maps and village views by Shaker mapmakers and artists of the nineteenth century. Emlen's book is an essential foundation for any study of Shaker architecture, but it does not purport to be a systematic analysis of building form, fabric, or function, nor does it address Shaker builders or the building process. The best general book on Shaker architecture is Julie Nicoletta, *The Architecture of the Shakers* (Woodstock, Vt.: Countryman Press, 1995), which is the first book organized around building types. The most informative section is the one on dwelling houses, based on her recent Ph.D. dissertation at Yale on the dwelling houses of Mount Lebanon. Another useful general book is William Lassiter's *Shaker Architecture* (New York: Bonanza Books, 1966). An important catalog of Historic American Buildings Survey (HABS) materials organized by communities is *Shaker Built: A Catalog of Shaker Architectural Records from the Historic American Buildings Survey, Washington, D.C.,* edited by John Poppeliers (Washington, D.C.: HABS, National Park Service, U.S. Department of the Interior, 1974), which includes HABS drawings of some New Lebanon, Watervliet, and Hancock Shaker buildings recorded in the 1930s, but provides little contextual analysis. A second general study by Herbert Schiffer, *Shaker Architecture* (Exton, Penn.:

Schiffer Publishing, 1979), is useful mostly for its drawings and pictures of sixteen Shaker communities.

In looking for sources of inspiration for Shaker architecture, writers have ranged far and wide. Robert F. W. Meader, "Reflections on Shaker Architecture," *Shaker Quarterly* 6, no. 2 (summer 1966), 35–44, is wildly speculative. With no effort to document his claims, Meader attributes Shaker community planning to the European "double monastery" tradition (for men and women). Peter Vogt, "The Shakers and the Moravians: A Comparison of the Architecture of Their Settlements," *Shaker Quarterly* 21, no. 3 (fall 1993), 79–97, is a thoughtful footnoted study that shows striking similarities between the Shaker and Moravian communities.

Studies of individual communities have highlighted two Shaker builders. Shaker master builder Moses Johnson, credited with the design and construction of eleven Shaker meetinghouses, and Micajah Burnett, the master builder of the Pleasant Hill, Kentucky, Shaker community, have been featured in *Antiques* articles by Marius B. Peladeau, "The Shaker Meeting Houses of Moses Johnson," and James C. Thomas, "Micajah Burnett and the Buildings at Pleasant Hill" (*Antiques* 98, no. 4 [October 1970], 594–599; 600–605). "The Architecture of the Shakers," by D.M.C. Hopping and Gerald R. Watland, was the first article on the subject to be published in *Antiques* (vol. 72, no. 4 [October 1957], 335–559). Edward Deming Andrews published a booklet on Moses Johnson, *A Shaker Meeting House and Its Builder* (Hancock, Mass.: Shaker Community, 1962). Robert P. Emlen, "Raised, Razed, and Raised Again: The Shaker Meetinghouse at Enfield, New Hampshire: 1793–1902," *Historical New Hampshire* 30 (fall 1975), features a single Johnson meetinghouse that burned in 1902. In 1984 Hancock published a general history of its village restoration written by Amy Bess Miller, *Hancock Shaker Village/The City of Peace: An Effort to Restore a Vision, 1960–1985* (Hancock, Mass.: Hancock Shaker Village, 1984). Of the guidebooks on individual sites, Hancock's is the most extensive, providing solid descriptive information on surviving structures, as well as many historical photographs of Hancock buildings. See John Ott, *Hancock Shaker Village: A Guidebook and History* (Hancock, Mass.: Shaker Community, 1976).

The only article on Shaker architecture to suggest a theoretical framework is A. Donald Emerich's "American Monastic; or, The Meaning of Shaker Architecture" in *Journal of the Victorian Society in America* 11, nos. 3–4 (1992), 3–11. Emerich interprets Shaker architecture as the tangible expression of Shaker theology, and in that sense his article is a modern architectural version of Edward Deming

Andrews and Faith Andrews's *Religion in Wood: A Book of Shaker Furniture* (Bloomington: Indiana University Press, 1966).

Although all of these studies of Shaker architecture contribute to our knowledge, several limitations are apparent. First, the studies are either nontheoretical or work from theoretical assumptions to the buildings, rather than developing hypotheses based on building research. Second, the authors are generally searching for masterpieces of Shaker design, the origins of Shaker style, and identifiable master builders, rather than seeking to understand the overall Shaker building process or Shaker buildings in their historical and cultural contexts. Third, the authors base their conclusions primarily on surviving buildings and HABS photos and drawings, rather than conducting the archaeological and documentary research necessary to provide information on the entire buildings corpus of a given community. A notable exception is the work of David R. Starbuck, who has published many studies of Canterbury's historic mill system, including "The Archaeology of Canterbury Shaker Village," *New Hampshire Archaeologist* 21 (1980), 67–79; "Canterbury Shaker Village: Archaeology and Landscape," *New Hampshire Archaeologist* 31 (1990), 1–163; *Canterbury Shaker Village: An Historical Survey,* 2 vols. (Durham: University of New Hampshire, 1983); "Documenting the Canterbury Shakers," *Historical New Hampshire* 43, no. 1 (1988), 1–20; and "The Shaker Mills in Canterbury, New Hampshire," *Journal of the Society for Industrial Archaeology* 12, no. 1 (1986), 11–38. Exemplary studies of individual Shaker buildings include E. Blaine Cliver, *The Carpentry Shop: An Historic Structure Report* (Canterbury, N.H.: Shaker Village, Inc., 1989); Robert P. Emlen, "The Great Stone Dwelling at Enfield, New Hampshire," *Old Time New England* 69, nos. 3–4 (winter/spring 1979), 69–85; and Jerry V. Grant, *Noble But Plain: The Shaker Meetinghouse at Mount Lebanon* (Old Chatham, N.Y.: Shaker Museum and Library, 1994). On the subject of Shaker community planning and building, Dolores Hayden's *Seven American Utopias: The Architecture of Communitarian Socialism.* Cambridge, Mass.: MIT Press, 1976, is still the classic reference work.

Andrews, Edward Deming. *The Gift to Be Simple: Songs, Dances and Rituals of the American Shakers.* 1940. Reprint, New York: Dover Publications, 1962. Aaron Copland discovered the Shaker song "Simple Gifts" from pages of this book.

———. *The People Called Shakers: A Search for the Perfect Society.* 1954. Reprint, New York: Dover Publications, 1963. A general history of the Shakers.

———. *Community Industries of the Shakers.* Reprint Services Corporation, 1993. A classic in the field.

Andrews, Edward Deming, and Faith Andrews. *Shaker Furniture: The Craftsmanship of an American Communal Sect.* 1937. Reprint, New York: Dover Publications, 1964. The interpretation of Shaker culture found in the black-and-white photographs in this book, by William F. Winter, and the Andrewses' accompanying text had a seminal role in shaping the public's image of the Shakers when this book was first published in 1937.

———. *Religion in Wood: A Book of Shaker Furniture.* 1966. Reprint, Bloomington: Indiana University Press, 1982.

———. *Visions of the Heavenly Sphere: A Study in Shaker Religious Art.* Charlottesville: University Press of Virginia, 1969. The first full-length treatment of "gift" drawings, with reproductions and checklist.

———. *Fruits of the Shaker Tree of Life: Memoirs of Fifty Years of Collecting and Research.* Stockbridge, Mass.: Berkshire Traveller Press, 1975. This book, by two pioneering scholars and collectors, contains information on diverse subjects, including Shaker herb lore, prints depicting the Shakers, Shaker work in the Index of American Design, and early exhibitions of Shaker objects.

———. *Work and Worship among the Shakers.* 1974. Reprint, New York: Dover Publications, 1982. The chapter "Shaker Inventions and Improvements" contains the most complete list of Shaker gadgetry.

Beale, Galen, and Mary Rose Boswell. *The Earth Shall Blossom: Shaker Herbs and Gardening.* Woodstock, Vt.: Countryman Press, 1991. Includes chapters on the seed industry, the medicinal herb industry, medical practices, culinary and domestic use of herbs, and promotional catalogs.

Berry, Brian J. L. *America's Utopian Experiments: Communal Havens from Long-Wave Crises.* Hanover, N.H., and London: University Press of New England, 1992. Relates the demographic patterns of utopian groups to recurring periods of economic and social stress.

[Bishop, Rufus, and Seth Y. Wells, eds.] *Testimonies of the Life, Character, Revelations, and Doctrines of Mother Ann Lee and the Elders with Her . . . Second Edition.* Albany: Weed, Parsons, & Co., Printers, 1888. Facsimile reprint issued by the United Society at Sabbathday Lake, Maine. One of Shakerism's most important source documents, recounting Lee's sayings and oral accounts of her life.

Brewer, Priscilla J. *Shaker Communities, Shaker Lives.* Hanover, N.H., and London: University Press of New England, 1986. A study of Shaker social history and demographics.

Buchanan, Rita. *The Shaker Herb and Garden Book.* Boston: Houghton Mifflin Co., 1996. Focuses on the horticultural practices of the New Hampshire, New York, and Massachusetts Shaker villages.

Burks, Jean M. *Documented Furniture: An Introduction to the Collections* (of Canterbury Shaker Village). Canterbury, N.H.: Shaker Village, 1989.

Burns, Amy Stechler, and Ken Burns. *The Shakers: Hands to Work, Hearts to God. Their History and Visions from 1774 to the Present.* New York: Portland House, 1987. A companion to the Burnses' documentary of the same name.

Burns, Deborah E. *Shaker Cities of Peace, Love, and Union: A History of the Hancock Bishopric.* Hanover, N.H., and London: University of New England Press, 1993. Hancock bishopric included Hancock and Tyringham, Massachusetts, and Enfield, Connecticut.

Campion, Nardi Reeder. *Mother Ann Lee: Morning Star of the Shakers.* Hanover, N.H., and London: University Press of New England, 1990. A biography of Mother Ann Lee, useful despite a few factual errors and debatable points of interpretation.

Carr, Sister Frances A. *Shaker Your Plate: Of Shaker Cooks and Cooking.* Sabbathday Lake, Maine: United Society of Shakers, 1985. Authentic Shaker recipes from Sabbathday Lake and memories of various community members.

————. *Growing Up Shaker.* Sabbathday Lake, Maine: United Society of Shakers, 1995.

Chmielewski, Wendy E., Louis J. Kern, and Marlyn Klee-Hartzell. *Women in Spiritual and Communitarian Societies in the United States.* Syracuse, N.Y.: Syracuse University Press, 1993.

Cook, Harold E. *Shaker Music: A Manifestation of American Folk Culture.* Lewisburg, Penn.: Bucknell University Press, 1973.

Deignan, Kathleen. *Christ Spirit: The Eschatology of Shaker Christianity.* Metuchen, N.J., and London: The American Theological Library Association and the Scarecrow Press, Inc., 1992.

Emlen, Robert P. *Shaker Village Views: Illustrated Maps and Landscape Drawings by Shaker Artists of the Nineteenth Century.* Hanover, N.H., and London: University Press of New England, 1987. A thorough examination of maps of the Shaker communities produced by their members.

[Evans, Sister Jessie.] *The Story of Shakerism by One Who Knows.* East Canterbury, N.H.: Shakers, 1907.

Foster, Lawrence. *Religion and Sexuality: Three American Communal Experiments of the Nineteenth Century.* New York and Oxford: Oxford University Press, 1981. Foster examines the antebellum crisis in marriage and family life and alternatives in Shaker celibacy, Mormon polygamy, or Oneida "complex marriage."

————. *Women, Family, and Utopia: Communal Experiments of the Shakers, the Oneida Community, and the Mormons.* Syracuse, N.Y.: Syracuse University Press, 1991.

Frost, Eldress Marguerite. *The Shaker Story.* Canterbury, N.H.: Canterbury Shakers, n.d. [Penacook, N.H.: Hazen Printing Co., 1963].

Gordon, Beverly. *Shaker Textile Arts.* Hanover, N.H., and London: University Press of New England with the cooperation of the Merrimack Valley Textile Museum and Shaker Village, 1980. The most complete source for this medium.

Grant, Jerry V., and Douglas R. Allen. *Shaker Furniture Makers.* Hanover, N.H., and London: University Press of New England for Hancock Shaker Village, Pittsfield, Massachusetts, 1989. The first book to give detailed information about leading Shaker cabinetmakers.

Hall, Roger. *Love Is Little: A Sampling of Shaker Spirituals.* New York: Sampler Records, 1996. This songbook was written to accompany a recording of the same name that was produced by Roger Hall, who transcribed and arranged Shaker songs.

Historical New Hampshire Special Issue: Canterbury Shaker Village [*Historical New Hampshire* 48, nos. 2–3 (summer–fall 1993)]. Concord, N.H.: New Hampshire Historical Society, 1993.

Humez, Jean M., ed. *Gifts of Power: The Writings of Rebecca Jackson, Black Visionary, Shaker Eldress.* Edited with an introduction by Jean McMahon Humez. Amherst: University of Massachusetts Press, 1987.

————. *Mother's First-Born Daughters: Early Shaker Writings on Women and Religion.* Bloomington and Indianapolis: Indiana University Press, 1993.

Kassay, John. *The Book of Shaker Furniture.* Amherst: University of Massachusetts Press, 1980.

Kennedy, Gerrie, Galen Beale, and Jim Johnson. *Shaker Baskets and Poplarware.* Vol. 3 in the Shaker Field Guide Series. Stockbridge, Mass.: Berkshire House, 1992.

Kern, Louis I. *An Ordered Love: Sex Roles and Sexuality in Victorian*

Utopias. Chapel Hill: University of North Carolina Press, 1981.

Kesten, Seymour R. *Utopian Episodes: Daily Life in Experimental Colonies Dedicated to Changing the World.* Syracuse, N.Y.: Syracuse University Press, 1993.

Ketchum, William C., Jr. *Simple Beauty: The Shakers in America.* New York: Smithmark Publishers, 1996.

Kirk, John T. *The Shaker World: Art, Life, Belief.* New York: Harry N. Abrams, 1997. Kirk examines many aspects of Shaker society and shows how art, life, and belief were inseparably bound together. The book contains some brief but insightful remarks about affinities between Shaker and other design movements such as Arts and Crafts and Scandinavian Modern; Kirk also discusses contemporary artists whose work has been influenced by or parallels Shaker design.

Kitch, Sally L. *Chaste Liberation: Celibacy and Female Cultural Status.* Urbana and Chicago: University of Illinois Press, 1989.

Klamkin, Marian. *Hands to Work: Shaker Folk Art and Industries.* New York: Dodd, Mead & Company, 1972.

Kramer, Fran. *Simply Shaker: Groveland and the New York Communities.* Rochester, N.Y.: Rochester Museum and Science Center, 1991. This exhibition catalog is the best introduction to the material culture and history of the Groveland community.

Lassiter, William. *Shaker Architecture.* New York: Bonanza Books, 1966.

Lindsay, Eldress Bertha. *Seasoned with Grace: My Generation of Shaker Cooking.* Edited by Mary Rose Boswell. Woodstock, Vt.: Countryman Press, 1987. Includes recipes, memories, and insights of Bertha Lindsay, the last Canterbury Shaker eldress. Also contains a chronology and map of Canterbury Shaker Village, several articles by Mary Rose Boswell on Shaker dietary traditions and kitchen organization, and biographical entries on various Canterbury Shakers.

Lossing, Benson John. *An Early View of the Shakers.* Edited by Don Gifford. Hanover, N.H., and London: University Press of New England for Hancock Shaker Village, 1989. An illustrated and annotated reprint of Lossing's detailed eyewitness account of the New Lebanon, New York, Shaker colony published in *Harper's,* July 1857.

McGuire, John. *Basketry—The Shaker Tradition: History, Techniques, Projects.* New York: Sterling Publishing Co., 1989.

Meader, Robert F. W. *Illustrated Guide to Shaker Furniture.* New York: Dover Publications, 1972.

Melcher, Marguerite Fellows. *The Shaker Adventure.* Old Chatham, N.Y.: Shaker Museum, 1986. One of the best general histories of the movement.

Mercadante, Linda A. *Gender, Doctrine, and God: The Shakers and Contemporary Theology.* Nashville: Abingdon Press, 1990. Chronicles the development of Shaker conceptions of God and explores the implications of the Shakers' theological experimentation for Christianity today.

Milbern, Gwendolyn. *Shaker Clothing.* (Lebanon, Ohio: Warrenville County Historical Society, n.d. [1960s]).

Miller, Amy Bess. *Shaker Herbs: A History and a Compendium.* New York: Clarkson N. Potter, 1976. This classic herb book provides useful information on each Shaker community.

Miller, Amy Bess, and Persis Fuller. *The Best of Shaker Cooking.* New York: Macmillan General Reference, 1985. One of the best and most complete Shaker cookbooks.

Miller, M. Stephen. *Marketing Community Industries, 1830–1930: A Century of Shaker Ephemera.* New Britain, Conn.: M. Stephen Miller, 1988. This catalog accompanied an exhibition of the author's collection at the Hancock Shaker Village museum in Pittsfield, Massachusetts.

Morse, Flo. *The Shakers and the World's People.* New York: Dodd, Mead & Co., 1980. Presents excerpts from several hundred years of commentary about the Shakers.

Muller, Charles R. *The Shaker Way. Ohio Antiques Review,* 1979. With chapters on topics including Shaker and Danish Modern furniture and Victorian Shaker furniture.

Muller, Charles R., and Timothy D. Rieman. *The Shaker Chair.* Amherst: University of Massachusetts Press, 1992. The most complete study of the Shaker chair.

Murray, Stuart. *Shaker Heritage Guidebook: Exploring the Historic Sites, Museums, and Collections.* Spencertown, N.Y.: Golden Hill Press, 1994. An indispensable guide to Shaker sites and collections.

Nicoletta, Julie. *The Architecture of the Shakers.* Woodstock, Vt.: Countryman Press, 1995.

Patterson, Daniel W. *The Shaker Spiritual.* Princeton, N.J.: Princeton University Press, 1979. The most complete treatment of Shaker music.

———. *Gift Drawing and Gift Song: A Study of Two Forms of Shaker Inspiration.* Sabbathday Lake, Maine: United Society of Shakers, 1983. An important work on Shaker "gift" drawings.

Pearson, Elmer R., and Julia Neal. *The Shaker Image.* 2d ed., 1974.

Pittsfield, Mass.: Hancock Shaker Village, 1994. Contains pictures and biographical entries of several hundred Shakers.

Piercy, Caroline, and Arthur Tolve. *The Shaker Cookbook: Recipes and Lore from the Valley of God's Pleasure.* Bowling Green, Ohio: Gabriel's Horn Publishing Co., 1984.

Procter-Smith, Marjorie. *Women in Shaker Community and Worship: A Feminist Analysis of the Uses of Religious Symbolism.* Lewiston, Maine: Edwin Mellen Press, 1985. One of the most important feminist analyses of Shaker history.

———. *Shakerism and Feminism: Reflections on Women's Religion and the Early Shakers.* Old Chatham, N.Y.: Center for Research and Education, Shaker Museum and Library, 1991.

Promey, Sally M. *Spiritual Spectacles: Vision and Image in Mid-Nineteenth-Century Shakerism.* Bloomington: Indiana University Press, 1993. Provides a theoretical framework that relates the "gift" drawings and paintings to the evolution of Shaker society and spirituality during this period.

Richmond, Mary L. *Shaker Literature: A Bibliography,* vol. 1: *By the Shakers,* vol. 2: *About the Shakers.* Hancock, Mass.: Shaker Community, 1977. Volume 1 of this invaluable bibliography lists materials published by the Shakers and their apostates; volume 2 covers publications by the "world's people" about the Shakers.

Rieman, Timothy D. *Shaker: The Art of Craftsmanship.* Alexandria, Va.: Art Services International, 1995. This exhibition catalog focuses on the craftsmanship of Mount Lebanon, New York.

Rieman, Timothy D., and Jean M. Burks. *The Complete Book of Shaker Furniture.* New York: Harry N. Abrams, 1993. The best book on Shaker furniture. Identifies characteristics of a particular craftsman or community.

Robinson, Charles Edson. *The Shakers and Their Homes.* 1893. Reprint, Canterbury, N.H.: Shaker Village, in collaboration with the New Hampshire Publishing Company, Somersworth, N.H., 1976. Includes two firsthand accounts of trips to Canterbury made by the author in 1854 and 1892.

Rocheleau, Paul, and June Sprigg. *Shaker Built: The Form and Function of Shaker Architecture.* New York: Monacelli Press, 1994.

Sarle, Cora Helena. *A Shaker Sister's Drawings: Wild Plants Illustrated by Cora Helena Sarle.* New York: Monacelli Press, 1997. A facsimile of Sarle's exquisite drawings, each accompanied by Henry Clay Blinn's notations regarding botanical classification and plant usage.

Sasson, Diane. *The Shaker Spiritual Narrative.* Knoxville: University of Tennessee Press, 1983.

Schiffer, Herbert F. *Shaker Architecture.* Exton, Penn.: Schiffer Publishing, 1979.

Sprigg, June. *By Shaker Hands.* Hanover, N.H., and London: University Press of New England, 1975, 1990. This book portrays the ideals the Shakers strove to attain. The text is written with a touch of poetry and humor and is enriched by the author's drawings.

———. *Shaker Design.* New York: Whitney Museum of American Art; New York and London: W. W. Norton & Co., 1986. Catalog of the exhibition at the Whitney Museum of American Art. Views everyday objects made by the Shakers as artworks and specimens of masterful design.

———. *Simple Gifts: A Memoir of a Shaker Village.* New York: Alfred A. Knopf, 1998.

Sprigg, June, and Jim Johnson. *Shaker Woodenware.* Shaker Field Guide Series, vols. 1 and 2. Great Barrington, Mass.; Stockbridge, Mass.: Berkshire House, 1991, 1992. A series of guides for collectors. Volume 1 covers boxes, carriers, buckets, dippers, sieves, pails, and tubs; volume 2 addresses tools, equipment, and issues of authenticity.

Sprigg, June, and David Larkin. *Shaker: Life, Work, and Art.* Boston: Houghton Mifflin Co., 1987.

Starbuck, David R. *Canterbury Shaker Village: Archaeology and Landscape.* [special issue of *The New Hampshire Archaeologist* 31, no. 1]. New Hampshire Archaeological Society, 1990. Includes the first in-depth look at Canterbury's mill system.

Starbuck, David P., and Scott T. Swank. *A Shaker Family Album: Photographs from the Collection of Canterbury Shaker Village.* Hanover, N.H., and London: University Press of New England, 1998.

Stein, Stephen J. *Letters from a Young Shaker: William S. Byrd at Pleasant Hill.* Lexington: University Press of Kentucky, 1985.

———. *The Shaker Experience in America: A History of the United Society of Believers.* New Haven and London: Yale University Press, 1992. The most complete scholarly history of the Shakers.

Van Kolken, Diana. *Introducing the Shakers: An Explanation and Directory.* Bowling Green, Ohio: Gabriel's Horn Publishing Co., 1985.

Wertkin, Gerard C. *The Four Seasons of Shaker Life: An Intimate Portrait of the Community at Sabbathday Lake, Maine.* New

York: Simon and Schuster, 1986. A glimpse of modern Shaker life at the last surviving Shaker community.

Wetherbee, Martha, and Nathan Taylor. *Shaker Baskets.* Sanbornton, N.H.: Martha Wetherbee Basket Shop, 1993. The authors are master basketmakers who have spent years studying and reproducing Shaker basketry.

White, Anna, and Leila S. Taylor. *Shakerism: Its Meaning and Message.* Columbus, Ohio: Press of Fred J. Heer, 1904. [Facsimile reprint (n.d.) issued by the United Society of Shakers at Sabbathday Lake, Maine.] This classic history, written by two members of the Mount Lebanon "progressive wing," allows one to see how turn-of-the-century Shakers interpreted their own experience.

Whitson, Robley Edward. *The Shakers: Two Centuries of Spiritual Reflection.* New York; Ramsey, Ontario; and Toronto: Paulist Press, 1983.

INDEX

ILLUSTRATION CREDITS

All photographs copyright © Bill Finney except the following:
Pages 18–19, 41, 45, 129, 134, 203 (bottom) ❖ Photographs by Todd Buchanan.
Pages 99, 106, 125, 141, 203 (top), 206–207, 210, 211 ❖ Photographs by Scott T. Swank.
Page 146 ❖ Photograph by Graydon Wood.
Page 175 ❖ Photograph by Michael Fredericks.
Page 176 ❖ Photograph by Greg Heisey.
Page 177 ❖ Photograph by Dave Kutchukian.
Page 205 ❖ Photograph by John Boeckeler.

Sources for illustrations not listed in the captions are as follows:
Page 7 ❖ Tom Gillis for Richard Conway Meyer Architect.
Page 25 ❖ Tom Gillis/Scott Craven/
   Cory Neale for Richard Conway Meyer Architect.
Pages 26, 27 ❖ Tom Gillis/Cory Neale for Richard Conway Meyer Architect.